Submarine Cables Protection and Regulations

Utpal Kumar Raha · Raju K. D.

Submarine Cables Protection and Regulations

A Comparative Analysis and Model Framework

Springer

Utpal Kumar Raha
Rajiv Gandhi School of Intellectual Property Law
Indian Institute of Technology Kharagpur
Kharagpur, West Bengal, India

Raju K. D.
Rajiv Gandhi School of Intellectual Property Law
Indian Institute of Technology Kharagpur
Kharagpur, West Bengal, India

ISBN 978-981-16-3435-2 ISBN 978-981-16-3436-9 (eBook)
https://doi.org/10.1007/978-981-16-3436-9

This Springer imprint is published by the registered company Springer Nature Singapore Pte Ltd.
The registered company address is: 152 Beach Road, #21-01/04 Gateway East, Singapore 189721, Singapore

To our Parents

Preface

Submarine cables were laid on the seabed between land-based stations to facilitate the transmission of data, telecommunications, the Internet, etc.—a driving factor to the global economy and strategic tool in national security. Modern society may not be aware of cables' vulnerabilities posed by natural or anthropogenic forces and remains negligent to cable governance issues. Hence, laying, protection, and quick relinking of cables have become critical with timely approval (including that of national authorities) for cable operators and cable repairing ships to mobilize becoming crucial; yet, this remains broadly challenging in most jurisdictions.

Under the United National Convention on the Law of the Sea, 1982 (UNCLOS), the States' legal frameworks may have a significant role in ensuring the laying and protection of submarine cables. The present study deals with the submarine cable regime comprising international law, legal instruments on cables in the selected jurisdictions, and dedicated submarine cable regimes of Australia and New Zealand. It undertakes a comparative and analytical research method on available legal premises to ascertain the fundamental principles, doctrines, approaches, and existing legal standards on submarine cables.

It reveals that States' responses to their international obligations concerning cables vary among jurisdictions significantly. Available legal standards in many countries are no longer adequately addressing challenges in laying and protecting the submarine cable. However, they have indicated governance approaches such as imposing control on marine activities, prescribing dedicated authority, and obligations on cable injuries, building cooperation, and promoting awareness about the critical nature of cables. The potentials of these approaches are required to be enhanced further by definite actions. The submarine cable regimes of Australia and New Zealand are not free from the criticisms; however, they have made a significant contribution to the jurisprudence of national laws.

As a way forward, this study proposes a draft model legal framework for national instruments for the governance of submarine cables networks within their jurisdictions.

Kharagpur, India

Utpal Kumar Raha
Raju K. D.

Acknowledgments

We express our gratitude to the faculty members of the Rajiv Gandhi School of Intellectual Property Law, Indian Institute of Technology Kharagpur, for guidance, which has been a constant source of encouragement and flow of invaluable suggestions during the development of this book, without which this work would not have been possible. We consider ourselves blessed to work at this institution.

We would like to offer our gratitude to the teachers and other friends who had encouraged us to progress with this book proposal. The cooperation of Ms. Nupoor Singh is greatly appreciated.

We express indebtedness to our parents and other members of our family, who have always been with our side selflessly.

Utpal Kumar Raha
Raju K. D.

List of the International Conventions, Statues Other Arrangements

A. International Conventions

1. The Convention for the Protection of Submarine Cable March 14, 1884, TS 380.
2. Convention on the Continental Shelf, April 29, 1958, 499 UNTS 311.
3. Convention on the High Seas, April 29, 1958, 450 UNTS 11.
4. The United Nations Convention on the Law of the Sea December 10, 1982, 1833 UNTS 3.
5. The International Regulations for Preventing of Collisions at Sea October 20, 1972, 1050 UNTS 16.
6. The Protocol to the 1972 Convention on the Prevention of Marine Pollution by the Wastes and other Matter November 7, 1996, 2006 ATS 11.
7. Convention for the Protection of the Marine Environment of the North-East Atlantic, September 22, 1992, 32 ILM 1069 (1992).
8. Convention on Environmental Impact Assessment in a Transboundary Context (Espoo Convention) 1989 UNTS 309, 30 ILM 800 (1991).

B. National Statutes and Instruments and Other Arrangements

1. Australian Communication and Media Authority Act 2005 (No. 45, 2005) of Australia.
2. Canadian Environmental Assessment Act, 2012 (S.C. 2012, c. 19, s. 52).
3. Canadian Navigable Waters Act (R.S.C., 1985, c N-22).
4. French Code of Postal and Electronic Communications.
5. General Maritime Direction 2012 of Columbia.
6. Ghana Shipping (Protection of Offshore Operations and Assets) Regulations 2012.
7. Law of the People's Republic of China on the Administration of Sea Areas 2001 (No. 61).

8. National Environmental Policy Act of 1969 (42 U.S.C. §4321 et seq.).
9. Regulations on the Management of Laying Submarine Cables and Pipelines 1989 of China.
10. Regulations on the Protection of Submarine Cables and Pipelines 2004 of China.
11. Submarine Cables and Pipeline Protection Act 1963 (Act No. 61 of 1963) of Australia.
12. Submarine Cables and Pipelines Protection Act 1966 (1966 No 5) of New Zealand.
13. Submarine Cables and Pipelines Protection Act 1996 (Public Act 1996 No. 22) of New Zealand.
14. Telecommunications Business Law of Japan (Law No. 86 of December 25, 1984).
15. The Coastal Zone Management Act 1972 (CZMA) (16 U.S.C. 1451 et seq.).
16. The Directive, viz. On Strengthening the Protection of Submarine Cables and Ensuring the Safety of International Telecommunications 2007 of Vietnam.
17. The Law of Navigation 20.094, of Argentina.
18. The Marine and Coastal Access Act 2009 (MCAA) (c 23) of UK.
19. The Minister of Transportation Decision No. 94/ 1999 (Regulation of Submarine Cables 1999) of Indonesia.
20. The Submarine Cable Act, 29 February 1888, 47 US Code.
21. The Submarine Cable Deployment Guidelines 2010 of Singapore.
22. The Submarine Cable Repair Guidelines 2010 of Singapore.
23. The Submarine Telegraph Act, 1885 (c. 49) of UK.
24. The Telecommunication Act 1997 (No. 47, 1997) of Australia.
25. The Territorial Waters, Continental Shelf, Exclusive Economic Zone and other Maritime Zones Act, 1976, (ACT No. 80 Of 1976) of India.

Domestic Court Cases and Other Materials

Cases

Ninety-Four Consortium Cable Owners v Eleven Named French Fishermen, Tribunal de Grande Instance de Boulogne Sur Mer (1st Chamber) August 28, 2009, (File No 06/00229DG/LM).
Société Telus Communication v. Peracomo Inc., 2011 FC 494 (CanLII).
Peracomo Inc. v. Société Telus Communications, 2012 FCA 199 (CanLII).
Peracomo Inc. v. TELUS Communications Co., 2014 SCC 29 (CanLII),
Telefónica International Wholesale Services America (Tiws) and Others vs. Tamika S A. And Other, First Court of Appeals in Civil Matters, Official Notice 0003-000193/2015.

Reports

A. United Nations General Assembly

   a. United Nations General Assembly Resolution A/65/37a On Oceans And Law Of The Sea (U.N. GAOR, 65th Sess., 59th plenary meeting).

B. Other Reports

   a. Report on Reliability of Global Undersea Communications Cable Infrastructure (ROGUCCI), Issue I, (IEEE Communications Society and East West Institute, 2010).
   b. Report on Submarine Cable Information Sharing Project: Legislative Practices and Points of Contact, Asia-Pacific Economic Cooperation (APEC, 2011).
   c. Final Report 1: Separation, the Communications Security, Reliability and Interoperability Council IV, Working Group 8 ("WG8"), December 2014.
   d. Report on the Operation of the Submarine Cable Protection Regime—A Report on Five Years' Operation of Schedule 3A of the Telecommunications Act 1997, the Submarine Cable Protection Regime, September 2010.

About This Book

This book acknowledges that laying, quick relinking, and protecting submarine cables have become critical with timely approval for carriers and cable repairing ships and are most challenging in many jurisdictions. It identifies that a dedicated national instrument on submarine cable as a way forward is yet to be appreciated by many of the States, and presently, there is no model legal framework for national instruments on submarine cables available. To bridge these gaps, the book undertakes a systematic inquiry and analysis of the relevant authorities of submarine cable regimes. It consults existing literature on international law on cables and analyses specific principles and provisions on laying repair and maintenance of submarine cables and States' obligations towards protecting cables from vulnerabilities. It touches upon cable regulation in the deep sea concerning the International Seabed Authority and proposed biodiversity agreement. It indicates suitable measures on cable laying, etc., and security risks in the marine space beyond the national jurisdictions. To map States' response, it explores the domestic cable regimes, including both the selected jurisdictions and Australia and New Zealand, and analyses specific legal provisions and institutional setup, and demonstrates State practices, approaches, and loopholes in governance of the cable system within national jurisdictions. This book suggests adopting the spatial ocean management approach, dedicated regulatory authority, a competent enforcement agency, strict liability with exemplary punishment on cable damage, etc., and the cable system to strengthen the cable system's management. Finally, it arranges the fundamental premises of a common minimum framework for national instruments seeking coastal States' deliberations in implementing initiatives towards a robust law and policy for reliability, resiliency, and security of the cable system. The cable industries, pipeline, fishing, and shipping industries, academicians, government authorities and international bodies, and the maritime community worldwide are looking at the issues and challenges of submarine cable regimes, particularly national regimes, and suggestive remedial measures. Most respectfully, these stakeholders may find the present book unique, enriching the existing literature and a helpful reference.

Contents

About the Authors

Utpal Kumar Raha is a former Research Scholar at Rajiv Gandhi School of IP Law, IIT Kharagpur, India. His research interest is ocean law and policy. He has been writing in the area of underwater cable law and policy and maritime security, marine conservation in peer-reviewed journals and also presented research papers in conferences held in Asia and Europe. Before that, he has qualified for University Grand Commission National Eligibility Test in 2013, and masters in law from the Hidayatullah National Law University, Raipur, a reputed institution among the national law schools in India.

Raju K. D. is Professor of Law at Rajiv Gandhi School of IP Law, IIT Kharagpur, India. He has several books and book chapters to his credit in addition to papers in international journals. His research interests are WTO law, IP and competition law, and Law of the Sea, Air & Space.

Symbols and Abbreviations

APEC	Asia-Pacific Economic Cooperation
COLREGS	The Regulations for Preventing Collision at Sea, 1972
EEZ	Exclusive Economic Zone
EIA	Environment Impact Assessments
FAO	Food and Agricultural Organization
ICPC	International Cable Protection Committee
MPA	Marine Protected Area
OSPAR	The Convention for the Protection of the Marine Environment of the North-East Atlantic 1992
TW	Territorial Water
UNCLOS	United Nations Convention on the Law of the Sea 1982
UNEP	United Nations Environment Programme
UNODC	UN Office on Drugs and Crime
UN	United Nations

List of Tables

Chapter 1
Introduction

1.1 Background

Freedom of laying submarine cables is an essential component of the freedom of seas that intends to promote telecommunications *vis-a-vis* international communications.[1] Submarine cables (cables) are laid on the seabed between land-based stations to carry telecommunication, data, and the iInternet for multiple applications.[2] They facilitate telecommunications, and it is of vital importance to the global economy and national securities of all States.[3] To assist, promote, and regulate the activities relating to cables' laying, the international community has agreed on several instruments.[4] The international Convention on the Law of the Sea 1982 (UNCLOS) is the most important among them.[5] The State parties to this Convention also have obligations to support submarine cables' laying and protection in marine spaces within the national

[1]Freedom of the high seas is a right conferred on all States under international law that the high seas are open to all. Freedom to lay submarine cable and pipeline is one of the six freedoms of the high seas.

Article 87 of UNCLOS 1982 provides 'Freedom of the high seas

1. The high seas are open to all States, whether coastal or land-locked. Freedom of the high seas is exercised under the conditions laid down by this Convention and by other rules of international law. It comprises, inter alia, both for coastal and land-locked States:

(a) freedom of navigation;

(b) freedom of overflight;

(c) freedom to lay submarine cables and pipelines, subject to Part VI;

(d) freedom to construct artificial islands and other installations permitted under international law, subject to Part VI;

(e) freedom of fishing, subject to the conditions laid down in Section 2;

(f) freedom of scientific research, subject to Parts VI and XIII.'

For an overview of the international regime on submarine cables, see Burnett et al. [1].

[2]Starosielski [2].

[3]Beckman [3].

[4]Burnett et al. [1].

[5]Burnett et al. [1].

U. K. Raha and Raju K. D., *Submarine Cables Protection and Regulations*,
https://doi.org/10.1007/978-981-16-3436-9_1

maritime jurisdictions.[6] They are to respect other States' rights to lay submarine cables, however are entitled to take reasonable measures to regulate submarine cable operation (survey of the submarine cable route, laying, repairing, and maintenance of cable).[7]

Submarine cables are laid for the transmission of data, which sustains the Internet and e-communications.[8] These submarine cables carry massive data, internet, and voice across the ocean/seas connecting continents and countries, which is a driving factor behind the modern world.[9] Emerging technological developments are opening new windows of submarine cable uses to explore and exploit the undersea.[10] Besides the telegraph cables, submarine cables include submarine power cables and fiber optic telecommunication cables. Moreover, these cables are also used to collect data about ocean environments and called green cables.[11] These cables are nevertheless vulnerable and susceptible to damage from either anthropogenic or natural forces.[12] Natural hazards such as submarine landslides and sediment movability pose a severe risk to the cable system.[13]

These cables are exposed to other competing and conflicting marine uses and interests. Other marine interests and activities, including fishing, shipping, exploration, exploitation of marine resources, hinder and disrupt submarine cables. The laying of submarine cables is susceptible to interference caused by these activities. Submarine cables face obstructions from those marine affairs and related activities, especially in the coastal areas.

---

[6] Article 79 of UNCLOS 1982 provides 'Submarine cables and pipelines on the continental shelf.

1. All States are entitled to lay submarine cables and pipelines on the continental shelf, in accordance with the provisions of this article.

2. Subject to its right to take reasonable measures for the exploration of the continental shelf, the exploitation of its natural resources and the prevention, reduction and control of pollution from pipelines, the coastal State may not impede the laying or maintenance of such cables or pipelines.

3. The delineation of the course for the laying of such pipelines on the continental shelf is subject to the consent of the coastal State.

4. Nothing in this Part affects the right of the coastal State to establish conditions for cables or pipelines entering its territory or territorial sea, or its jurisdiction over cables and pipelines constructed or used in connection with the exploration of its continental shelf or exploitation of its resources or the operations of artificial islands, installations and structures under its jurisdiction.

5. When laying submarine cables or pipelines, States shall have due regard to cables or pipelines already in position. In particular, possibilities of repairing existing cables or pipelines shall not be prejudiced.'

[7] Davenport [4].

[8] Starosielski [2].

[9] Starosielski [2].

[10] Clark [5].

[11] Agarwala [6]. It states that "... new submarine cables laid for the dual purpose of telecommunication and data gathering and ... simply 'green cables', where a green cable system is defined as a fibre-optic submarine cable system equipped with sensors at regular intervals along the entire length of the cable."

[12] Pope et al. [7].

[13] Carter, and Burnett. [8].

These activities also pose threats of breakage and injuries to the cables.[14] Those marine activities around the coasts pose a severe threat of breakage or damages to cables besides natural phenomena. Risks to the submarine cable system also include the vulnerabilities of the cable landing stations on coasts.[15] Such marine activities also become a potential interference to cable operations.

Incidents of cable damage have severe implications on communication networks. Submarine mass movements pose severe threats to cables.[16] Several submarine cables were affected and damaged due to a massive undersea earthquake in Hengchun, Taiwan, in 2006.[17] Many of these cables were severed in 4000 m depth of this area. These damaged cables also include cable buried deep beneath the mud. The implications of this incident and losses to communication networks connecting countries such as Taiwan, Korea, Japan, Singapore, and Malaysia cannot be estimated. These countries almost lost their trading. The cable repair ships sharing 40% of the global strength took as many as seven weeks to complete the communication process. However, disruption on the Internet in these countries persisted for several weeks more.[18]

In 2007, Vietnam faced severe disruption of Internet services due to a cable cut by thieves,[19] hundreds of kilometers of submarine cables to sell it. The components of submarine cables have economic values. Thus, Vietnam faced disruptions in the provision of the Internet for three months and was forced to take recourse of satellites and land-based cables to provide the Internet. The cables' replacement cost was $ 5.8 million to Vietnam besides the loss of revenue from trade and communications.[20]

In 2008, anchors from the ship dragged off submarine cables on the north coast of Alexandria, which led to the breaking of five cables linking Europe, North Africa, and the Middle East.[21] Only one remained intact, and all these countries become dependent on only that cable. This incident affected the Internet services of more than 80 million people from the Middle East and Asia. It also disrupted Internet services in Egypt and Pakistan by 60 percent.[22] India also lost its westbound connection between 50 and 60%, which had implications on its vast outsourcing service sectors.[23]

The protection and preservation of submarine cable infrastructure are very vital for uninterrupted telecommunication services. Cable damage is caused due to negligence (primarily fishing, shipping, exploration, and exploitation activities) and intentional

---

14 Sunak [9].

15 Ross [10].

16 Pope et al. [7].

17 Qiu [11].

18 Qiu [11].

19 Staff Reporter [12].

20 Staff Reporter [12].

21 Singel [13].

22 Clark [5].

23 Sunak [9].

activities (shipping, theft, a threat from terrorist activities). The majority of the incidents of cable breaks are reported within the national coastal jurisdictions of States.[24] Another study on cable faults between 2010 and 2015 suggests that external human aggression causes most cable faults (90–95%). Among these total cable faults, the fishing shares over 40 percent and anchoring between 25 and 30 percent. Regarding the occurrence of the cable faults, most of the faults occur within shallow water (up to 300 m water depth), and 74–80% of the cable faults occur in water depths less than 200 and 500 m, respectively.[25]

Cable breaking leads to disruption of telecommunications and bandwidth which together result in multiple consequences. An injury to cable incurs a huge direct loss in repairing charges besides indirect loss due to disruption in telecommunication dependent transactions, etc.[26] In most cases, cable ships require to meet several compliances before proceeding to repair the damaged cables. Such requirements make the cable fixing process and the cable outage time lengthy.[27] The protection of submarine cables and the resolution and accommodation of potential conflicts among the competing marine activities have become more critical than ever.[28]

The submarine cable regimes play an essential role in addressing the said challenges associated with these cables. The international submarine cable regime is set out in the United Nations Convention of the Law of the Sea 1982 (UNCLOS), which intends to espouse the laying of cables in the seabed by accommodating numerous other marine activities and interests.[29] UNCLOS follows the spatial distribution of

[24]As a reference, see the cable repair data prepared by Verizon for the International Cable Protection Committee (ICPC), presented to the ICPC Plenary, Hamburg, on April 12, 2016, and calculated from data between January 2008 and December 2015. See Sugadev [14]. The present study, compiled by the author of the given article from different sources, reveals that every year one or more cable faults are reported in the following jurisdictions including India:

'Portugal, Thailand, Qatar, Singapore, Turkey, Belgium, India, and Vietnam—one or two;

Egypt, Saudi Arabia, South Africa, Libya, Greece, the United States, Iran, Spain, and France—two to four;

The United Arab Emirates, the Philippines, Malaysia, South Korea, Japan, and the Netherlands—four to six;

Italy—more than six; Indonesia—more than twelve;

The United Kingdom, and Taiwan—more than fourteen; and China—more than twenty-four.'

[25]Kordahi [15].

[26]Introduction, Submarine Cable Information Sharing Project: Legislative Practices and Points of Contact September 2011, Telecommunications and Information Working Group, 2012 APEC Secretariat [16].

[27]Davenport [4].

[28]Takie [17].

[29]Wagner [18].

ocean management.[30] It prescribes rights and obligations on its State parties for laying and protection of submarine cables accordingly.

In this connection, that Article 79 of UNCLOS 1982 provides that all States are entitled to lay cables in the continental shelf. Here, in addition to States, the phrase '*all States*' includes cable companies also.[31]

Therefore, the State parties to UNCLOS require to take measures for laying of the submarine cables along with associated activities such as submarine cable operation and protection within the national marine zones. The national laws complying with UNCLOS obligations and mandating other marine activities and interests within its marine spaces become crucial. Therefore, these laws and regulatory authorities have a significant role in advancing the laying and protection of telecommunication cables. These laws also needed to cope with emerging challenges to the laying and protecting cables, such as accommodation of deep-sea mining and cable activities in the 'Area.'[32]

The coastal activities are increasing day by day. Together with other economic activities such as energy exploration and exploitations, conservation measures, and intensification of other prospective utilities, both traditional marines use shipping, fishing, conservation measures, and intensification of other future utilities and have added to the existing marine uses.

The vulnerability of submarine cables heightened due to several issues such as coastal States' temptations for territorialization, negligent attitude, and lack of awareness about the critical nature of the submarine cables.

Thus, coastal States' submarine cable law and its regulatory regime have a significant role in bringing stability to the cable systems. The present research deals with an essential question of whether the existing national regime on submarine cables is adequate to support cables' laying and protection (Fig. 1.1).

1.2 Submarine Cables

The Encyclopaedia of Public International Law defines submarine cable as 'means of communication laid on the seabed between two terminal points.' Submarine cables are of two types:[33] (i) submarine power cable for the transmission of energy,

---

[30] See Raha and Raju [19] '... the nations of the world deliberated upon the law relating to the seas. The deliberations from 1973 to 1982 resulted in the United Nations Convention on the Law of the Sea (the UNCLOS). The three UNCLOS Conventions formulated substantive laws with regard to territorial jurisdiction of States to the water in and around their land, created mechanisms for the protection of these waters, as also to give freedom to countries to access these waters so as to aid trade, commerce, communication and passage.'

[31] Clause 1 of Article 79 of UNCLOS provides that *all States are entitled to lay submarine cables and pipelines on the continental shelf, in accordance with the provisions of this article.*

[32] Kroon [20].

[33] Carter et al. [21].

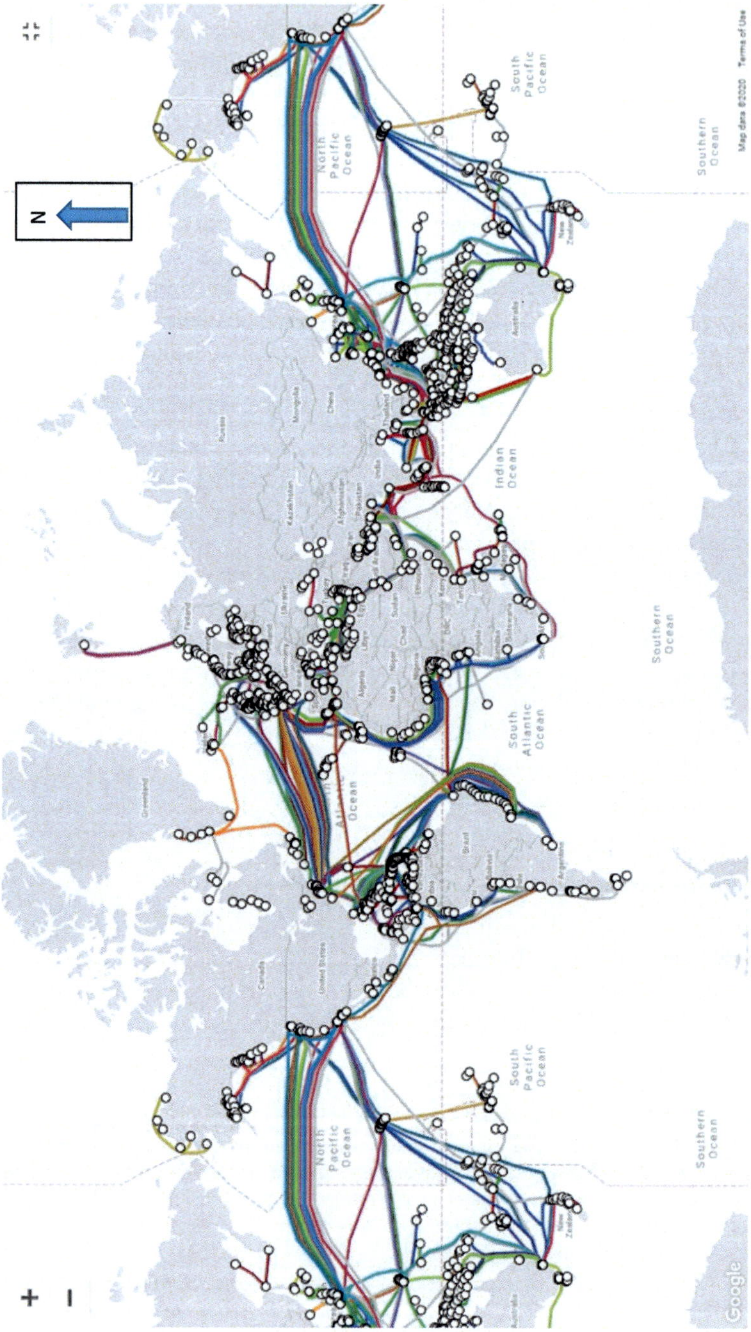

Fig. 1.1 Global submarine cable map. *Source* TeleGeography https://www.submarinecablemap.com/

and (ii) fiber optic telecommunication cables for the transfer of data and voice.[34] Besides, these cables are increasingly in use in marine scientific data collection.[35] Despite the internet-dependent nature of our world, a thorough understanding of the e-communication infrastructure has emerged only recently. Besides the need for high-bandwidth, the demand for cable increases with undersea oceanographic research, digital technology in oil and gas exploration,[36] ocean observatories[37] and offshore energy parks, and green energy.[38] These fibre optic and power cable-based systems support the ocean observatories, increasing application in marine research, climate/ocean change, natural hazards, and resource assessment.[39] Further, there is an emerging application of submarine cables, known as green cables used for collecting oceanographic data or marine scientific data.[40]

Submarine cables are the most sought after marine business after offshore energy extraction, global shipping, and naval expenditures.[41] There is a dramatic growth in the submarine cable industry.[42] And the submarine cable industry has shown immense potential to grow further.[43] Today, education, health, banking, share market, trade, insurance, entertainment, addressing emergencies, national security-related activities, and the like intensely rely on telecommunication systems,[44] comprising more than 200 independent international cables.[45] There is no doubt these 'unseen and unsung cables are the true skeleton and nerve of our world communication system, linking all countries together in a fiber-optic web.'[46] Cables have become the arteries carrying the lifeblood of communication. However, major cable damage produces significant losses, direct and indirect.[47] A cable represents numerous stakeholders,

---

[34]Davenport [22].

[35]Davenport [23].

[36]Malecki and Wei [24].

[37]Malecki and Wei [24].

[38]Waltz [25].

[39]Carter and Burnett [8].

[40]Agarwala [26]. See also, Article 112—Right to Lay Submarine Cables and Pipelines, 261–264 *at* 64, in Myron [27] (herein after known as the UNCLOS Commentary) and it States 'As noted by the ILC in its Commentary on its draft articles, the reference to cables 'applies not only to telegraph and telephone cables, but also to high-voltage power cables' [28].

[41]Wrathall [29].

[42]Malecki and Wei [24].

[43]Malecki and Wei [24].

[44]'Cyberspace, in the physical form of undersea fiber-optic cables, carries an even greater value for trade [than shipping goods] through financial transactions and information.' Greenleaf, and Amos [30].

[45]Burnett et al. [1].

[46]U.N. GAOR [31].

[47]For example, following the model, a fault in all landing points in Australia would entail direct costs (for cable repair) of US$ 2.2 million and indirect economics cost of US$ 3169 million mostly due to the loss of 100% of international Internet traffic. See Economic Impact of Submarine Cable Disruptions, 42 (2012).

in case of its breakage gives rise to hue and cry globally. The UN General Assembly has recognized the subsea cable system as 'critical communication infrastructure'.[48]

1.3 Law on Submarine Cables

The international law relating to the high seas revolves around three basic principles, *among other things:* (i) freedom of the high seas, (ii) territorial sovereignty, and (iii) common heritage of mankind; all these principles encompass submarine cable.[49] Among these, the principle of territorial sovereignty and freedom of the high seas apply to the coastal sea and the high seas, respectively. The principle of the common heritage of mankind applies to the rest of the sea, known as the 'Area.'

The principles of freedom of sea confer privilege on States to engage in submarine cable operation in the high seas as defined traditionally. The territorial waters attract sovereignty principles. Lastly, the principle of 'common heritage of mankind' applies to the submarine cable operations in the 'Area.' These principles, therefore, establish the spatial distribution of jurisdictions over marine space by prescribing the rights and obligations of States concerning the submarine cables.[50]

International law on submarine cables has its origin in the nineteenth century. First, the Convention for the Protection of Telegraph Cable was adopted in 1884 (the

---

[48]G.A. Res. 65/37 [32].

[49]Art 2 of the UNCLOS 1982 provides 'Legal status of the territorial sea, of the air space over the territorial sea and of its bed and subsoil

1. The sovereignty of a coastal State extends, beyond its land territory and internal waters and, in the case of an archipelagic State, its archipelagic waters, to an adjacent belt of sea, described as the territorial sea

2. This sovereignty extends to the air space over the territorial sea as well as to its bed and subsoil.

3. The sovereignty over the territorial sea is exercised subject to this Convention and to other rules of international law.'

Art 87 of the UNCLOS 1982 provides 'Freedom of the high seas

1. The high seas are open to all States, whether coastal or land-locked. Freedom of the high seas is exercised under the conditions laid down by this Convention and by other rules of international law. It comprises, inter alia, both for coastal and land-locked States:

(a) freedom of navigation;

(b) freedom of overflight;

(c) freedom to lay submarine cables and pipelines, subject to Part VI;

(d) freedom to construct artificial islands and other installations permitted under international law, subject to Part VI;

(e) freedom of fishing, subject to the conditions laid down in Section 2;

(f) freedom of scientific research, subject to Parts VI and XIII.

2. These freedoms shall be exercised by all States with due regard for the interests of other States in their exercise of the freedom of the high seas, and also with due regard for the rights under this Convention with respect to activities in the Area.'

Art 136 UNCLOS1982 provides 'Common heritage of mankind-

The Area and its resources are the common heritage of mankind.'

[50]Tanaka [33].

Cable Convention).[51] It had prescribed obligation on States for breakage of telegraph cables in the high seas.[52] It had limited application, and its mandates bind only a limited number of States and apply to submarine telegraph cables in the high seas only. Most of the State parties have not implemented this Convention.

Next, the 1958 Geneva Convention on the law of the sea codifies the 'freedom of laying of submarine cables' and adopted three more provisions than the Cable Convention that prescribes punishment for breaking or injuring cables beyond the territorial water.[53] These provisions have been endorsed in the 1982 UNCLOS *ad verbatim.* The Cable Convention 1884, the Geneva Convention 1958, and the UNCLOS 1982 comprise primary international law on submarine cables.[54]

The relevant provisions of the UNCLOS concerning submarine cables represent the customary international law.[55] However, it may not be the same in the case of the Cable Convention provisions not contained in the UNCLOS since these provisions lack wide acceptance.[56]

Along with these Conventions, the Regulations for Preventing Collision at Sea, 1972 (COLREGS),[57] and the Protocol to the 1972 Convention on the Prevention of Marine Pollution by the Wastes and other Materials, 1996, comprise the international legal regime for submarine cables.[58]

Nevertheless, the substantive international submarine cable regime is set out in UNCLOS, which prescribes rights and obligations on both coastal States' and non-coastal States' over the submarine cables in the established maritime zones.[59]

Presently, international law on submarine cable applies to submarine communication cables as well as power cables. The UNCLOS spatial distribution of ocean governance prescribes that States have sovereignty over the territorial water (TW) and sovereign rights over the exclusive economic zones (EEZ) and continental shelves.[60] Therefore, the coastal States' rule of law deals with the cable operation in TW. The coastal States have sovereign rights and enjoy certain rights and jurisdictions over the EEZ and continental shelves' submarine cables. The EEZ and the continental shelves denote the same geographical area to a large extent and are overlapping jurisdictions.

---

[51] Burnett, et al. [1].

[52] Keye [34] and Burnett [35].

[53] Continental Shelf Convention [36] and High Seas Convention [37].

[54] UNCLOS [38].

[55] Roach [39].

[56] Beckman [3].

[57] International Regulations for Preventing Collisions at Sea to the Convention for the Regulations for Preventing Collisions at Sea 1972 which provides rules to govern among other issues the operations of ships including cable ships. These include preventive measures.

[58] The Protocol to the Convention on the Prevention of Marine Pollution by Dumping of Wastes and Other Matter 1972 (London Convention). '*Dumping* does not include abandonment in the sea of cable placed for a purpose other than the mere disposal thereof' (Article 1, paragraph 4.2.3).

[59] Beckman [40].

[60] Raha and Raju [41].

The State parties to UNCLOS enjoy the freedom of laying and the protection of cables beyond and adjacent to the territorial waters.[61] UNCLOS relies on coastal States' discretion on cable governance within the territorial waters where the latter enjoy sovereignty.

Article 58 of UNCLOS deals with exclusive economic zones (EEZ), which recognize States' right to enjoy the freedom to lay submarine cables and other internationally lawful use of the sea and freedom of the high Seas within EEZ. Article 87 defines the freedom of high Seas and entitles the States to lay cables beyond EEZ. Article 112 recognizes States' rights of cable operators in the 'high seas and the Area.'

The States also have rights to lay cables on the continental shelves under Article 79 of the UNCLOS, known as continental shelves regimes. These States also should exercise these rights due to the rights and entitlements of other States, which have specific rights and jurisdictions in the EEZ and continental shelves, where they enjoy sovereign rights. The following paragraphs attempt to illustrate the challenges of the present and prospective submarine governance in the respective marine zones.

The submarine cable operation in both EEZ and continental shelves is subject to coastal States' legal, regulatory, and conservation measures. For instance, cable operators incur a 'fee' for laying cables in the EEZ of Malta; and permits are necessary for laying cables in the EEZ of both India and China.[62]

These are few examples of the creeping jurisdiction of coastal States' extended authority over their marine spaces. The definitions of the terms like 'reasonable measures' and 'internationally lawful use of sea' are not consistent, generating claims and counterclaims among States.[63] In short, these restrictions are causing an unnecessary delay in the laying of submarine cable and its operations within EEZ and continental shelves.

Submarine cable operations within the national jurisdictions require to must meet various regulatory measures such as approvals from authorities, including defense, coast guards, shipping, fisheries, customs, environment, etc. Environment Impact Assessments (EIA), conservation zones, etc., also added burdensome requirements

---

[61] Art 58 of UNCLOS 1982 provides 'Rights and duties of other States in the exclusive economic zone

1. In the exclusive economic zone, all States, whether coastal or land-locked, enjoy, subject to the relevant provisions of this Convention, the freedoms referred to in article 87 of navigation and overflight and of the laying of submarine cables and pipelines, and other internationally lawful uses of the sea related to these freedoms, such as those associated with the operation of ships, aircraft and submarine cables and pipelines, and compatible with the other provisions of this Convention.

2. Articles 88–115 and other pertinent rules of international law apply to the exclusive economic zone in so far as they are not incompatible with this Part.

3. In exercising their rights and performing their duties under this Convention in the exclusive economic zone, States shall have due regard to the rights and duties of the coastal State and shall comply with the laws and regulations adopted by the coastal State in accordance with the provisions of this Convention and other rules of international law in so far as they are not incompatible with this Part.'

[62] Davenport [4].

[63] Beckman [3].

to the process for laying cables. The lack of clarity in such an approach and relevant guidelines or instructions also becomes additional difficulties to the cable operations.

The cable operators need to send cable ships to cable damage for immediate repairing and re-establish the communications. It requires quick approval for the cable ship to proceed toward the spot of damage to repair and restore operations. The lengthy approval process generally causes a delay in cable repairing and slows down of communication speed.

The existing legal and regulatory measures, however, have little incentive for the protection of submarine cables. The coastal States are under obligation to adopt provisions for protecting the submarine cables, to protecting the submarine cables, criminalizing the culpable act of causing damage to the cable, and prescribing appropriate liability on the convict. A State may exercise such jurisdictions on its citizens and/flag vessels. Indeed, much depends on the coastal State law. In the absence of adequate law prescribing appropriate liability against cable, the damage increases its susceptibility, and no illegality is ascribed in case of breakage or injury to cable. The reviewing and developing submarine cable regimes also depend on the regulatory authorities of the coastal State.

The submarine cable regime also remains a neglected area of concern for international organizations. UN bodies on the law of the sea hardly have any dedicated authority to deal with submarine issues in their regular agendas.

However, in recent times, few developments show that few international organizations, including the UN, are interested in submarine cable regimes.[64] Besides, international non-governmental bodies like International Cable Protection Committee (ICPC), Asia-Pacific Economic Cooperation (APEC), and few academic institutions and other institutes are engaged in research work relating to submarine cables.[65]

Regarding national regimes on submarine cables, an illustration may help underscore the degree of complexities that the cable operators face to lay cables in the seabed within the national jurisdictions. The cable carriers must take permission from several Indian authorities before laying cables within Indian maritime zones. The same applies to a cable repair ship. In both pre-cable repair and post-repair operations, it is necessary to obtain permission from various Indian authorities.

National security is the paramount concern of any country; it may be the reason behind such a cumbersome and lengthy procedure to obtain permission in India. In many States, several authorities and government departments together deal with the submarine cables operations. These government departments on communications focus on technical standards and standardization of networks but the issues of the development of submarine cable legal regimes. Whatever so maybe the reason, inadequacy, lack of transparency, and complexities are the distinctive features in most domestic cable regimes in most jurisdictions except in Australia and New Zealand.

Australia and New Zealand have adopted specific laws to deal with issues relating to submarine cables. The Protection of Submarine Cables and Pipelines Act 1996 of New Zealand prohibits activities in the protected areas assigned for cable protection,

[64] G. A. Res. 65/37, *Supra* note 48.

[65] Davenport [4].

and it prescribes liability for acts of cable damage. It also provides a detailed procedure for the enforcement of the same. The Submarine Cables and Pipeline Protection Act 1963 and Schedule 3A of the Telecommunication Act 1997 regulate submarine cables in Australian waters. The Australian Communication and Media Authority Act 2005 establishes the Australian Communication and Media Authority (ACMA) mandate to declare protection zones for submarine cables of national significance and grant permits to install submarine cables in Australian waters. Both of these legislations prescribe provisions for penalties and enforcement too.

1.4 Primary Problem with the Submarine Cable System

The global economy and security are increasingly interdependent on telecommunication. The submarine cable system must be supported by a better cable regime to ensure its safety and resiliency, which is inevitable for telecommunication transmissions. The problem underpinning the laying of cable is that the legal and institutional mechanism for its protection is weak and inadequate.

In many States, the legal instrument on submarine cables suffers from inadequacy, ambiguities, and arguably going against international law. Most of the issues and challenges related to cables occur within States' national jurisdictions, notably within territorial waters. However, most countries do not have specific and clear legal measures for laying and protecting cables. Thereby cables' susceptibility to damage and injury continues. Within national jurisdictions, the cable operators have to meet additional requirements, including measures relating to the environment, permit, shipping, and local crew, which hamper urgent cable repair operations. This permission process delays cable installations and operations, and it appears to be a significant source for prospective disputes. Most of the countries' national legislation does not address accidental and intentional damage to cables. Therefore, the absence of clear legal measures on submarine cables at the domestic level appears to impede the cable operator and a free telecommunication flow.

1.5 Literature Review Revealing the Protection and Regulation Challenges of the Submarine Cable System

In the early twentieth century, Higgins emphasized the significant prospect of the submarine cables and acknowledged international law's principle—'*submarine cables of neutrals are inviolable*'.[66] Since then, the importance of cables continued. While discussing the importance of the international rule of law, Oxman noted that all agendas such as reducing terrorism, poverty, unemployment, promotion of

[66]Higgins [42].

trade, transportation, education, and much more depend on strengthening the rule of law concerning international communications, including submarine cable communication.[67] There is a detailed study representing the idea of the submarine cable infrastructure. How cables are laid, repaired, and maintaining and cables use.

Most importantly, Douglas Burnett, Tara Davenport, and Robert Beckman have introduced the submarine cables system in detail.[68] Starosielski has also given an overview of the cable system.[69] Jenette has given an idea about the countries that dominate the internet.[70] Daniel has explained that the cable system has been instrumental to States' economic and political achievements.[71]

Moreover, Oxman has also noted that the submarine cable operation is subjected to the traditional challenges of ocean use, i.e., a conflict between 'exclusive use' and 'inclusive use'.[72] Then, J. Ashley Roach states that the freedom of laying submarine cables on the high sea is a century-old principle.[73] Beckman indicated the potential consequences of significant submarine cable damage on the global economy and security. According to him, the cable system protection from various marine activities such as fishing, shipping, and theft is a significant concern to the cable operators.[74] Warthall clearly warned that a substantial gap in law for cables was increasingly enhancing cables' vulnerability. The author dealt with the issue in detail. He elaborated on the reasons for cable damage such as opacity of the submarine environment and stealth avoiding detection and prosecution, use of unarmed undersea vehicles (UUV), lack of domestic legislation for cable injury, physical structure away from public notice, and the inapplicability of law on piracy and terrorism.[75] However, another recent study suggests that nations could also leverage these UUV to protect their submarine cable infrastructure.[76]

Backman has explicitly stated that submarine cable regulation in the EEZ is a gray area in the law of the sea. He has identified the ambiguities in existing legal regimes, especially in UNCLOS, by saying that in the EEZ, cable operators' freedom of laying cable is subject to coastal States' reasonable measures.[77] The scope of the 'reasonable measures' is not clear. Few coastal States are increasingly regulating submarine cable operation in the manner as against the freedom to lay and repair submarine cables. This author argues that such regulations are inconsistent with the UNCLOS.[78] The measures adopted by coastal States increasingly restrict cable

67 Oxman [43].

68 Burnett et al. [1].

69 Starosielski [2].

70 Ruiz and Barnett [44].

71 Headrick and Griset [45].

72 Oxman [43].

73 Roach [39].

74 Beckman [3].

75 Wrathall [29].

76 Clark [5].

77 Beckman [40].

78 Beckman and Davenport [46].

operation in EEZ. To Mudric, an important question is what comprises 'reasonable measures'?[79] Davenport continued to explain the issue and stated that coastal States' measures like permit, the environmental law as the case may be, restricting other States' freedom, and 'lawful use of sea' in EEZ might not be reasonable the opinion of those subjected.[80] He also raised concern for cable regulation in the high seas. His work revealed a lack of coordination between cable operators and the International Seabed Authority (ISA) in cable protection in the high seas. Recent works deal with the interactions between cables and marine biodiversity in the area beyond the national jurisdictions in detail.[81] Further, Logchem has emphasized the issues of submarine cable regulations in the disputed areas.[82]

Burnett compared the provisions for cables provided by three instruments, namely the 1884 Cable Convention, UNCLOS, and COLREGS. He found that the old Cable Convention provisions were more focused and provided detailed implementation procedures for cable damage.[83] He identified that besides law on piracy and terrorist activities on cable, the Cable Convention's provisions providing a detailed procedure for cable protection could be adopted.

Kordahi has shown that the majority of the cable faults occurred within the national jurisdictions.[84] Other studies have also held that cables close to shore are becoming more vulnerable. Various authors also argued for coastal States' extended penal jurisdiction. Takei highlights the littoral States' jurisdiction over the offense of cable breaks. He explicitly explained for coastal States' authority that is more extensive over the offenders (cable break) irrespective of his nationality (quasi-universal jurisdiction) and promoting zonal management approaches through by revision of existing Convention or adopting a new one. Further, he highlighted the need for different cable use laws, given the optical fiber cable used for the Internet needs more protection. After analyzing the legal regime for submarine cable beyond the territorial waters, the author further highlighted that a victim State, suffered from cable fault, could not initiate a legal course against the offender who was not subjected to its jurisdiction.[85]

Most importantly, a need to improve the existing cable regime or new legal standards and preventive measures for submarine cables has become a common argument in the available literature. Wagner highlighted the need for adequate international cable protection policies and stringent domestic laws complying with relevant provisions of the UNCLOS to improve a degree of cable protection.[86] Keye argued for creating prohibited areas for anchoring to protect cables and extended jurisdiction

---

[79]Mudric [47].

[80]Davenport [4].

[81]Burnett and Carter [48]. See Friedman [49]. See also Davenport [50].

[82]Logchem [51].

[83]Burnett [35].

[84]Kordahi [15].

[85]Takei [17].

[86]Wagner [18].

with the coastal States.[87] Both Soons[88] and Beckman emphasized a new Convention or an additional protocol to the SUA Convention. For Beckman, this is to treat 'the willful and intentional destruction or damage of submarine telecommunications cables or its infrastructure' as an internationally punishable crime.[89] Beckman argued for an amendment in piracy provisions and adopting a new Undersea Infrastructure Protocol (SUA). Coffen-Smout and Herbert, in particular, highlighted the need for more effective domestic laws for cable operation and its protection.[90]

There is no dedicated international lead agency for submarine cables. Dusan has explored to bring reform in ITU.[91] There is an argument that submarine cable governance may be improved under the umbrella of lead agencies at both the global and national levels. According to Takei, efforts for the improvement of existing submarine cable regime may be initiated through the organizations like the IMO (possessing competence to conduct global initiative for ocean governance), the UNGA through the UNDOALOS (extended review of existing laws and policies), the ISA (monitoring and information sharing with ICPC), and the regional bodies like APEC.[92] Some authors also argued for the nodal agency at the national level to ensure effective cable governance.

The book edited by Douglas Burnett, Tara Davenport, and Robert Beckman presents various submarine cable governance issues.[93] The book explains the growth, importance, and legal and policy challenges of the modern world's submarine cable system. First, it describes the cable industry's infrastructural development and network, submarine cables' importance to the global economy and security, and legal challenges to the cable operator. Then, it provides an overview and legal analysis of the international legal regime regulating underwater communication cable networks.

In this book, the authors have highlighted that the existing legal regime is not sufficient for present-day cable operation and argues for a comprehensive cable protection regime. The discussion continues with the cable operators' specific issues such as the cable route survey, laying of cable, and repair and maintenance of the damaged cables. This part reflects legal ambiguities and challenges relating to the law and practices involved with the cable operator. According to the authors, such legal gaps have become the source of future conflicts. The authors argue for common international and national laws for cable operation and protection of submarine cables from both natural and anthropogenic causes. Besides, these underwater cables are used for other purposes. Such as carrying electricity, military information, and facilitating offshore platform and renewable energy (wind)-related activities and those issues have been dealt with in the last section of the book, which comprises the

[87] Kaye [34].

[88] Soons [52].

[89] Beckman [53].

[90] Coffen-Smout and Herbert [54].

[91] Schuster [55].

[92] Takei [17].

[93] Burnett et al. [1].

essential incidents covering the growth of the submarine cable industry and the relevant excerpts of treaty provisions on cables. There are also studies dealing with the emerging use of 'green cables' in collecting marine data and related legal challenges concerning the permission for such a data procurement process and its ownership. While dealing with the 'green cables', Agarwala has emphasized achieving clarity about the ownership of the data obtained from marine scientific research in an area beyond the national jurisdictions.[94]

The necessity for an effective submarine cable regime is increasingly getting priority in international and regional meetings. The UNGA called upon States to protect fiber optic submarine cables following international law and mutual dialogue and for cooperation among States and the relevant regional and global organizations.[95] Similarly, the APEC Ministerial Meeting 2010 acknowledged the need for continued efforts to enhance submarine cables' protection. Further, the ROGUCCI Report, in giving priority to timely cable repair, appeals to nation-States for standard cable policies.[96]

From the Indian perspective, Rapp, Gady, Singh, and Rauscher stated that secure submarine cable infrastructure is vital to India's national security and India's ability to emerge as one of the world's few cyber superpowers.[97] However, India's approval process for cable repair operation is complicated. In India, cable repair ships require approval from seven authorities before the cable repair operation. The authors note that such a lengthy process is due to India's concern for national interests and security. According to the authors, the Indian government has recognized the criticality of a reliable undersea cable network to the Indian economy and security. It is considering the adoption of guidelines to improve the cumbersome process. The article focuses on the process of framing such guidelines. According to the authors, such an approach must address vital interests, including national security, immigration, customs, economics, and safety and environmental concerns. Further, according to these authors, India's maritime strategy must include the new priority for undersea cables' protection and care. After considering ICPC's suggestions for timely repair, the authors argue for pre-approval and lead the agency to improve the Indian approval process.

Anjali Sugadev also noted that India is located in a strategically and geographically significant position in the international cable map. However, India's critical role in a stable submarine cable system is not supported by its complex cable regulatory system that causes delayed approval for cable repairing. The article analyzes India's cable regime in the context of UNCLOS. India's cable repair regulatory regime comprises the MZI Act, guidelines, and notifications. However, according to the

[94]Agarwala [26].

[95]G.A. Res. 65/37.

[96]Rauscher [56].

Recommendation 2 'Nation-State governments should implement policies and procedures to provide timely approval to authorized cable ships seeking permission to repair damaged undersea communications cables.' *Ibid., at* 105.

[97]Rapp et al. [57].

author, India's cable repair regime, especially for EEZ, is arguably not in line with the UNCLOS provisions. The article represents India's approval process for cable repair in detail concerning the respective authorities involved therein. While dealing with the cable repair process, the author identified inconsistencies between India's practice and international standards. Likewise, a study by ICPC shows that India takes 50 days (average) for permission for repair, which is against the average international practice. Considering some standard cable repair processes in other jurisdictions, the study argues that India needs a specific set of rules for submarine cables, consistent with the international standards.[98]

1.6 Objectives of the Study

The challenges of the submarine cable operation and its protection are lingering for many years. However, the current literature review reveals a dearth of literature that deals with the fundamental principles of the law of the sea governing submarine cables. The available minimum literature on the law regulating submarine cables highlights the international aspect of the issue. There are not many literature sources that focus on the comparative study of national submarine cable regimes. Most of the authors argue for the dedicated national instrument to deal with the laying and protection of submarine cables within the national jurisdictions. Presently, there is no model legal framework for submarine cables available. Therefore, this study sought to address the following:

1. To analyze critical principles and instruments of international law of the sea relating to submarine cable operation and protection;
2. To identify commonalities and gaps in the legal instruments on cables in selected jurisdictions;
3. To undertake a comparative study between the dedicated laws and regulations on Australia and New Zealand submarine cables;
4. To suggest a model legal framework for cable operation and its protection.

1.7 Research Methodology

A doctrinal method is used to inquire into legal principles, doctrines, rules, and other measures governing cables to ascertain consistency, coherence, efficiency, and stability in the submarine cable regime. A comparative and analytical research method has been adopted to analyze the available legal premises on cables to evaluate the existing legal standards. These cable regimes' essential parameters will be the basis for developing a model legal framework for national instruments on cable.

[98] Sugadev [14].

The first research question has been probed through an analytical method of research. It deals with the broader principles of the law of the sea concerning submarine cables and relevant provisions set out in UNCLOS, 1982. Other international instruments on submarine cables have also been examined for this purpose. Thus, it provides the fundamental parameters of the international regime on submarine cables. The following two consecutive research questions are devoted to national instruments, arrangements, and specific cable legislation.

States' responses in the enforcement of their international obligations on cables vary from jurisdictions to jurisdictions. Many States for cable governances offer notification, regulations, orders, directives, guidelines, etc. Such instruments are widely known as secondary instruments and arrangements. *These States and their cable-related secondary instruments and arrangements represent a homogeneous group. This group of countries will be regarded as other jurisdictions/selected jurisdictions for this study.* However, Australia and New Zealand have enacted *dedicated legislation* that comprehensively deals with cables—*forming a distinct cable regime*. Thus, the national laws on submarine cables represent two categories of cable regimes.

The second research question focuses on cable regimes of selected jurisdictions/*other jurisdictions*. It follows both representative and advanced legal systems criteria in choosing these jurisdictions. It explores several cable-related instruments and undertakes a comparative analysis of the measures in those instruments. It intends to identify the basic parameters of these instruments.

The third research question of the study carries out a comparative analysis of the *dedicated submarine* cable regimes in Australia and New Zealand.

The present study is adopted with anticipation to ascertain the essential provisions of these cable-related secondary instruments and dedicated legislations. These provisions may provide crucial guidance in developing a draft model framework for national instruments on submarine cables.

The final research question will follow the synthesis of all the methods mentioned above to develop a model legal framework for national instruments on submarine cables. The manuscript follows the citation style as set out in Blue Book (19th eds.).

1.8 The Scope of the Study

The study primarily deals with the legal aspect of the submarine cable operation and the submarine cable system's security. The work does not include private law aspects (such as contract, insurance, prices) relating to the submarine cables.

1.9 Chapterization

Chapter 2 of this study deals with the analysis of the principles of the law of the sea and specific provisions of the international law on laying and the protection of submarine cables to highlight relevant rights and corresponding obligations of the State parties as set out under these laws. It intends to identify and underscore the ambiguities in the current international submarine cable regimes, which remained rudimentary to cope with the present challenges to the cable operation and ignored by the international institutions.

Chapter 3 focuses on the other submarine cable regimes in the selected jurisdictions (chosen across the continents and discussed in detail). It outlines these legal and regulatory measures and will point out that these regimes are creating a barrier to the laying of cables and creating a barrier to the laying of cables and patently inadequate for the protection of cables within the national jurisdictions.

Chapter 4 deals with the dedicated national legislation on submarine cables of Australia and New Zealand, respectively. A comparative analysis of these national legislation outlines how these States have been complying and responding to their international obligations and have become a pioneer in suggesting submarine cable regimes—an example for other countries.

Chapter 5 aims to provide a suggestive legal framework in implementing the law for cables within the national maritime jurisdictions. It seeks to frame a model legal framework, which could address concerns associated with submarine cables' safety and reliability, maybe a ready reference to the States in strengthening their submarine cable regimes.

References

1. Burnett, D., Davenport, T., & Beckman, R. (2013). Overview of the international legal regime governing submarine cables. In D. Burnett Douglas (Ed.), *Submarine cables: The handbook of law and policy* (pp. 6–90). Martinus Nijhoff Publication.
2. Starosielski, N. (2015). Introduction. In N. Starosielski (Ed.), *The undersea network* (pp. 1–25). Duke University Press.
3. Beckman, R. (2010). Submarine cables—A critically important but neglected area of the law of the sea. 7th International Conference on Legal Regimes of Sea, Air, Space and Antarctica (ISIL Conference), New Delhi. https://cil.nus.edu.sg/wp/wp-content/uploads/2010/01/Beckman-PDF-ISIL-Submarine-Cables-rev-8-Jan-10.pdf. Accessed 7 January 2017.
4. Davenport, T. (2012). Submarine communications cables and law of the sea: Problems in law and practice. *Ocean Development & International Law, 43,* 201–242.
5. Clark, B. (2016). Undersea cables and the future of submarine competition. *Bulletin of the Atomic Scientists, 74,* 234–237.
6. Agarwala, N. (2018). "Green cables"—Development, opportunities and legal challenges: Part I. *Maritime Affairs: Journal of the National Maritime Foundation of India, 14,* 49–62.
7. Pope, E., et al. (2017). Which earthquake triggers damaging submarine mass movements: Insights from the global submarine cable breaks? *Marine Geology, 384,* 131–146.
8. Carter, L., & Burnett, D. (2015). Subsea Telecommunication. In *Routledge handbook of ocean resources and management* (pp. 349–365). Routledge.
9. Sunak, R. (2017). Undersea cables-indispensable, insecure. Policy Exchange. https://policyexchange.org.uk/publication/undersea-cables-indispensable-insecure/. Accessed 14 November 2019.

10. Ross, M. (2014). Understanding interconnectivity of the global undersea cable communications infrastructure and its implications for international cyber security. *SAIS Review of International Affairs, 34,* 141–155.
11. Qiu, W. (2011, March 19). Submarine cables cut after Taiwan earthquake in Dec 2006. *Cable Networks.* https://www.submarinenetworks.com/news/cables-cut-after-taiwan-earthquake-2006. Accessed 12 December 2019.
12. Staff Reporter. (2017, June 8). Cable theft coasts Vietnam $6M, Ho Chi Minh City, Vietnam. *Photonics Media.* https://www.photonics.com/Articles/Cable_Theft_Costs_Vietnam_6M/a29904. Accessed 12 December 2019.
13. Singel, R. (2008, January 31). Fiber optic cable cuts isolate millions from internet, future cuts likely. *WIRED.* https://www.wired.com/2008/01/fiber-optic-cab/. Accessed 11 October 2017.
14. Sugadev, A. (2016). India's critical position in the global submarine cable network: An analysis of Indian law and practice on cable repairs. *Indian Journal of International Law, 56,* 173–200.
15. Kordahi, M. E. (2016). Global trends in submarine cable system faults. *Emerging Subsea Networks. SubOptic,* 1–7.
16. Introduction, Submarine Cable Information Sharing Project: Legislative Practices and Points of Contact September 2011, Telecommunications and Information Working Group, 2012 APEC Secretariat.
17. Takie, Y. (2012). Law and policy for international submarines cables: An Asia-Pacific perspective. *Asian Journal of International Law, 2,* 205–233.
18. Wagner, E. (1995). Submarine cables and protections provided by the law of the sea. *Marine Policy, 19,* 127–136.
19. Raha, U. K., & Raju, K. D. (2017). The Enrica Lexie case at the permanent court of arbitration: An analysis. *Indian Journal of International Law, 56,* 221–238.
20. Kroon, D. (2018). Due regard in the high seas: The tension between submarine cables and deep seabed mining. *Australian International Law Journal, 24,* 35–57.
21. Carter L., Burnett D., Drew S., Marle G., Hagadorn L., Bartlett-McNeil D., & Irvine N. (2009). Submarine cables and the oceans—Connecting the world. UNEP-WCMC Biodiversity Series No. 31. ICPC/UNEP/UNEP-WCMC.
22. Davenport, T. (2013). The installation of submarine power cables under UNCLOS: Legal and policy issues. *German Yearbook of International Law, 56,* 107–148.
23. Davenport, T. (2013). Submarine communications cables and science: A new frontier in ocean governance? In H. N. Scheiber (Ed.), *Science technology, and new challenges to ocean law* (pp. 209–252). A Law of the Sea Institute Publication.
24. Malecki, E. J., & Wei, H. (2009). A wired world: The evolving geography of submarine cables and the shift to Asia. *Annals of the Association of American Geographers, 99,* 360–382.
25. Waltz, E. *Offshore wind may power the future.* https://www.scientificamerican.com/article/offshore-wind-may-power-the-future/. Accessed 21 February 2017.
26. Agarwala, N. (2019). "Green cables"–Development, opportunities and legal challenges: Part II. *Maritime Affairs: Journal of the National Maritime Foundation of India, 15,* 93–107.
27. Myron H. Nordquist (Eds.). (2014). UN convention on the law of the sea commentary 1982 Online. Center for Oceans Law and Policy, University of Virginia.
28. Report of the International Law Commission covering the work of its eighth session (A/3159), article 27 Commentary, para. (4), II YB ILC 1956, *at* 253, 278.
29. Wrathall, L. R. (2011). *The vulnerability of subsea infrastructure to underwater attack: Legal shortcomings and the way forward, 12,* 224–257.
30. Greenleaf, J., & Amos, J. (2013). *A new naval era.* U.S. Naval Institute Proceedings.
31. U.N. GAOR, 65th Sess., 59th plen. mtg. at 4, U.N. Doc. A/65/PV.59 (Dec. 7, 2010). Economic Impact of Submarine Cable Disruptions. 2012. 42.
32. G.A. Res. 65/37, 121 (December 7, 2010).
33. Tanaka, Y. (2012). *The international law of the sea.* Cambridge University Press.
34. Keye, S. (2007). International measures to protect oil platforms. *Pipelines, and Submarine Cables from Attack, Tulane Maritime Law Journal, 31,* 377–423.

35. Burnett, D. (2011). *The 1884 international convention for protection of submarine cables provisions not in UNCLOS deserve attention now*. http://cil.nus.edu.sg/wp/wp-content/uploads/2011/04/Douglas-Burnett_1884_International_Convention_for_Protection_of_Submarine_Cables_Provisions_Not_in_UNCLOS_De1.pdf. Accessed 15 February 2017.
36. Continental Shelf Convention. (1958). Convention on the Continental Shelf, 29 Apr 1958, 499 UNTS (1964).
37. High Seas Convention. (1858). Convention on the High Seas, 29 Apr 1958, 450 UNTS (1963).
38. UNCLOS. (1982). The United Nations Convention on the Law of the Sea December 10, 1982, 1833 UNTS 3.
39. Roach, J. A. (2014). Today's customary international law of the sea. *Ocean Development & International Law, 45*, 239–259.
40. Beckman, R. (2010b). 1982 UNCLOS: A legal framework for cooperation between cable companies and coastal States, *International Cable Protection Committee (ICPC) Plenary Meeting*, Mauritius.
41. Raha, U. K., & Raju, K. D. (2019). Critical telecommunication cable infrastructure under the law of the sea convention (UNCLOS 1982). *National Capital Law Journal, 17*, 65–75.
42. Higgins, A. P. (1921–1922). Submarine cables and international law. *British Year Book of International Law, 2*, 27–33.
43. Oxman, B. H. (1996). The rule of law and the United Nations Convention on the Law of the sea. *Europian Journal of International Law, 7*, 353–371.
44. Ruiz, J. B., & Barnett, G. A. (2015). Who owns the international internet networks? *The Journal of International Communication, 21*, 38–57.
45. Headrick, D. R., & Griset, P. (2001). Submarine telegraph cables: Business and politics, 1838–1939. *The Business History Review, 75*, 543–578.
46. Beckman, R., & Davenport, T. (2012). *The EEZ regime: Reflections after 30 years, securing the ocean for the next generation*. LOSI Conference Papers, pp.1–41. https://www.law.berkeley.edu/files/Beckman-Davenport-final.pdf. Accessed 22 May 2017.
47. Mudric, M. (2010). Rights of states regarding underwater cables and pipelines. *Australian Resources and Energy Law Journal, 29*, 235–255.
48. Burnett, R., & Carter, L. (2017). International submarine cables and biodiversity of areas beyond national jurisdiction—The cloud beneath the sea. *Brill Research Perspectives in the Law of the Sea, 1*, 1–75.
49. Friedman, A. (2017). Submarine telecommunication cables and a biodiversity agreement in ABNJ: Finding new routes for cooperation. *The International Journal of Marine and Coastal Law, 32*, 1–35.
50. Davenport, T. (2018). The high seas freedom to lay submarine cables and the protection of the marine environment: challenges in high seas governance. *Symposium on Governing High Seas Biodiversity, American Journal of International Law Unbound, 112*, 139–143.
51. Logchem, Y. V. (2014). Submarine telecommunication cables in disputed maritime areas. *Ocean Development and International Law, 45*, 107–122.
52. Soons, A. (2009). Criminal jurisdiction over persons damaging submarine cables. *CIL Workshop on Submarine Cables and the Law of the Sea.*
53. Beckman, R. (2009). A new international convention or a protocol. *CIL Workshop on Submarine Cables and the Law of the Sea.*
54. Coffen-Smout, S., & Herbert, G. J. (2000). Submarine cables: A challenge for ocean management. *Marine Policy, 24*, 441–448.
55. Schuster, D. B. (2015, June). International telecommunication union—150 years of history: Adaptation to change and the opportunity for reform. *IEEE Communications Magazine—Communications Standards Supplement*.
56. Rauscher, K. F. (2010). Reliability of Global Undersea Communications Cable Infrastructure (ROGUCCI) (The Report, Issue I). www.ieee-rogucci.org. Accessed 21 March 2017.
57. Rapp, R. J., Gady, F. S., Parmar, S. S., & Rauscher, K. F. (2012). India's critical role in the reliance of the global undersea communications cable infrastructure. *Strategic Analysis, 36*, 375–383.

Chapter 2
Submarine Cables: Key Principles and International Law of the Sea

2.1 Background

> "In 1854, a letter to the Secretary of the Navy, Lieutenant Matthew Fontaine Maury commented on the feasibility of a telegraph cable between Newfoundland and Ireland. He said, 'insofar as the bottom of the sea is concerned, it can be done.' He followed, however, with 'I feel that the greatest difficulties will not be in the deep sea but after reaching the shallows at either end of the line.' A pioneer oceanographer of his time, Lieutenant Maury's statement was truly prophetic. Since the first transoceanic cables were laid, the primary cause of their failure has been physical damage, primarily resulting from conflicting uses of the relatively shallow continental shelves ' … at either end of the line'."[1]

Before this transatlantic telegraph cable between Newfoundland and Ireland, an incident where a fisherman cut the first submarine cable laid across the English Channel between Dover and Calais in 1850 had informed about the protection of this cable.[2] The laying of telegraph cables on the ocean's seabed had its initial challenges unique of its kind.[3] Despite its problems, there is a dramatic growth in the submarine cables industry in the following hundred years.[4] Today, most parts of the globe are connected by submarine cables.[5] This chapter evaluates the role of the current international regime in facilitating and bringing stability to this submarine cable system.

Submarine cables traverse different marine zones to connect continents, regions, and countries. Thus, submarine cable-related activities become subjects of multiple jurisdictions and to adjust with other competing marine activities. The laying of cables is a marine activity and other marine interests and activities, including fishing, shipping, exploration, and exploitation of marine resources. The submarine cable operations are exposed to potential conflicts posed by the said competing for marine

---

[1] Wagner [1].

[2] Huurdeman [2].

[3] Chandler [3].

[4] Malecki and Wei [4].

[5] Carter et al. [5].

U. K. Raha and Raju K. D., *Submarine Cables Protection and Regulations*,
https://doi.org/10.1007/978-981-16-3436-9_2

activities. Conflicting national interests, the cable system's critical nature, etc., are mounting a continuous challenge to laying and protecting cables. The Law of the Sea—a legal order of the maritime spaces and domestic laws—seeks to regulate and accommodate all marine activities to facilitate cable operation.

The international submarine cable regime comprises the Cable Convention 1884 and the Law of the Sea Conventions besides regulations that deal with signal and maintenance of minimum distance between vessels.[6] In reality, the current international regime on submarine cable is set out in the United Nations Convention on the Law of the Sea, 1982 (UNCLOS).[7] The submarine cable regime in UNCLOS is to meet both recent and potential challenges of the law of the sea. Such as the competing and conflicting national interests concerning laying and protection of the cable system. Therefore, the current cable regime meets the existing and emerging challenges.[8] Therefore, it is pertinent to undertake an inquiry into this submarine cable regime given highlighting whether it is adequate to ensure stability in the cable system.

In line with its first objective, the current research intends to analyze the fundamental principles and instruments of international law on laying and protecting submarine cables. It discusses and answers the research question, i.e., what is the prevailing submarine cable regime as set out in the UNCLOS, 1982, and other arrangements dealing with issues relating to cable operation and protection? With a brief discussion on the development, significance, and challenges to the modern submarine cable infrastructure, this chapter will focus on *first* the analysis of the fundamental principles of international law and the relevant legal provisions on submarine cables and *second* the issues of adequacy of the current submarine cable regime. This research aims to ascertain appropriate international regimes' sources on submarine cables and identify its fundamental principles and parameters. It will help in the development of a model legal framework for national instruments on submarine cables.

2.2 Growth, Importance, and Challenges to the Submarine Cable Infrastructure

In 1866, it was the first occasion when transatlantic telegraphic cables established a link between Ireland and Newfoundland.[9] During the British regime, Calcutta, Bombay, and Madras were important presidencies of India. In 1869, London was connected with Bombay,[10]Madras, and Calcutta was connected with London in

[6]Burnett, et al. [6].

[7]Burnett, et al. [6].

[8]Agarwala [7].

[9]Hayes [8].

[10]Huurdeman [2].

1870.[11] The best part of the nineteenth century British had dominated the cable industry and contributed to the exponential expansion of undersea communication networks.[12] Later, many other companies from America, French, Germany, etc., had joined the competition in laying cables.[13]

In the 1920s, usually, 200 words could have been transmitted in a minute.[14] Speedy communication immensely helped the intercontinental trade and security interests, and thus, underwater cable infrastructure continued to progress.[15] In the 1930s–1960s, other means of quick communication systems like radio and telephone got priority.[16] In particular, the satellite becomes more suitable than submarine cables.[17] However, the development of fiber optic cables in the 1980s, and the Internet system in the 1990s, heralded a new era in the global telecommunication system.[18] Among countries, America owns 39 percent of the international Internet traffic backbone, followed by Sweden (16 percent), China 10 and Japan (10 percent each), and Italy and India (7 percent each).[19] It indicates geopolitical and economic significance too.[20] The advancement of the modern telecommunication system is ever-growing.[21]

The General Assembly Resolution reminded the world community that the optical submarine cables transmitted most of the world's data and communications.[22] It declared the importance of cables to the global economy and all States' national security and its vulnerability to willful or accidental damage. It further appreciated various research works and workshops urging the coastal States to adopt laws to protect undersea cable systems. The United Nations General Assembly (UNGA) ultimately recognized the subsea cable system as 'critical communication infrastructure' and as vitally important to the global economy and all States' national security. The effort to recognize the importance of submarine cable could also be noticed when the Asia-Pacific Economic Cooperation (APEC) Ministerial Meeting

---

[11]The Indo-European Telegraph Company [9].

[12]Headrick and Griset [10].

[13]Headrick and Griset [10].

[14]Submarine cable was laid in 1902. Again first underwater telephone cable service connected San Francisco and Oakland in 1884. The following years with the developing technologies and efforts, transatlantic telephone cable in 1956 and fiber optic cables in 1988 were placed in service.

[15]"…cables should be regarded as international utility agencies because their linking up with land telegraphs gives them an infinite radius of action." See Higgins [11].

[16]Headrick and Griset [10]. See also Carter [5].

[17]J. Crispin et al. [12].

[18]Ash, *The Development of Submarine Cables, in* Burnett et al. [6].

[19]Ruiz and Barnett [13].

[20]Winseck [14].

[21]Winseck [14]. Douglas R. Burnett et al. [6]. Also two distinct technological convergences have caused the proliferation of fiber optic cables: (1) the blurring of a point to point communication and broadcasting; and (2) the convergence of telecommunications, computing, and entertainment into a common digital form. See Wrathall [15].

[22]G.A. Res. 65/37 [16].

2010 stated: 'International submarine cables are an essential enabler for regional economic integration.'[23]

2.3 Laying and Protection of Submarine Cable—Requirement of Regulation on Marine Affairs

Concern for laying and protecting submarine cables from other marine activities has been continuing since the beginning of the subsea communication design.[24] As this critical infrastructure's economic significance grows, the motivation to hold it has also become risky.[25]

2.4 Fundamental Principles and International Instruments on Submarine Cables

The international submarine cable regime comprises the principles of the law of the sea, international agreements, and other arrangements. The scheme of the law of the sea is developed under three principles, *among other things*, freedom of the sea, territorial sovereignty, and the common heritage of mankind. Among codified laws, there is the Cable Convention 1884, Law of Sea Conventions (three Conventions of the law of the sea, UNCLOS 1958, 1960, and 1982), along with the Regulations for Preventing of Collision at Sea, 1972 (COLREGS) and the Protocol to the 1972 Convention on the Prevention of Marine Pollution by the Wastes and other Materials, 1996.[26]

Regarding the customary international law on a submarine cable, there is a wide acceptance that UNCLOS's relevant provisions have attained the status of customary international law.[27] However, the provisions of the Cable Convention 1884 not included in UNCLOS are arguably not the customary law, given those provisions lack wide acceptance.[28]

---

[23]"Submarine Cable Information Sharing Project: Legislative Practices and Points of Contact, September 2011. Telecommunications and Information Working Group, March 2012, Asia Pacific Economic Cooperation (APEC)" [17].

[24]"I feel that the greatest difficulties will not be in the deep sea but after reaching the shallows at either end of the line." Wagner [1]. Wagner's statement turned out "prophetic".

[25]Wrathall [15].

[26]Brown [18]. The Protocol to the Convention on the Prevention of Marine Pollution by Dumping of Wastes and Other Matter 1972 (London Convention). '*Dumping* does not include abandonment in the sea of cable placed for a purpose other than the mere disposal thereof' (Article 1, paragraph 4.2.3).

[27]Roach [19].

[28]Beckman [20].

This analysis will progress according to the adopting years of the relevant Conventions. Regarding the fundamental principles, it is noted that the traditional principles of the law of the sea have been modified and set out in UNCLOS. This chapter will deal with these principles concerning the laying and protection of submarine cable accordingly.

2.5 Convention for the Protection of Telegraph Cables 1884 (the Cable Convention 1884)

British cable companies approached their government for redressal in the backdrop of the multiple incidents of telegraph cable breaks in the 1880s by the fishing vessels in the North Sea region. Thereby, the first Convention for the Protection of Telegraph Cable was adopted in 1884 (the Cable Convention).[29] It came into operation in 1888 with the ratification of 40 States (only Japan from Asia).[30] Most importantly, it imposed obligations on the breaking of telegraph cables in the high seas.

At the time of the ratification of this Convection, there was no clarity about the limit of territorial water (3 nm in some European Countries). Historically private companies engage with cable operation and enjoy the freedom of laying cable on behalf of their States.

The Cable Convention comprises seventeen Articles. Article 1 of the Convention deals the cable beyond the territorial waters.

Regarding the protection of cables, the most important provisions of the Convention are Articles 2 and 3, which deal with the civil and criminal liabilities against cable breaking.[31] Article 3 declares the responsibility of State parties granting a concession of landing submarine cables and the parties to adopt maximum effort to secure protection of cable tracks and their dimensions. And, Article 2 prescribes both criminal and civil liability for activities likely to cause interruption or obstruction to the telegraph communication. However, the erring party may avoid liability provided lifesaving effort for the crew or their ship results the cable injury. While laying cables, the cable owners' activities may cause damage to the existing cables. Therefore, Article 4 deals with the liability of such an erring cable owner.[32]

---

[29] Renault [21].

[30] Burnett, et al. [6].

[31] Article II of the Cable Convention 1884 provides.

"It is a punishable offence to break or injure a submarine cable, willfully or by culpable negligence, in such manner as might interrupt or obstruct telegraphic communication, either wholly or partially, such punishment being without prejudice to any civil action for damages.

This provision does not apply to cases where those who break or injure a cable do so with the lawful object of saving their lives or their ship after they have taken every necessary precaution to avoid so breaking or injuring the cable. & Article III—The High Contracting Parties undertake that, on granting a concession for landing a submarine cable, they will insist, so far as possible, upon proper measures of safety being taken, both as regards the track of the cable and its dimensions".

[32] Article IV of the Cable Convention provides.

The Convention also provides a supportive measure for the fishing community. It awards indemnity if the fisherman sanctifies his fishing nets and gears to avoid cable injury (Article 7).[33] In releasing fishing nets and gears which have already caught the cable, fishing vessels brake cables. Thus, this provision is an effective measure to limit cable injuries by compensating the fishermen.

Articles 8–11 of the Convention deals with its implementing procedures. The Convention recognizes the owning country of the erring vessel as a trial based on the principle of personal jurisdiction (Article 8). It prescribes the summary proceedings for the quick disposal of the offense (Article 11). It saves belligerents' freedoms and does not restrict Belligerents' rights (Article 15).

It is to note that the Cable Convention 1884 prescribes essential provisions on the protection of cables and cable ships and its detailed implementing procedures by Articles 5, 6, and 10. All of these provisions still hold good and are essential to this research too. Its features are discussed below under the heading 'Ambiguities in the International Regime on Submarine Cables and the Way Forward.'

The Cable Convention 1884 has limited application. Its mandates bind only a limited number of States and apply to submarine telegraph cables in the high seas.[34] Moreover, this Convention's implementation has been poor due to inadequate domestic laws that fail to define cable break as illegal in their respective jurisdictions.[35] There was nothing to deter fishing and other vessels from avoiding cable breaks. However, a comparative analysis (provided below) of the three Conventions' relevant provisions, namely Cable Convention 1884, Geneva Convention 1958, and COLREGS 1972,[36] UNCLOS 1982, will reveal the merit of the Cable Convention.

2.6 The League of Nations Conference for the Codification of International Law 1930 at the Hague (Hague Conference)

Scholars from a few non-governmental and academic bodies argue for the codification of international law, including the law of the sea, in the early part of the twentieth century. Since the 1920s, international conferences under the League of Nations become a powerful means for the codification of international law.[37] In this

"The owner of a cable who, on laying or repairing his cable, breaks or injures another cable, must bear the cost of repairing the breakage or injury, without prejudice to the application, if need be, of Article II of the present Convention".

[33] Article VII of the Cable Convention 1884.

[34] Kaye [22].

[35] Coffen-Smout and Herbert [23].

[36] International Regulations for Preventing Collisions at Sea to the Convention for the Regulations for Preventing Collisions at Sea 1972 which provides rules to govern among other issues the operations of ships including cable ships. These include preventive measures.

[37] See UN Documents Concerning Development and Codification of International Law [24].

regard, the League of Nations Conference for the Codification of International law 1930 at the Hague (Hague Conference) was an important initiative.[38] *First*, it recognizes the State's sovereignty over its coastal waters. Thus, the cable operation and the protection of existing cables within these waters become subject to coastal States.'[39] *Second,* the Conference also recognizes the innocent passage of the foreign vessels. Therefore, it also acknowledges the cable repairing ships' rights of innocent passage in the coastal waters.[40]

2.7 UNCLOS I—1958

After the Second World War, the Cable Convention became the basis for consideration of submarine cable regulations by the International Law Commission (ILC).[41] The ILC, after much debate, concluded that though there was a specific Convention dealing with submarine cables, it was necessary to recognize and codify the '*Freedom of laying of submarine cables.*' In this respect, it is worth quoting the following:

In 1950, the ILC first recognized the principle that all States were entitled to lay submarine cables on the high seas. When it was first discussed in the ILC at its second session, it was even commented that, since the right to lay submarine cables had never been questioned, there was no need to explicitly mention it in any convention on the topic. However, the Commission agreed that, while the principle of freedom to lay submarine cables had never been challenged, it was essential to include it in any convention on the issue.[42]

Three provisions of the Cable Convention on cable breaking were included in the Geneva Conventions on the Law of the Sea 1958.[43] Geneva Convention on the High Sea 1958 (High Sea Convention 1958) provides Articles 26–30 that deal with the issue of the submarine cables.[44]

The term 'high seas' under this High Sea Convention 1958 means all parts of the sea that are not included in the territorial sea or the internal waters of a State.[45]

---

[38]Tanaka [25].

[39]Miller [26].

[40]Kraska [27].

[41]Beckman [20].

[42]Davenport [28]. See "Report of the International Law Commission on its Second Session," Official Records of the General Assembly, Fifth Session, Supplement No. 12 (A/1316), Doc. No A/CN.4/34 (1950), at 384. See also Comments of Judge Hudson and Mr. Spiropolous, *Yearbook of the International Law Commission*, Vol. I, Doc. A/CN.4/Ser.A/1950, 199 (1950).

[43]Takie [29].

[44]High Seas Convention [30].

[45]Article 1 of the Convention. The Geneva Conference of the Law of the Sea which is also known as UNCLOS I adopted 1. The Convention on the Territorial Sea and the Contiguous Zone, 2. The Convention on the High Seas, 3. The Convention on Fishing and Conservation of the Living Resources of the High Seas, 4. The Convention on the Continental Shelf, and 5. The Optional Protocol of Signature concerning the Compulsory Settlement of Disputes.

Article 2 of the Convention declares that the high sea is open to all nations within the limit and recognizes, with other freedom of laying of the submarine cables and pipelines. The provisions, in reality, codify the age-old principle of the freedom of the high seas.

The high sea freedoms are subject to limitations, which are again to strike a balance among mutual entitlements of the high sea States. Beyond the restrictions imposed by the High Sea Convention 1958, those freedoms could also subject to the other rules of international law. Article 26 of the High Sea Convention 1958 empowers all the States explicitly to lay submarine cables and pipelines on the high seas' seabed. Under the provision, the coastal States may take reasonable measures to conduct exploration of the continental shelf. The exploitation of its natural resources obliges the coastal States otherwise not to impede submarine cables' laying or maintenance.[46] The cable owner is also required to pay due regard to others' rights of cable operation therein.

Articles 27–29 of this High Sea Convention 1958 deal with protecting the submarine cables and imposing an obligation on breaking of cables on the high sea. These provisions replicate Articles 2, 4, and 7 of the Cable Convention 1884 (discussed above). Moreover, Article 30 of the Geneva Convention 1958 saves the application of the Cable Convention 1884.[47] It provides as the provisions of this Convention shall not affect Conventions or other international agreements already in force, as between States Parties to them.

The Geneva Conventions 1958 was the first international instrument on the law of the sea with extensive global support (in comparison with some parties to the Cable Convention 1884).[48] These Conventions widen the scope and application of the submarine cable regime to include protecting the telephone cables and the high-voltage power cables.[49]

2.8 UNCLOS II—1960

The second United Nations Conference on the Law of the Sea was held in 1960. It primarily dealt with the issues of the territorial waters' outer limits (UNCLOS II) and remained undecided. Therefore, in this context, a discussion on UNCLOS 1960 is unnecessary.

---

[46]Article 4 of the Continental shelf Convention 1958 also provides that "subject to its right to take reasonable measures for the exploration of the continental shelf and the exploitation of its natural resources, the coastal State may not impede the laying or maintenance of submarine cables or pipe lines on the continental shelf".

[47]Article 30 of the Geneva Convention [31].

[48]Continental Shelf Convention [32] and High Seas Convention [30].

[49]Mudric [33].

2.9 UNCLOS III 1982–The Laying and Protection of Submarine Cables

The State parties adopted the comprehensive mandate for marine affairs, i.e., the Constitution of the law of the sea (UNCLOS) in 1982. UNCLOS included the relevant provisions of the Geneva Convention on submarine cable, *ad verbatim*.[50] The applicable provisions on cables, provided with the UNCLOS, represent the primary international regime on laying and protecting submarine cables.

Indeed, the fundamental principles and provisions of international law on submarine cables set out in UNCLOS.[51] UNCLOS prescribes both coastal States' and non-coastal States' rights and obligations concerning submarine cables' laying and protection. According to UNCLOS's established maritime zones, it prescribes coastal States' rights and responsibilities on submarine cables. The remainder of this section will deal with UNCLOS's principles and provisions concerning the laying and protection of submarine cables.

For ages, the principle of freedom of sea applies to accommodate marine activities in the deep sea that also hold submarine cables. The vast ocean is open to all States' actions. Simultaneously, the coastal State exercises sovereign authority over the waters close to its shore. Therefore, the principle of sovereignty applies to the cable within the limited waters near the coasts. Lately, these principles of the law of the sea are starched by various dimensions like change in ocean use, newly immerged States', etc. After serious deliberations over the years, the world community agreed to revise these existing principles to give way to the other third principle of the law of the sea, i.e., the principle of the common heritage of mankind through UNCLOS 1982. Therefore, three broad principles apply to all activities, including cable in the marine zones under UNCLOS. The sovereignty principle refers to the waters near to coast (territorial waters up to 12 nm toward the sea). *Secondly,* the principle of freedom of seas applies to the waters beyond the territorial waters and EEZ up to 200–350 nm maximum (depending on the continental shelf of the coastal States that comes under the national jurisdiction). In the EEZ, States enjoy sovereign rights, and other States have freedom of high seas with certain limitations—a sui generis regime. Beyond the limit of national jurisdictions, the seabed and ocean floor and subsoil thereof is known as the 'Area,' which comes under the third principle of the common heritage of mankind. These laws of the sea jurisdictional arrangements have a significant role in submarine cable governance. Submarine cables traverse all over the ocean, and thus, the laying and protection of submarine cables attract all of these three principles of the law of the sea.

State under UNCLOS has the authority to regulate all activities occurring in its territorial water. A coastal State has sovereignty over its adjacent waters up to 12 nautical miles (nm) recognized as territorial waters (TW)[52] and the air

---

[50] UNCLOS [34].

[51] For an overview on international law on submarine cables, see, Mensah [35].

[52] Article 3, UNCLOS 1982.

space above and the seabed and subsoil below.[53] Similarly, the archipelagic State[54] has sovereignty over its archipelagic waters within its archipelagic baselines. The sovereignty of the coastal State extends to these waters. Thus, activities related to submarine cables in this water are subject to national laws and regulations. However, coastal States' authority over their territorial waters is not absolute. Through Article 2 [3] of the UNCLOS, States have agreed to exercise their sovereignty over their territorial waters in compliance with other provisions of UNCLOS and different rules of international law. Foreign ships are entitled to innocent passage through the territorial waters.[55] For innocent passage, the passage must be continuous and expeditious, and it must not engage in any activity not having a direct bearing on the passage. All of the measures have implications on cables related activities.

Regarding cables, note that a ship's passage engaged in the laying of cables in territorial water does not qualify for the innocent passage. Submarine cable operation within territorial water is subject to national laws. Further, coastal States may adopt necessary laws and regulations to regulate innocent passage to protect the submarine cables.[56] Therefore, in the territorial water, domestic rules apply to cable operators, and cable companies need to take permits, licenses, and other permissions under coastal States' regulations.

Following UNCLOS, the coastal State may adopt measures for regulating the laying of cables in its territorial water. Still, the main problem lies in its procedure and additional requirements with which the cable companies are compelled to comply. For example, cable companies need to make an application for permits and licenses for cable operation. In most of these cases, several domestic authorities are involved with such an approval process. These may include approval from defense authorities, national security authorizations, environmental permits, permits for construction, land use, etc.

Additionally, the cable companies may necessarily need to take permission from maritime authorities. Different countries have inadequate and complex submarine cable regulatory system. These regulatory requirements result in undue delay in cable operation and become a barrier to communication's free flow. Further, there is an emerging additional requirement for Environmental Impact Assessment (EIA) to lay cables on the seabed.[57] The EIA prescribes other requirements such as technical information, environmental accreditation, environmental review, and comprehensive analysis, including consultation of different stakeholders.

Moreover, the rationality and legality of the EIA are not free from doubts. A study suggests that the submarine cable operation has minimal or no impact on the marine

[53]Article 2 (2), UNCLOS 1982.

[54]An archipelagic State is any internationally recognized State or country that comprises a series of islands that form an archipelago. The term is defined by the United Nations Convention on the Law of the Sea to define what borders such States should be allowed to claim.

[55]Article 17, UNCLOS 1982.

[56]Article 21, UNCLOS 1982.

[57]OSPAR [36].

environment.[58] Further, coastal States' need to promote their shipping industry leads to demanding foreign cable companies to use local vessels and employ local crew members for cable operation within its territorial water. Such requirements are not always tenable as the cable operation needs skilled crews and a specialized vessel that may not be available in the locality. Such conditions can cause unnecessary inconvenience to the cable operator.[59]

Article 21 of the Convention empowers the coastal States to adopt the law to protect the submarine cables in their jurisdiction.[60] However, the significant point concerning the cable system's security is that the provision does not oblige the coastal States to enact legislative measures to protect the submarine cables therein. Under UNCLOS, domestic law's adoption for cables' security lies in the State's discretion. In practice, many of the coastal States do not adopt regulations for this purpose. Such an arrangement under UNCLOS results in a gap in the law to protect submarine cables in TW.

Another area of ambiguities relates to States' authorities to survey the cable route and data obtained through the marine scientific research beyond national jurisdictions.[61] Legal responses to the cable route survey and collection of data beyond the TW are under study.[62] Does the cable route survey cover the marine scientific research, or who won marine data from marine spaces beyond national jurisdictions?[63]

Traditionally, marine spaces beyond the TW are regarded as high seas, where a State free to lay submarine cables. UNCLOS also establishes different zones over marine space beyond the TW. From baseline, these zones are extended as Contiguous Zone (24 nm), Exclusive Economic Zone (EEZ) (200 nm), the high seas, and the Area. In addition to this, the ocean floor is called the continental shelf up to 200 nm or beyond. The EEZ is a marine zone of *sui generis,* acknowledging primarily coastal States' economic interests therein. The continental shelf is the seabed and subsoil of the submarine areas that extend beyond its territorial sea through the natural prolongation of its land territory to the outer edge of the continental margin.[64]The continental shelf of a coastal State comprises the seabed and subsoil of the submarine areas that extend beyond its territorial sea throughout the natural prolongation of its land territory to the outer edge of the continental margin, or to a distance of 200 nautical miles from the baselines from which the breadth of the territorial sea is measured where the outer edge of the continental margin does not extend up to that distance". These spaces come under the continental shelf regime. The EEZ regime and the continental shelf regime up to 200 nm apply concurrently to the same geographical area. Beyond the EEZ, the water column and its seabed and subsoil

[58]Malecki and Wei [4].

[59]Davenport [28].

[60]Article 21, UNCLOS.

[61]Davenport [37].

[62]Ibid.

[63]Agarwala [7].

[64]Article 76 (1) of UNCLOS 1982 provides "Definition of the continental shelf-.

are regarded as the high seas and the *Area*. These regimes attract submarine cable operation on the ocean floor of these zones.

The point is that the submarine cables laid on the seabed of this marine space attract the laws of both the EEZ regime and the continental shelf regime.[65] In the EEZ, the coastal States have sovereign rights to explore and exploit living and non-living natural resources of the waters and jurisdiction over specified matters.[66] In the continental shelf, it has sovereign rights to explore the continental shelf and exploit the natural resources, minerals on the seabed, and subsoil.[67] In the EEZ regime, the coastal States' jurisdiction has been explicit. The coastal State's sovereign

---

[65]Brown [18].

[66]Article 56 of UNCLOS 1982 provides "Rights, jurisdiction and duties of the coastal State in the exclusive economic zone.

1. In the exclusive economic zone, the coastal State has:

(a) sovereign rights to explore and exploit, conserving and managing the natural resources, whether living or non-living, of the waters superjacent to the seabed and of the seabed and its subsoil, and with regard to other activities for the economic exploitation and exploration of the zone, such as the production of energy from the water, currents and winds;

(b) jurisdiction as provided for in the relevant provisions of this Convention with regard to:

(i) the establishment and use of artificial islands, installations and structures;

(ii) marine scientific research;

(iii) the protection and preservation of the marine environment;

(c) other rights and duties provided for in this Convention.

2. In exercising its rights and performing its duties under this Convention in the exclusive economic zone, the coastal State shall have due regard to the rights and duties of other States. It shall act in a manner compatible with the provisions of this Convention.

3. The rights set out in this article with respect to the seabed and subsoil shall be exercised in accordance with Part VI".

[67]Article 76 of UNCLOS 1982 defines "the continental shelf.

"1. The continental shelf of a coastal State comprises the seabed and subsoil of the submarine areas that extend beyond its territorial sea throughout the natural prolongation of its land territory to the outer edge of the continental margin, or to a distance of 200 nautical miles from the baselines from which the breadth of the territorial sea is measured where the outer edge of the continental margin does not extend up to that distance".

See also Article 77 of UNCLOS "Rights of the coastal State over the continental shelf

1. The coastal State exercises over the continental shelf sovereign rights for the purpose of exploring it and exploiting its natural resources.

2. The rights referred to in paragraph 1 are exclusive in the sense that if the coastal State does not explore the continental shelf or exploit its natural resources, no one may undertake these activities without the express consent of the coastal State.

3. The rights of the coastal State over the continental shelf do not depend on occupation, effective or notional, or on any express proclamation.

rights for exploring the continental shelf confer with the jurisdiction to regulate such activities.[68]

Article 87 of the Convention provides that the freedom of laying submarine cables is a freedom of the high seas.[69] With the combined reading of Article 87 and Article 58 (2), it becomes clear that the freedom of laying submarine cables applies in the EEZ.[70] The result is that there are two provisions, i.e., Article 58 and Article 79, affirming other States' rights to laying submarine cables within the EEZ of a coastal State.[71] Notably, these provisions clarify that the freedom of the laying of cables includes maintenance and repairs operation. Together with these entitlements, the States, while exercising their freedom of laying submarine cables, must comply with

---

4. The natural resources referred to in this Part consist of the mineral and other non-living resources of the seabed and subsoil together with living organisms belonging to sedentary species, that is to say, organisms which, at the harvestable stage, either are immobile on or under the seabed or are unable to move except in constant physical contact with the seabed or the subsoil".

[68] For an overview, see, Burnett [38].

[69] Article 87of UNCLOS 1982 provides "Freedom of the high seas.

1. The high seas are open to all States, whether coastal or land-locked. Freedom of the high seas is exercised under the conditions laid down by this Convention and by other rules of international law. It comprises, *inter alia*, both for coastal and land-locked States:

(a) freedom of navigation;

(b) freedom of overflight;

(c) freedom to lay submarine cables and pipelines, subject to Part VI;

(d) freedom to construct artificial islands and other installations permitted under international law, subject to Part VI;

(e) freedom of fishing, subject to the conditions laid down in Section 2;

(f) freedom of scientific research, subject to Parts VI and XIII.

2. All States shall exercise these freedoms with due regard for the interests of other States in their exercise of the freedom of the high seas, and also with due regard for the rights under this Convention with respect to activities in the Area".

[70] Article 58 of UNCLOS provides "Rights and duties of other States in the exclusive economic zone.

1. In the exclusive economic zone, all States, whether coastal or land-locked, enjoy, subject to the relevant provisions of this Convention, the freedoms referred to in article 87 of navigation and overflight and of the laying of submarine cables and pipelines, and other internationally lawful uses of the sea related to these freedoms, such as those associated with the operation of ships, aircraft and submarine cables and pipelines and compatible with the other provisions of this Convention.

2. Articles 88–115 and other pertinent rules of international law apply to the exclusive economic zone in so far as they are not incompatible with this Part.

3. In exercising their rights and performing their duties under this Convention in the exclusive economic zone, States shall have due regard to the rights and duties of the coastal State and shall comply with the laws and regulations adopted by the coastal State following the provisions of this Convention and other rules of international law in so far as they are not incompatible with this Part".

[71] Article 79 of UNCLOS 1982 provides "Submarine cables and pipelines on the continental shelf.

the other provisions of the Convention.[72] The fundamental of the freedom of laying of submarine cables (Article 87) within the EEZ and continental shelf (Article 79) and beyond the outer limits of the continental shelf on the seabed of the high seas (Article 112) requires careful analysis.

Article 79 of UNCLOS has improved the provisions set out in Article 4 of the Convention on the Continental Shelf 1958[73] and Article 26 of the Convention on the High Seas 1958,[74] developed on the ILC draft. Regarding paragraph 2 on States' rights to take reasonable measures, in its Commentary, ILC has noted….

> 'The coastal State is obliged to permit the laying of cables and pipelines on the floor of its continental shelf, but….it can impose conditions as to the route to be followed, in order to prevent undue interference with the exploitation of the natural resources of the seabed and subsoil….'[75]

Coastal State authority on its continental shelf has been acknowledged and forwarded further by China during the 1973 session of the Seabed Committee of UNCLOS. It proposed the following addition to this provision….

> 'The delineation of the course for laying submarine cables and pipelines on the continental shelf by a foreign State is subject to the consent of the coastal State.'[76]

---

1. All States are entitled to lay submarine cables and pipelines on the continental shelf, in accordance with the provisions of this article.

2. Subject to its right to take reasonable measures for the exploration of the continental shelf, the exploitation of its natural resources and the prevention, reduction and control of pollution from pipelines, the coastal State may not impede the laying or maintenance of such cables or pipelines.

3. The delineation of the course for the laying of such pipelines on the continental shelf is subject to the consent of the coastal State.

4. Nothing in this Part affects the right of the coastal State to establish conditions for cables or pipelines entering its territory or territorial sea, or its jurisdiction over cables and pipelines constructed or used in connection with the exploration of its continental shelf or exploitation of its resources or the operations of artificial islands, installations and structures under its jurisdiction.

5. When laying submarine cables or pipelines, States shall have due regard to cables or pipelines already in position. In particular, possibilities of repairing existing cables or pipelines shall not be prejudiced".

[72] Article 58 and Article 79, UNCLOS 1982.

[73] Article 4 of the Continental Shelf Convention 1958 provides 'Subject to its right to take reasonable measures for the exploration of the continental shelf and the exploitation of its natural resources, the coastal State may not impede the laying or maintenance of submarine cables or pipelines on the continental shelf.'.

[74] Article 26 of High Seas Convention 1958 provides.

'1. All States shall be entitled to lay submarine cables and pipelines on the bed of the high seas.

2. Subject to its right to take reasonable measures for the exploration of the continental shelf and the exploitation of its natural resources, the coastal State may not impede the laying or maintenance of such cables or pipelines.

3. When laying such cables or pipelines the State in question shall pay due regard to cables or pipelines already in position on the seabed. In particular, possibilities of repairing existing cables or pipelines shall not be prejudiced.

[75] Article 79—Submarine Cables and Pipelines on the Continental Shelf (II), 908–917 *at* 910–911, in Nordquist [39] (herein after known as the UNCLOS Commentary 2014).

[76] UNCLOS Commentary 2014.

Coastal States' enhanced competence on its continental shelf, territory, and territorial sea regarding cables and pipelines also proposed by the USA and suggested the following addition to this provision…

> 'Nothing in this article shall affect the jurisdiction of the coastal State over cables and pipelines constructed or used in connection with the exploration or exploitation of its continental shelf or the operations of an installation under its jurisdiction, or its right to establish conditions for cables or pipelines entering its territory or territorial sea.'[77]

The said proposal also acknowledges the coastal States' competence in adopting reasonable measures to prevent pollution.[78] Finally, the Informal Composite Negotiating Text (ICNT) represented the provision's final form and renumbered 79.[79] Indeed, Article 79 deals with both submarine cables and pipelines and deserves a thorough analysis.[80] This provision begins with the phrase 'All States.'

> 'The expression 'All States' on paragraph 1 (and in Article 112) is not to be read restrictively. In practice many submarine cables and pipelines are privately owned, and are laid by corporations or other private entities. The term therefore refers to the right of States or their nationals to lay cables and pipelines.'[81]

States' freedom of laying submarine cables on other States continental shelf is restricted 'in accordance with the provisions of this article' as provided in Paragraphs 2–5 of this provision.

> …Paragraph 1 affirms, in a form appropriate for the continental shelf, the provisions of Article 87, paragraph 1(c), by which the freedom of the high seas includes the freedom to lay submarine cables and pipelines 'subject to Part VI.' The phrase 'subject to Part VI' in Article 87 incorporates the limitations on the freedom that are contained within the provisions of Article 79.'[82]

'The laying' in paragraph 2 refers to 'new cables and pipelines' and maintenance' denotes both new and existing cables and pipeline.' Paragraph 2 of the provision has provided that coastal States may adopt reasonable measures to reduce and control pollution from pipelines. Paragraph 3 relates to 'the delineation of the course for laying submarine pipeline' and not cables. Paragraph 4 affirms coastal States' authority to establish conditions and jurisdictions of cables on its continental shelf. First, 'the right of the coastal State to establish conditions for cables or pipelines entering its territory or territorial sea'; second, 'jurisdiction over cables and pipelines constructed or used in connection with the exploration of its continental shelf or exploitation of its resources or the operations of artificial islands, installations, and structures under its jurisdiction.' Coastal States rights conform to its sovereignty over its territory, and territorial sea and jurisdiction relate to a the continental shelf concerning the natural resources and analogous to Articles 77 and 80.[83] Article 77

77 UNCLOS Commentary 2014.

78 UNCLOS Commentary 2014.

79 A/CONF.62/WP.10 (ICNT [40], article 79, VIII Off. Rec.1, 17. Ibid., *at* 909 and 915.

80 Beckman [20].

81 UNCLOS Commentary 2014.

82 The UNCLOS Commentary 2014.

83 UNCLOS Commentary 2014.

requires coastal States' consent to explore or exploit the natural resources of the continental shelf.[84] And, Article 80 deals with the artificial island, installations, and structures on the continental shelf.[85]

In this connection, the interesting question is the scope of coastal State' 'conditions' under the first part of paragraph 4. It appears that the coastal State has the competence to impose such additional conditions on the cables within its territorial sea only.[86] Indeed, coastal States have jurisdiction over submarine cables within its EEZ or continental shelf if such cables are 'related to the exploration of its continental shelf or exploitation of its resources or the operations of artificial islands, installations, and structures under its jurisdiction.'

For the protection of existing cables on the continental shelf, paragraph 5 sounds cautious for laying new cables, requiring new cables, requiring 'due regard' toward the cable already positioned. Further, the laying of new cables takes account the possibility of the repairing and maintaining the old cables, and it must not cause interference and prejudice to the latter.

A similar provision is provided concerning the archipelagic waters by Article 51, paragraph 2 and Article 112, paragraph 2 for cables (discussed below) on 'seabed of the high seas beyond the continental shelf.'[87] Further, Articles 113–115 deal with the breaking or injury of cables (discussed below) and apply to the cables on the continental shelf beyond the territorial sea's outer limits. These provisions apply to the cables within the exclusive economic zone by Article 58 when the coastal State establishes the exclusive economic zone. The cables on the continental shelf beyond the exclusive economic zone's outer limits attract high seas provisions. '….If the coastal States have not established an exclusive economic zone, Articles 113–115 directly apply….. to….cables …..on the continental shelf.'[88]

Article 112 applies to the cables beyond continental shelf's outer limits that affirms' all the States to lay submarine cables ….. on the bed of the high seas

---

[84]Article 77 of UNCLOS 1982 provides for '*Rights of the coastal State over the continental shelf.*

1. The coastal State exercises over the continental shelf sovereign rights for the purpose of exploring it and exploiting its natural resources.

2. The rights referred to in paragraph 1 are exclusive in the sense that if the coastal State does not explore the continental shelf or exploit its natural resources, **no one may undertake these activities without the express consent of the coastal State.**

3. The rights of the coastal State over the continental shelf do not depend on occupation, effective or notional, or on any express proclamation.

4. The natural resources referred to in this Part consist of the mineral and other non-living resources of the seabed and subsoil together with living organisms belonging to sedentary species, that is to say, organisms which, at the harvestable stage, either are immobile on or under the seabed or are unable to move except in constant physical contact with the seabed or the subsoil.'

[85]Article 80 of UNCLOS 1982 provides for '*Artificial islands, installations and structures on the continental shelf*—Article 60 applies *mutatis mutandis* to artificial islands, installations and structures on the continental shelf.'.

[86]Beckman [20].

[87]UNCLOS Commentary 2014.

[88]UNCLOS Commentary 2014.

beyond the continental shelf.'[89] 1. All States are entitled to lay submarine cables and pipelines on the bed of the high seas beyond the continental shelf. 2. Article 79, paragraph 5, applies to such cables and pipelines.' In compression to its predecessor (the Convention on the High Sea 1956), it reaches its present form in the sixth session [41].[90] Articles 79 and 112 provide different treatments for cables. The latter deals with the cables 'on the seas bed's beyond the continental shelf'—two regimes of the high seas and the continental shelf.[91] More specifically,

The reference to the bed of the high seas' beyond the continental shelf' is equivalent to 'beyond the limits of national jurisdiction.' In effect, it refers to the Area.'[92]

Article 112 conforms with Article 87 (c), which is again subjected to Part VI (the Continental Shelf regime). Article 79, paragraph 5 (as mentioned above) has sought to control the rights provided under Article 112 (paragraph 2). States' obligations toward the old cables are also in conformity with Article 87, paragraph 2 –

'These freedoms shall be exercised by all States with due regard for the interests of other States in their exercise of the freedom of the high seas and also with due regard for the rights under this Convention concerning activities in the Area.'

Thus, UNCLOS imposes several requirements for cable operators. They avoid causing damage to the existing cables (as mentioned above), interferences with coastal States' sovereign rights, and *reasonable measures* (regulations adopted by the coastal State to regulate its activities) therein.

UNCLOS also obliges the coastal States to exercise their rights and jurisdictions within EEZ due to the other States' entitlements on submarine cables.[93] On some of the occasions, the Convention further restricts States' rights (both coastal and non-coastal) under *other rules of international law,* which also apply to submarine cable operation.[94]

An important question is whether the 'reasonable measures,' as provided by UNCLOS, affirm all coastal States' rules in its EEZ on other States' cable operations.[95] Measures like environmental requirements adopted by the coastal States in their EEZ may not be reasonable to the cable operators. There are incidents where coastal States extended mandates prescribed for the pipeline to cables; nevertheless, the pipelines are undoubtedly distinct from cables. Delineation of the pipeline requires coastal States' consent (Article 79, paragraph 3). However, coastal States are also extending such requirements for the submarine cable route. The incidents are where coastal States ask cable companies for annual fees for laying cables that

---

[89] Article 112 of UNCLOS 1982 provides *Right to lay submarine cables and pipelines.*

[90] A/CONF.62/WP.10 [41], article 79, VIII Off. Rec.1, 20.

[91] Ibid., UNCLOS commentary on Article 112-Right to lay submarine cables and pipelines, 261–265 *at* 263.

[92] UNCLOS Commentary 2014.

[93] Treves [42]. See also Kroon [43].

[94] Article 58 (1), UNCLOS [34].

[95] Raha [44].

do not even enter its territorial waters.[96] The cable repair operation in the EEZ is also subject to coastal States' consent requirements. It is not clear about the issue of whether such measures are reasonable or not. Coastal States' concern for their marine environment is developing another practice. There is a recent trend to extend domestic environmental laws to cable operations. These marine regulations include measures for specific environmental control on Special Areas of Conservation (SACs) and Maritime Protected Areas (MPAs).[97] Application of such environmental standards to cable operation may not be reasonable under UNCLOS as the cable operator has minimal or no impact on the marine environment.[98]

These are also examples of creeping jurisdiction and coastal States' extended authority over their marine spaces. The interpretations of the phrases like '*reasonable measures*' and '*internationally lawful use of sea*' are not uniform. In particular, the application of '*due regard*' in balancing the competing interests between the laying submarine cables and emerging mining activities in the 'Area' is not free from doubt.[99] These generate claims and counterclaims among States, and in particular, these restrictions can cause interference and unnecessary delay to the submarine cable operation.

The protection of submarine cable infrastructure in the EEZ and continental shelf is another area of utmost importance today. There are two issues here, i.e., the protection of cable repairing ships and the protection of submarine cables. The vessels engaged in marine activities such as fishing activities may interfere with the cable ships and their cable operation. Here, the competing marine space and use, i.e., to catch fish and repair cables, is a problem.

A fishing vessel engaged in fishing may cause the cable ship to engage with the cable repair operation. Such interference may be a hindrance to the cable repairing process and delay the relinking of telecommunication. The Cable Convention provides measures to avoid such interventions. It requires that the other ships maintain a minimum distance from cable ships, provided an arrangement is made by giving advance notice by cable ships to the local guards of the area of cable operation.[100] The 1972 COLREGES also requires cable ships to show signal and sound

---

[96]Beckman and Davenport [45].

[97]OSPAR [36].

[98]Carter [5].

[99]Kroon [43].

[100]Article 5 of the Cable Convention provides "Vessels engaged in laying or repairing submarine cables shall conform to the regulations as to signals which have been, or maybe, adopted by mutual agreement among the High Contracting Parties, with the view of preventing collisions at sea.

When a ship engaged in repairing a cable exhibits the said signals, other vessels which see them, or are able to see them, shall withdraw to or keep beyond a distance of one nautical mile at least from the ship in question, so as not to interfere with her operations.

Fishing gear and nets shall be kept at the same distance.

Nevertheless, fishing vessels which see, or are able to see, a telegraph-ship exhibiting the said signals, shall be allowed a period of 24 h at most within which to obey the notice so given, during which time they shall not be interfered with in any way.

The operations of the telegraph-ships shall be completed as quickly as possible".

to keep other vessels, especially fishing vessels, away from cable ships in operation. However, the UNCLOS did not include these measures of the Cable Convention.

Nevertheless, cable repairing ships follow the mandate as provided by the COLREGES. However, the coastal States neglect to implement these mandates, and the other vessels continue to cause interventions to the cable ships in its cable repair process. Thus, the coastal States may take appropriate measures in strengthening the protection of cable ships.[101]

The protection of cable is a matter of real concern in the EEZ. Three provisions of the Cable Convention prescribing a penalty for breaking or injury of submarine cable were integrated to the Convention on the High Seas 1958 and then in UNCLOS by Articles 113–115. They prescribe the State's liability to adopt measures to protect cables beyond the outer limits of the TW and within the EEZ and continental shelf. It obliges States to criminalize the breaking or injury of submarine cables by their subjects over whom it has jurisdiction. These provisions prescribe a cable owner's liability for breaking an existing cable and award for indemnity for sacrificing fishing net, fishing gear, etc., to avoid cable damage. All of these provisions also require a careful analysis that begins with Article 113.

Article 113 provides that willful breaking or injuring of submarine cables is an offence and imposes an obligation on States to adopt laws and regulations prescribing punishment for willful breaking or injuring cables by ships or individuals whom it has jurisdiction.[102] Compared to its predecessors, as provided in the 1884 Cable Convention and Convention on the High Seas 1958,[103] Article 113 has a wide scope. In addition to the 'willful or culpable negligent' of breaking or injury of cable, it added 'conduct calculated or likely to result in such breaking or injury.' The former implies some criminal activity on the ship or individual to attract national laws and regulations. Its origin, the Declaration on the Protection of Submarine Cables and Pipelines 1886, stated that

---

[101] Sun [46].

[102] Article 113 of UNCLOS 1982 provides for '*Breaking or injury of a submarine cable or pipeline and States* —Every State shall **adopt the laws and regulations** necessary to provide that the breaking or injury by a ship flying its flag or by a person subject to its jurisdiction of a submarine cable beneath the high seas done wilfully or through culpable negligence, in such a manner as to be liable to interrupt or obstruct telegraphic or telephonic communications, and similarly the breaking or injury of a submarine pipeline or high-voltage power cable, shall be a punishable offence. **This provision shall apply also to conduct calculated or likely to result in such breaking or injury.** However, it shall not apply to any break or injury caused by persons who acted merely with the legitimate object of saving their lives or their ships, after having taken all necessary precautions to avoid such break or injury.'.

[103] Article 27 of the High Seas Convention 1958 provides.

'Every State shall take the necessary legislative measures to provide that the breaking or injury by a ship flying its flag or by a person subject to its jurisdiction of a submarine cable beneath the high seas done wilfully or through culpable negligence, in such a manner as to be liable to interrupt or obstruct telegraphic or telephonic communications, and similarly the breaking or injury of submarine pipeline or high-voltage power cable shall be a punishable offence. This provision shall not apply to any break or injury cause by persons who acted merely with the legitimate object of saving their lives or their ships, after having taken all necessary precautions to avoid such break or injury.'

> 'in regard to the term 'wilfully' -It is understood that the imposition of penal responsibility…does not apply to cases of breaking or of injuries [to cables] occasioned accidentally or necessarily in repairing a cable, when all precautions have been taken to avoid such breaking or damages'.[104]

Regarding the standard of 'culpable negligence,' ILC 1956 commentary relating to damage of unmarked cable provides.'

> 'Obviously, if the presence of the cable or pipeline has not been adequately marked, there can be no question of 'culpable negligence' on the part of navigators…'[105]

Then, the additional mandate of Article 113 relates to the conduct of a ship or individual 'calculated or likely to result in' cable breaking or injury. Thus, it applies and makes such behavior as 'intended or attempted' to break or injure cables-a punishable offence.'[106] The enforcement of offence under this provision applies to the cables within EEZ (through Article 58) and continental shelf. This provision and following national law maintains the nationality and flag States' jurisdictions and does not apply to the foreign ships or individuals allegedly involved in breaking or injuring submarine cables. Thus, it maintains the penal jurisdiction provided Article 97[107] and enforcement jurisdiction provided under Article 94, paragraph 7.[108] The 'incident of navigation' under Article 97 includes 'incidents involving damage to a submarine cable…..'.[109] Following Article 94, paragraph 7, a State should undertake 'an inquiry into every incident of navigation' including alleged conduct of 'willful or culpable negligent' or 'calculated or likely to result in' the breaking or injury of submarine cables involving a ship flying its flag.[110] The offence under Article 113 may be avoided on the ground of 'any break or injury caused by persons who acted merely with the legitimate object of saving their lives or their ships after taking all necessary precautions to avoid such break or injury.'

---

[104]UNCLOS Commentary 2014 on Article 113—*Breaking or injury of a submarine cable or pipeline and States, at* 269.

[105]UNCLOS Commentary 2014 *at* 269–270.

[106]UNCLOS Commentary 2014 *at* 270.

[107]Article 97 of UNCLOS 1982, provides '*Penal jurisdiction in matters of collision or any other incident of navigation and States.*

1. In the event of a collision or any other incident of navigation concerning a ship on the high seas, involving the penal or disciplinary responsibility of the master or of any other person in the service of the ship, no penal or disciplinary proceedings may be instituted against such person except before the judicial or administrative authorities either of the flag State or of the State of which such person is a national.'

[108]Article 94, Paragraph 7 of UNCLOS 1982 provides.

'Each State shall cause an inquiry to be held by or before a suitably qualified person or persons into every marine casualty or incident of navigation on the high seas involving a ship flying its flag and causing loss of life or serious injury to nationals of another State or serious damage to ships or installations of another State or to the marine environment. The flag State and the other State shall cooperate in the conduct of any inquiry held by that other State into any such marine casualty or incident of navigation.'

[109]UNCLOS Commentary 2014 on Article 113—*Breaking or injury of a submarine cable or pipeline and States, at* 269.

[110]UNCLOS Commentary 2014 *at* 269.

Article 114 imposes the liability on the State to adopt laws and regulations to ensure the individuals on which it has jurisdiction must meet 'the cost of repairs' in case they damage existing cable of another owner while engaged in laying cables which are within the EEZ (through Article 58) and the continental shelf.[111] This provision has provided that national law would apply to its subjects only, i.e., cable owners. The fouling cable owner under this provision shall have civil liability. The liability of a person on damaging cable is limited to the 'cost of the repairs' and does not include replacing the cost of damaged cables and the financial loss incurred by the victim cable owner.[112]

Lastly, Article 115 promotes and encourages compensation seeking support from the marine community to avoid potentially breaking or injuring cables.[113] 'An anchor, a net, or any other fishing gear' may catch cable—a potential source of cable damage. The owner of these gears, etc., which have already entangled cable, may sacrifice them to avoid cable damage. Article 115 obliges the State to adopt a law to ensure that such sacrifice and incurred losses are indemnified. Responsibility for indemnification of the benefited cable arises if 'the owner of the ship has incurred a loss of an anchor, a net or any other fishing gear in avoiding injury to a submarine cable provided he has taken all reasonable precautionary measures beforehand.'[114] Such measures include any measures the legitimate objective of which is to save the lives of crew members or the ship itself.'[115] The national law may provide detailed procedures for claiming this indemnity in detail. Further, like Articles 113 and 114, regarding States enforcement jurisdiction, Article 115 follows the nationality principles, and jurisdiction of a ship flying its flag applies to the cable within the EEZ (through Article 58) and the continental shelf.[116] Much of the implementation of UNCLOS's obligation on the protection of cables and indemnity issues, compensation rest on the State parties.

Lack of implementation of UNCLOS provisions mentions above weakens the deterrent elements, and the fishing, shipping, and other marine activities hardly care

---

[111] Article 114 of UNCLOS 1982 provides *'Breaking or injury by owners of a submarine cable or pipeline of another submarine cable or pipeline and States.*

Every State shall adopt the laws and regulations necessary to provide that, if persons subject to its jurisdiction who are the owners of a submarine cable or pipeline beneath the high seas, in laying or repairing that cable or pipeline, cause a break in or injury to another cable or pipeline, they shall bear the cost of the repairs.'

[112] UNCLOS Commentary 2014 on Article 114—*'Breaking or injury by owners of a submarine cable or pipeline of another submarine cable or pipeline and States,* 271–274 at 273–274.

[113] Article 115 of UNCLOS 1982 provides *'Indemnity for loss incurred in avoiding injury to a submarine cable or pipeline and States.*

Every State shall adopt the laws and regulations necessary to ensure that the owners of ships who can prove that they have sacrificed an anchor, a net or any other fishing gear, in order to avoid injuring a submarine cable or pipeline, shall be indemnified by the owner of the cable or pipeline, provided that the owner of the ship has taken all reasonable precautionary measures beforehand.'

[114] UNCLOS Commentary 2014 on Article 115—*Indemnity for loss incurred in avoiding injury to a submarine cable or pipeline and States,* 257–278 *at* 277.

[115] UNCLOS Commentary 2014 *at* 277.

[116] UNCLOS Commentary 2014 *at* 277–278.

about the safety of the cables. The cable operators are helpless and compelled to bear an enormous cost for the cable repair operation. It is time to rethink whether such a loss is limited only to the cable operators?

Further, there is theft of submarine cables. Whether theft of cable is piracy under the law of the sea? Whether piracy, as defined under Article 101 of the Convention, includes the act of the theft of submarine cable? The answer is not clear. Therefore, the legal treatment of the theft of submarine cable is uncertain. There is a concern for the safety of the critical submarine cable infrastructure from terrorist activities. One incident of a terrorist attack against any chokepoint of the undersea network may cause severe interruption to data's telecommunication and traffic. Such an incident will severely impact the international economy and security and may create a hue and cry globally.[117]

The recent development in the sea law indicates negotiation on the area beyond national jurisdictions (ABNJ) and its biodiversity is going on. It may have an impact on high sea submarine cable operation. According to a study, suggest that a new agreement on ABNJ may formalize a flexible and cooperative approach with the cable industry to accommodate both the cable operation and the environment concerns to a limited extent.[118]

2.10 International Institutional Framework Dealing with the Submarine Cables

A dedicated international organization has a significant role in developing the law and policy measures in a given area. It to be noted that there is no international author with a dedicated agenda on the submarine cable regime. Among the international institutions, first, the International Telegraph Union (ITU) was founded in 1865 to manage affairs related to the telegraph. Later the agency concentrated on the standardization of telecommunication.[119] Further, the ITU members and their divergent interests also have remained a hurdle to realize the potential of this organization for quite a long time.[120] Under the UN's umbrella, the International Maritime Organization (IMO) was responsible for dealing with international shipping activities, which included cable ships. Other relevant international organizations like the United Nations Office of Legal Affairs/ Division for Ocean Affairs and the Law of the Sea (UNDOALOS) and Food and Agriculture Organization (FAO) were also responsible for ocean affairs, including underwater cables. However, none of those organizations has a dedicated agenda for submarine cable operations. In the absence of a lead agency, supervision and review of submarine cable operation arguably remained poor. Thereby, international submarine cable governance continues to be

[117] Wrathall [15].

[118] Friedman [47].

[119] See, Jayakar [48].

[120] SchusterJune [49].

impaired. The recent developments show that submarine cable issues are increasingly getting attention from international organizations, including the UN.[121] In the recent past, international non-governmental bodies like International Cable Protection Committee (ICPC), regional authorities like Asia-Pacific Economic Cooperation (APEC), and research under the academic institutes and other institutes are increasingly getting involved with research work and workshops related to submarine cables.[122] The absence of a lead agency has become a hurdle to the submarine cable regime's development process.

This is to note further that there may be a potential conflict between the freedom of laying cables and other freedoms such as mining and bottom trawling in the 'common heritage of mankind' set out in UNCLOS. There is no independent authority who is competent to resolve conflicts relating to the laying of cables in the *Area*. An international body such as the ISA has limited competency and may regulate to the extent submarine laying relates to the mining in the *Area*. Indeed, the regulation of submarine cables in the 'Area' is a regulatory gap. To fill this regulatory gap, several relevant bodies under UN-Ocean (DOALOS, FAO, UNESCO, UNEP, CBD, ISA, and International Hydrographic Organization/IHO) and ICPC may seek recourse of the cooperation or coordination. Such coordination may extend to the regional fisheries management organizations and sea programs, which are again under the FAO and UNEP.[123] It is to note that ICPC has developed a draft convention layout for strengthening the regime on the protection and repair of submarine cables.

2.11 Draft Convention for the Protection and Repair of Submarine Cable Infrastructure[124]

The International Cable Protection Committee (ICPC) has noted that the current international cable regime has become insufficient in facilitating in laying and protecting submarine cables. It identifies that the States, *firstly*, are lagging in enforcing their obligations under UNCLOS and interfering with other States' rights; *secondly*, they remain negligent to the cable infrastructure's vulnerabilities posing by human aggressions in particular theft and terrorism.

Therefore, ICPC has suggested a draft agreement under the UNCLOS framework for extended protection and repair of submarine cables. The ICPC is the worlds' largest body comprising the cable operators and States as well.[125] The salient features of these draft measures are as follows.

[121] G.A. Res. 65/37, 121 [16].

[122] Davenport [28].

[123] Takie [29].

[124] International Cable Protection Committee Draft on '**Convention for the Protection and Repair of Submarine Cable Infrastructure**' 2008. (ICPC restricted access).

[125] The ICPC [50].

UNCLOS has recognized the freedom of communication, including the freedom of communication through submarine cables. This communication system is increasingly becoming essential and has become a critical infrastructure to the modern economy and security. Therefore, States need to adopt a robust cable protection mechanism and confer special status to the cable repair vessels. The international community is to 'ensure that the world's communications are robust, reliable, and repairable.'

Article 1 deals with the definition and scope of specific terminologies such as 'submarine cables' and 'repair ship.' It defines 'submarine cable means an undersea cable system landing in two or more State or between a State and an island of that State.' This definition is essential as the existing international cable regime does not explain these undersea cables. The commentary to this draft also explains that the submarine cable includes the landing stations in each country and all of the components in and between the landing stations, terminal equipment, land cable from the landing station to the beach, the submarine cable, optical amplifiers, and repeaters branching units and spares. In short, this definition intends to protect the integrated submarine cable system.

Article 2 deals with the objects clause of this proposed agreement, which intends to ensure the reliability, resiliency, and security of the world's submarine cable infrastructure through enforcement at the national levels. Article 3 affirms that this agreement will be interpreted in accord with the UNCLOS provisions.

Articles 4–7 of this draft provide that a cable repair ship should enjoy the right of innocent passage. According to Article 4, a cable repair ship engaged with repair and maintenance either stopped or anchored within territorial sea should attract the innocent passage regime under UNCLOS. Suppose the coastal State may agree on giving innocent passage treatment to the cable repairing ship to reduce the lengthy permit process to ensure immediate communication relinking by quickly repairing a damaged cable. Article 5 requires a cable operator to give pertinent information to the affected States' local authorities to enhance the repairing operation's transparency. Articles 6 and 7 provide an obligation to both of the cable ships to follow signaling measures, etc., and a coastal State to support cable ships to complete quick repairing.

Articles 8–10 of this draft provide essential measures for protecting submarine cable and the enforcement. Article 8 urges the State to enact laws and issue regulations to strengthen submarine cable protection initiatives. Such measures are required to design to deter or prevent threats to cable injury. Both actual and attempt acts of cable injury attract this provision. However, such measures do not apply during wartime. Article 9 deals with the enforcement of these provisions. It states on the application of Article 10 of the Cable Convention 1884 that it provides details about the implementation and collection of cable damage evidence. It provides that the warships or ships, specially commissioned for this purpose, may target both vessels, either in suspicion of cable damage or likely to cause cable damage. Lastly, Article 10 of this draft urges all the States to initiate extended cooperation and coordination through participation to prevent, deter, and address intentional hostilities to the submarine cable infrastructure.[126]

Another important provision of this draft is Article 11, which deals with the settlement of disputes. It provides that the parties to both of this agreement and UNCLOS will follow the UNCLOS dispute settlement mechanism. However, parties only agreed to this agreement may choose any means of dispute settlement provided under Article 287 of UNCLOS that deals with the dispute settlement mechanism. It also clarifies any dispute settlement mechanism will apply relevant provisions of UNCLOS, Paris Convention, and this agreement for resolving any dispute.[127] It is to be noted that according to Article 297, paragraph 1(a), a dispute concerning the freedom of laying of submarine cables within the EEZ or continental shelf and on the bed of the high seas is subjected to Part XV, Section 2, which provides compulsory binding dispute settlement procedures.[128]

2.12 Ambiguities in the International Regime on Submarine Cables and the Way Forward

In his scholarly work, Backman explicitly stated that submarine cable regulation in the EEZ is a grey area in the law of the sea, and the State should adopt appropriate measures to strengthen the cable regime.[129] It is also pertinent to deal with other ambiguities in the existing international law on submarine cables to determine possible mitigating measures. As discussed above, the global submarine cable regimes are represented by the Cable Convention 1884, and the Geneva Convention 1958, and UNCLOS 1982.[130] A comparative analysis of all of these Conventions' relevant provisions will help identify the appropriate measures that the States may adopt to facilitate laying and the protection of cables (Table 2.1).

As discussed above, only three provisions of the Cable Convention 1884 had been adopted in the following Conventions, including UNCLOS. The rest of the provisions of the Cable Convection 1884 is limited only to the parties to it. Those provisions do not bind the non-parties to the Cable Convention. Some of those provisions still hold effective. For example, UNCLOS prescribes an obligation for breaking or injury of cables in general. A clear procedure may necessary for its effective implementation.

---

[126]Takie [29].

[127]Ibid.

[128]Article 297 [1](a) of UNCLOS 1982 pfovides—'when it is alleged that a coastal State has acted in contravention of the provisions of this Convention in regard to the freedoms and rights of navigation, overflight or the laying of submarine cables and pipelines, or in regard to other internationally lawful uses of the sea specified in article 58;' Ibid, UNCLOS Commentary on Article 79—Submarine Cables and Pipelines on the Continental Shelf (II), 908–917 at 17 and Ibid, UNCLOS commentary on Article 112-Right to lay submarine cables and pipelines, 261–265 at 65 and *Ibid*, Backman, *at* 11–12.

[129]Beckman [51].

[130]Mensah [35].

Table 2.1 Articles on the protection of submarine cables set out in the Cable Convention, High Sea Convection, and UNCLOS, respectively

Cable Convention 1884	Geneva Convention 1958	UNCLOS 1982
2	27	113
4	28	114
7	29	115

In this respect, Cable Convection suggests implementing procedures that may apply to the enforcement of Article 113 of UNCLOS.[131]

Article 115 of the UNCLOS prescribes indemnity for the cost of the sacrificed anchor or fishing gear.[132] However, UNCLOS is silent on the procedure on indemnity. In this respect, Article 7 of the Cable Convention provides the process in detail.[133] To establish a claim to such compensation, a statement, supported by the evidence of the crew, should, whenever possible, be drawn up immediately after the occurrence; and the master must, within 24 h after his return to or next putting into port, make a declaration to the proper authorities. The latter shall communicate the information to the consular authorities of the country to which the owner of the cable belongs." It says that *first* the proof of the loss of the fishing nets and gear must be in written form and with corroboration of the crew. Second, the statement is required to be lodged with the consular authorities of the cable owner within 24 h of the vessel's arrival in the first port after such loss. In this respect, the following study is worth mentioning[134]

> "The Article 7 requirement has been implemented widely by the cable industry by the use of toll-free 24/7 phone numbers, displayed on cable awareness charts distributed at no cost to mariners, that allow the mariner to contact the cable owners while the vessel is at sea or in port.[135] It is an industry custom and practice that an affidavit form of claim statement is then provided for the vessel's master to complete and submit for evaluation. If the mariner is not able to determine who the cable owner is, the coast guard or captain of the port may receive the claim and forward it to the cable owner."[136]

---

131 Burnett [38].

132 Article 115 of the UNCLOS 1982 provides "Every State shall adopt the necessary laws and regulations. It must ensure that the owners of ships who can prove that they have sacrificed an anchor, a net or any other fishing gear, to avoid injuring a submarine cable or pipeline, shall be indemnified by the owner of the cable or pipeline, provided that the owner of the ship has taken all reasonable precautionary measures beforehand".

133 Article VII—"Owners of ships or vessels who can prove that they have sacrificed an anchor, a net, or other fishing gear to avoid injuring a submarine cable, shall receive compensation from the owner of the cable.

134 Burnett [38].

135 ICPC Recommendation No. 5, Issue 7A (Standardization of Cable Awareness Charts). Copies of this and other ICPC recommendations can be obtained free of charge from the International Cable Protection Committee (ICPC) upon request (www.iscpc.org).

136 ICPC Recommendation No. 6, Issue 8A (Recommended Actions for Effective Cable Protection (Post Installation)).

Douglas Burnett has identified that the principle Articles 5, 6, and 10 of the Cable Convention 1884, which are absent in UNCLOS, still hold good for today's cable operation. He further recommended that these Articles' utility be considered for use in other international instruments to fill current UNCLOS regime gaps. Now, it is appropriate to look into those provisions.

Article 5 of the Cable Convention 1884 deals with the issues of preventive measures involved with keeping the area of cable operation free from interference by other vessels engaged in that vicinity.[137] The article has five components. First is the free operation of the cable ship engaged in laying or repairing of submarine cables. It prescribes an obligation on the parties to agree upon specific signals used by these vessels to avoid collisions at seas. The second component specifically mentions maintaining the distance between the other ships and cable ships engaged in cable repairing activities. It urged other vessels that if it notices such signals indicating a vessel involved in repairing a cable, the former must withdraw to or keep at a distance of one nautical mile at least so as not to interfere with her operation. It deals with the vessels and urges the fishing vessels to keep fishing gear and nets at the same distance in the third part of the article. The next part of this provision addresses the concern for existing fishing nets and gears, and other vessels in the prospective area of cable operation. It says that at least 24 h before engaging in cable operation in an area, a notice is required to give coastal States and coast guard authorities about the scheduled arrival of the cable ship and related activities. It provides a reasonable opportunity for the fishing vessels to remove their fishing nets and gear and maintain the required minimum distance. The cable vessels are prohibited from interfering with the fishing vessel within the said period of 24 h. Lastly, the cable operators are required to complete the cable operation as quickly as possible.

In practice, the State must engage its coast guard authorities to communicate and notice the mariners. For service of such notice, it is communicated to the vessel operators and fishing associations engaged in a particular area of cable operation. Additionally, the cable operators deploy an industry contract patrol vessel in advance of the cable work to request that fishing gear and fishing net to remove from the intended place of cable operation.[138]

[137]Article V of the Cable Convention "Vessels engaged in laying or repairing submarine cables shall conform to the regulations as to signals which have been, or maybe, adopted by agreement among the High Contracting Parties, with the view of preventing collisions at sea.

[138]Burnett [38].

Though UNCLOS does not provide such measures, the Convention on the International Regulations for Preventing Collisions at Sea 1972 (COLREGS) prohibits other vessels from interfering with a cable ship engaged in cable operation. Rules 27 and 18 are the most important provisions to avoid collision between cable ships and other vessels. Rule 27 provides that a cable ship engaged with the cable operator is considered a 'vessel restricted in its ability to maneuver.'[139] Here, the vessels with

[139]Rule 27 of COLREGS provides.

"*(a).* A vessel not under command shall exhibit:

(i). two all-round red lights in a vertical line where they can best be seen;

(ii). two balls or similar shapes in a vertical line where they can best be seen;

(iii). when making way through the water, in addition to the lights prescribed in this paragraph, sidelights and a stern light.

(b). A vessel restricted in her ability to maneuver, except a vessel engaged in mine clearance operations, shall exhibit:

(i). three all-round lights in a vertical line where they can best be seen. The highest and lowest of these lights shall be red, and the middle light shall be white;

(ii). three shapes in a vertical line where they can best be seen. The highest and lowest of these shapes shall be balls and the middle one a diamond;

(iii). when making way through the water, a masthead light or lights, sidelights, and a stern light, in addition to the lights prescribed in sub-paragraph (i);

(iv). when at anchor, in addition to the lights or shapes prescribed in sub-paragraphs (i) and (ii), the light, lights or shape prescribed in Rule 30.

(c). A power-driven vessel engaged in a towing operation such as severely restricts the towing vessel and her tow in their ability to deviate from their course shall, in addition to the lights or shapes prescribed in Rule 24(a), exhibit thelights or shapes prescribed in subparagraphs (b)(i) and (ii) of this Rule.

(d). A vessel engaged in dredging or underwater operations, when restricted in her ability to maneuver, shall exhibit the lights and shapes prescribed in subparagraphs (b)(i), (ii) and (iii) of this Rule and shall also, when an obstruction exists, exhibit:

(i). two all-round red lights or two balls in a vertical line to indicate the side on which the obstruction exists;

(ii). two all-round green lights or two diamonds in a vertical line to indicate the side on which another vessel may pass;

(iii). when at anchor, the lights or shapes prescribed in this paragraph instead of the lights or shape prescribed in Rule 30.

(e). Whenever the size of a vessel engaged in diving operations makes it impracticable to exhibit all lights and shapes prescribed in paragraph (d) of this Rule, the following shall be exhibited:

(i). three all-round lights in a vertical line where they can best be seen. The highest and lowest of these lights shall be red, and the middle light shall be white;

cable operators have considered a vessel restricted in its ability to maneuver.'[140] Rule 27, in brief, mandates the cable ships to show appropriate lights at night and shapes during the day so that vessels in the area are aware of its restricted maneuverability status. In practice, cable ships adhere to these requirements with almost religious dedication.[141] Another necessary provision of the Convention is Rule 18, which mandatorily asks another vessel, especially fishing vessels, to stay out of the way of the cable ship.[142] However, it is to note that maintaining a distance between cable ships and other vessels is very general. It does not provide keeping any mandatory distance between these vessels. Due to the lack of clear rules, vessels may travel even very close to the cable ships. It is a weak and *prima facie* defective measure to avoid collision or interference in vessels' respective engagement.

On the contrary, Article 5 provides the distance between cable ships and other vessels must be at least one nautical mile. In reality, the ship engaged with the cable operation engages large areas in its operation with long cables and equipment. Simultaneously, fishing vessels are also involved with very long fishing nets ranging from the vicinity's vast area. It requires a noticeable and measurable distance between vessels.

(ii). a rigid replica of the International Code flag "A" not less than 1 m in height. Measures shall be taken to ensure their all-round visibility.

(f). A vessel engaged in mine clearance operations shall in addition to the lights prescribed for a power-driven vessel in Rule 23 or to the lights or shape prescribed for a vessel at anchor in Rule 30 as appropriate, exhibit three all-round green lights or three balls. One of these lights or shapes shall be exhibited near the foremast head and one at each end of the foreyard. These lights or shapes indicate that it is dangerous for another vessel to approach within 1000 metres of the mine clearance vessel.

(g). Vessels of less than 12 metres in length, except those engaged in diving operations, shall not be required to exhibit the lights and shapes prescribed in this Rule.

(h). The signals prescribed in this Rule are not signals of vessels in distress and requiring assistance. Such signals are contained in Annex IV to these Regulations."

140The term "vessel restricted in her ability to maneuver" means a vessel which from the nature of her work is restricted in her ability to manoeuvre as required by these Rules and is therefore unable to keep out of the way of another vessel. The term "vessels restricted in their ability to maneuver shall include but not be limited to:

(i) a vessel engaged in laying, servicing or picking up a navigation mark, submarine cable or pipeline;

(ii) a vessel engaged in dredging, surveying or underwater operations; (iii) a vessel engaged in replenishment or transferring persons, provisions or cargo while underway;

(iv) a vessel engaged in the launching or recovery of aircraft;

(v) a vessel engaged in mine clearance operations;

(vi) a vessel engaged in a towing operation such as severely restricts the towing vessel and her tow in their ability to deviate from their course".

See also Burnett [38].

141Burnett [38].

142Rule 18 of the COLREGS provides."Except where Rules 9, 10 and 13 otherwise require:

(a). A power-driven vessel underway shall keep out of the way of:

(i). a vessel not under command; *(ii).* a vessel restricted in her ability to maneuver; *(iii).* a vessel engaged in fishing;

(iv). a sailing vessel.

(b). A sailing vessel underway shall keep out of the way of:

Therefore, considering Article 5 of the Cable Convention's utility, there is a practical urgency to have a specific mention of a certain distance between vessels. And, it could be achieved through an amendment in COLREGS Rule 18 (c), which relates to fishing vessels, with the following addition

"(iii) If the vessel restricted in her ability to maneuver is a cable ship, the fishing vessel and its gear shall keep one nautical mile away."[143]

Then use of an identifier, i.e., a buoy in a cable repair area, represents the area's sensitivity and awareness of other vessels to keep away. Article 6 of the Cable Convention provides the significance of buoy use to represent the position of the cables.[144] The provision urges the other vessels and fishing nets and gears to be beyond a distance of one-quarter of a nautical mile at least from said buoys. Therefore, the specific mention of a definite distance as provided with this article is still hold rational, and it can be added to the COLREG Rule 18 (c) through an amendment-

"(iv) If the vessel observes a cable repair buoy, the fishing vessel shall keep the vessel and its gear one-quarter of a nautical mile away."[145]

Article 10 of the Cable Convention 1884 strengthens the implementation of the mandate of the Convention. Indeed,

It provides the procedure for evidence collection on alleged an act of cable breaks. Article 113 of the UNCLOS provides the liability of cable damage.[146] The provision criminalizes the actual damage and the action, which is an attempt to cause damage

---

(i). a vessel not under command; *(ii)*. a vessel restricted in her ability to maneuver; *(iii)*. a vessel engaged in fishing.

(c). A vessel engaged in fishing when underway shall, so far as possible, keep out of the way of: *(i)*. a vessel not under command; *(ii)*. a vessel restricted in her ability to maneuver.

(d).

(i). Any vessel other than a vessel not under command or a vessel restricted in her ability to maneuver shall, if the circumstances of the case admit, avoid impeding the safe passage of a vessel constrained by her draught, exhibiting

the signals in Rule 28. *(ii)*. A vessel constrained by her draught shall navigate with particular caution having full regard to her special condition.

(e). A seaplane on the water shall, in general, keep well clear of all vessels and avoid impeding their navigation. In circumstances, however, where a risk of collision exists, she shall comply with the Rules of this part.

(f).

(i). A WIG craft shall include when taking off, landing and in flight near the surface, keep well clear of all other vessels and avoid impeding their navigation; *(ii)*. a WIG craft operating on the water surface shall comply with the Rules of this Part as a power-driven vessel.

[143]Burnett [38].

[144]Article VI of the Cable Convection provides "Vessels which see, or can see, the buoys showing the position of a cable when the latter is being laid, is out of order, or is broken, shall keep beyond a distance of one-quarter of a nautical mile at least from the said buoys. Fishing nets and gear shall be kept at the same distance".

[145]Burnett [38].

[146]Article 113 of the UNCLOS 1982 provides "Every State shall adopt the necessary laws and regulations. It should ensure that the breaking or injury by a ship flying its flag or by a person subject to its jurisdiction of a submarine cable beneath the high seas done wilfully or through

to the resulting cable interruption in communication. As usual, it does not speak about the procedure of obtaining evidence of the offense. It is noted that in the ocean, the erring crew is, in most cases, are the witness. They are required to be testified to obtain evidence on the technical report detailing the vessels' position when the cable was broken. Both comprise the vital evidence for proving the guilt. For this purpose, authoritative persons need to board on the erring vessels to access the vessel's documents and crews in question. However, UNCLOS is silent in this regard. However, as mentioned above, the Cable Convention's member parties agreed on a procedure that allows authorized officers of the War Ship to board on the erring ships to conduct the necessary evidence collection operation through Article 10.[147] After boarding, the officer may scrutinize the ships' necessary papers like a logbook, etc., and conduct an investigation. At the end of the investigation, everything that starts from the boarding should be reduced into a report which is again required to be signed by the erring vessel's crew. Then the copy of the report is submitted before the court of trial in facilitating the judicial process.

Further, it is not clear that Article 101 of UNCLOS that deals with piracy applies to the incident of cable theft. Moreover, the UNCLOS is silent regarding users of the terrorists' attack on the submarine cables and its consequences. Commentators have identified underwater cable infrastructure—an *Achilles heel* that is vulnerable to piracy and terrorist attack.[148] In both of the cases, UNCLOS does not provide clear measures. As beyond the territorial waters, UNCLOS allows only ship boarding of a vessel involved with piracy, slavery, or non-showing of a flag.

The existing submarine cable protection measures are not adequate to address the intentional breaking or injury of cables. It has been explained that these provisions

culpable negligence, in such a manner as to be liable to interrupt or obstruct telegraphic or telephonic communications, and similarly the breaking or injury of a submarine pipeline or high-voltage power cable, shall be a punishable offence. This provision shall also apply to conduct calculated or likely to result in such breaking or injury. However, it shall not apply to any break or injury caused by persons who acted merely with the legitimate object of saving their lives or their ships, after having taken all necessary precautions to avoid such break or injury".

[147] Article 10 of the UNCLOS 1982 provides "Offences against the present Convention may be verified by all means of proof allowed by the legislation of the country of the court. The officers commanding the ships of war, or ships specially commissioned for the purpose by one of the High Contracting Parties, may find a reason to believe that an infraction of the measures provided for in the present Convention has been committed by a vessel other than a vessel of war. They may demand from the captain or master the production of the official documents proving the nationality of the said vessel. The fact of such document having been exhibited shall then be endorsed upon it immediately.

Further, formal statements of the facts may be prepared by the said officers, whatever may be the nationality of the vessel incriminated. These formal statements shall be drawn up in the form and in the language used in the country to which the officer is making them belongs; they may be considered, in the country where they are adduced, as evidence following the laws of that country. The accused and the witnesses shall have the right to add, or to have added to that, in their language, any explanations they may consider useful. These declarations shall be duly signed".

[148] Gady [52], See Henry F. Cooper [53]. See also Tsuruoka [54].

are lagging *firstly,* lack of implementation; *secondly*, minimal penalty stick to the principle of the perpetrators' personality, and lastly, no enforcement jurisdictions.[149]

As stated above, UNCLOS provisions set out in Articles 113–115 for the protection of submarine cables beneath the high seas, in the EEZ, and on the continental shelf beyond the TW's outer limits not adequate to address terrorist attacks on cables.[150] Among these, Article 114 deals with the breaking or injury by owners of a submarine cable or pipeline of another submarine cable or pipeline and Article 115 on indemnity for loss incurred in avoiding injury to a submarine cable or pipeline. Article 113 prescribes for the breaking or injuries to the submarine cables.[151] In principle, it may apply to the 'willful act of the breaking or injury' of submarine cables.[152] It does not mean that this provision would apply in the protection of submarine cable from the act of terrorism. Article 113 is inadequate for the act of destruction of submarine cable from terrorist activities. It appears that it applies to the activities linked with the regular exercise of marine activities and does not take account of sabotage by an act of terrorism and use of the flag of convenience for deliberate cable breaking.[153] Implementing this provision, a State enacts provision imposing penalties of monetary fine, which may deter the negligent act of marine activities leading to cable injury; however, it is substantially inappropriate to counter an act of terrorism of cable destruction or damage.

The next limitation relates to the State's criminal jurisdiction, which is based on the nationality principle.[154] The implementing States under Article 113 exercise jurisdictions over the perpetrators who are its nationals or are found on board a vessel is flying its flag. Thus, a State is clueless to the terrorists who are foreign nationals and acted from an alien vessel engaged in the destruction or damage of submarine cables on the continental shelf even if she has law under Article 113. The enforcing State is also handicapped since it has no competence under Article 113 to deploy its warship in collecting evidence and holding the perpetrators liable.[155] Furthermore, the victim States' authority over the alleged willful act of the foreign nationals or flagship beyond territorial sovereignty leading interference to its telecommunication is relatively weak irrespective of the jurisdiction on the principle of passive nationality.[156] The potential threat of terrorism against the submarine cable was not in the minds of the UNCLOS drafters or any other international instruments. Therefore, States competence to exercise their criminal jurisdictions over terrorism against critical communication cables has remained unaddressed.[157]

---

[149]Davenport [28]. See also Takie [29].

[150]Backman [20].

[151]Article 113 of UNCLOS 1982.

[152]Davenport [28].

[153]See also Keye [22] *at* 422.

[154]Keye [22] *at* 419.

[155]Keye [22] *at* 419.

[156]Keye [22] *at* 419.

[157]Keye [22] *at* 223.

The mandate under Article 113 and following national law conferring criminal jurisdiction on the nationality principle may be appropriate for accidental damage or injury of submarine cables. This mandate is significantly inadequate to counter willful human aggression amounting to terrorist activities on critical submarine cable infrastructure: the terrorism Conventions and the SUA Convention's provisions on intervention by a third State maybe a way forward.[158]

Indeed there is no instrument to address an act of terrorism on submarine cables on the line of the Protocol for the Suppression of Unlawful Acts against the Safety of Maritime Navigation (SUA protocol) or its 2005 Amendment.[159] There may be an Undersea Infrastructure Protocol defining areas of responsibility and permissible jurisdiction over a critical cable system to bridge this security gap.[160] The IMO may take such initiative to bring a protocol conferring State a strong basis for its naval forces to supervise critical cables and boarding a suspicious vessel. Most importantly, the UN Office on Drugs and Crime (UNODC), together with States, may take the initiative for developing an agenda at the UN platform leading to the adoption of such an instrument. The proposed instrument or protocol may impose an obligation on the State to undergo the submarine cable registration process and acknowledge States' competence to protect submarine cables analogous to its rights to defend its flagships.[161]

The next basis of States' action responding to terrorism against submarine cables may be related to establishing a single point of contract to monitor behavior threatening submarine cable. Such a single-point contract may be facilitated by the institutions such as ICPC, regional cable committees, and coastal security authorities and reduced to an intergovernmental arrangement. Lastly, States may acknowledge the establishment of protection zones for the submarine cables for specific purpose (discussed further in Sect. 4.5, Chap. 4).

Regarding the determination of the offence of terrorism of submarine cables, it is necessary to consider the other existing 'UN terrorism Conventions.'[162] Among existing UN terrorism Conventions, the offence of terrorist attack on submarine cables attracts the International Convention for the Suppression of Terrorist Bombing 1997. It states 'it is an offence to unlawfully and intentionally use an explosive or lethal device against an infrastructure facility with the intent to cause extensive destruction of such facility or where such destruction results in or are likely to result in major economic loss.' The submarine cable communication system comes under the preview of 'an infrastructure facility' as it is a public or privately owned facility

---

158Keye [22] *at* 223.

159Wrathall [15] *at* 245.

160Wrathall [15] *at* 250.

161Wrathall [15] *at* 250.

162The Convention for the Suppression of Unlawful Seizure of Aircraft 1970; Convention for the Suppression of Unlawful Acts against the Safety of Civil Aviation, 1971; Protocol for the Suppression of Unlawful Acts of Violence at Airports Serving International Civil Aviation, supplementary to the Convention for the Suppression of Unlawful Acts against the Safety of Civil Aviation, 1988; Convention for the Suppression of Unlawful Acts against the Safety of Maritime Navigation, 1988 and its Protocol 2005. See Burnett et al. [6].

that provides or distributes services.[163] However, such a mandate is limited to the terrorist activities against cable by bombing and not applied to other means such as cutting of cables. The objective of a potential instrument would be to address offence linked with the person who 'intentionally cause destruction or damage of critical submarine cable infrastructure by punishing such offences as an action of the criminals.' It requires States to provide a mechanism to ensure prosecution of such offence irrespective of the place or nationality of the persons or vessels involved with the sabotage of submarine cables.

Therefore, irrespective of the involvement of the terrorist group or with a terrorist motive or purpose, an act of 'destruction or damage of critical submarine cable infrastructure' would be considered as an offence if it is done 'unlawfully and intentionally.' The gravity of such offence would be greater than that of the offence under Article 113. Then, the State parties shall ensure the enforcement of the alleged offence of terrorism against the cable system. They require to adopt a law imposing severe punishment for 'intentionally causing destruction or damage to the critical submarine cable infrastructure' amounting to terrorist activities. They need to exercise jurisdiction over the offence and the perpetrators (person or vessels) irrespective of their nationality and place of offence. The State in whose jurisdiction the perpetrators are physically present may take them into custody. Then, it may extradite the perpetrators to the appropriate State for prosecution.[164] In precise, such measures may authorize States to exercise jurisdictions over the offense of terrorism against cable systems. Those perpetrators must have no safe haven. They will be either tried or extradited for trial.

Therefore, the present international cable regime on submarine cable has several limitations. This regime nevertheless set out the fundamental principles of laying and the protection of submarine cables. These principles are the freedom of laying cables and the protection of cables. They also establish measures to control other marine activities to limit their interference to the cable operation and prescribe certain standards for other vessels regarding signals, prior notice, maintaining distances, etc. Lastly, they also prescribe detailed guidelines regarding the implementation of these provisions. In precise, the international regime's principles and parameters on cables suggest the essential basis for a proposed draft legal framework national instrument on submarine cables.

Regarding environmental standards and submarine cable operation on high seas, there may be a cooperative approach between cable carriers and the concerned authorities, even though there is no certainty about the impact of cable operation on the marine environment.[165] Moreover, exclusion of cable operation from the biodiversity and high seas marine standards may not be tenable.[166] However, there is a compelling

---

[163] Burnett, et al. [6] *at* 292.

[164] Burnett, et al. [6] *at* 290–293.

[165] Davenport [55].

[166] Friedman [47].

argument representing the submarine cable industry's' position on marine biodiversity concerns concerning the cable in area beyond the national jurisdictions.[167] It emphasis that new environmental standards on the cable may be an additional burden to the cable operators, given the submarine cables have a minimum impact on the marine environment. Therefore, a new instrument on marine biodiversity (if adopted) could exclude cables to accommodate the freedom of laying submarine cables harmoniously.[168]

2.13 Summary

The international submarine cable regime set out in UNCLOS declares the principle of Freedom of the Laying of Submarine Cables and associated activities. It prescribes provisions conferring rights and imposing liabilities on the States parties to adopt a measure for cables accordingly. However, UNCLOS is no longer adequate to ensure the submarine cables system security and reliability, which has become the critical communication infrastructure—the backbone of telecommunications and the internet.

Firstly, UNCLOS follows the principle of State sovereignty within TW and does not obligate State parties to adopt the law on cables within TW. Thus, the submarine cable governance within TW rests on States' discretions. There, in the absence of a clear law, cable breaking may not be illegal, and laying the cable is also challenging.

Secondly, the issues with the submarine cable regimes are not promoted by international organizations, including the organization related to the law of the sea.

Thirdly, though UNCLOS has prescribed obligations on the States concerning laying and protecting cables within EEZ and beyond, these international obligations have not been implemented effectively in many national jurisdictions.

Fourthly, the UNCLOS regime on submarine cables mostly remains silent on addressing deliberate human aggressions on submarine cables. The existing principle of protecting cables is focused on risks to cables from the regular marine users engaged in marine activities; however, it does not deal with the cable system's security threats posed by piracy and maritime terrorism. Finally, the international regime on cables prescribes several principles and parameters—which are the primary basis for a proposed draft legal framework for national instruments on submarine cables.

In continuation of the international regime's shared principles and parameters, the following two consecutive chapters will analyze and compare the relevant national instruments and dedicated legislations on submarine cables. It will help in identifying the basic premise of the existing submarine cables standards. As mentioned in the research methodology above, Chap. 3 of this study deals with a homogeneous group of jurisdictions that are yet to adopt dedicated national instruments on cables. And, the

---

167 Burnett and Carter [56].

168 Burnett and Carter [56], *at* 62.

following Chap. 4 will deal with the States that have already adopted comprehensive legal and regulatory systems on submarine cables.

References

1. Wagner, E. (1995). Submarine cables and protections provided by the law of the sea. *Marine Policy, 19,* 127–136.
2. Huurdeman, A. (2003). *The worldwide history of telecommunications.* Wiley.
3. de Chandler, C. F. (1922). Submarine telegraph cables. *Scientific American, 127,* 91–92.
4. Malecki, E. J., & Wei, H. (2009). A wired world: The evolving geography of submarine cables and the shift to Asia. *Annals of the Association of American Geographers, 99,* 360–382.
5. Carter, L., Burnett, D., Drew, S., Marle, G., Hagadorn, L., Bartlett-McNeil, D., & Irvine, N. (2009). *Submarine cables and the oceans—Connecting the world* (UNEP-WCMC Biodiversity Series No. 31). ICPC/UNEP/UNEP-WCMC.
6. Burnett, D., Davenport, T., & Beckman, R. (2013). Overview of the international legal regime governing submarine cables. In D. Burnett (Ed.), *Submarine cables: The handbook of law and policy* (pp. 6–90). Martinus Nijhoff Publication.
7. Agarwala, N. (2019). "Green cables"—Development, opportunities and legal challenges: Part II. *Maritime Affairs: Journal of the National Maritime Foundation of India, 15,* 93–107.
8. Hayes, J. (2008). A history of transatlantic cables. *IEEE Communications Magazine*, pp. 42–48.
9. The Indo-European telegraph company. *History of the Atlantic Cable & Undersea Communications.* http://atlantic-cable.com/CableCos/Indo-Eur/index.htm. Accessed 24 February 2018.
10. Headrick, D. R., & Griset, P. (2001). Submarine telegraph cables: Business and politics, 1838–1939. *The Business History Review, 75,* 543–578.
11. Higgins A. P. (1921–1922). Submarine cables and international law. *British Year Book of International Law, 75,* 27–33.
12. Crispin, J., Cummins, J. M., Emus, R., & reyna, J. (1985). satellites versus fibre optic cables. *International Journal of Satellite Communications, 3,* 217–220.
13. Ruiz, J. B., & Barnett, G. A. (2015). Who owns the international internet networks? *The Journal of International Communication, 21,* 38–57.
14. Winseck, D. (2017). The geopolitical economy of the global internet infrastructure. *Journal of Information Policy, 7,* 228–267.
15. Wrathall, L. R. (2011). The vulnerability of subsea infrastructure to underwater attack: Legal shortcomings and the way forward. *Sandeago International Law Journal, 12,* 224–257, 228.
16. G.A. Res. 65/37, 121 (December 7, 2010).
17. "Submarine Cable Information Sharing Project: Legislative Practices and Points of Contact, September 2011. Telecommunications and Information Working Group, March 2012, Asia Pacific Economic Cooperation (APEC)." https://www.apec.org/Meeting-Papers/Sectoral-Ministerial-Meetings/Telecommunications-and-Information/2010_tel. Accessed 21 February 2018.
18. Brown, E. D. (1992). The significance of a possible EC EEZ for the law relating to artificial islands, installations, and structures, and cables and pipelines, in the exclusive economic zone. *Ocean Development and International Law, 23,* 115–144.
19. Roach, J. A. (2014). Today's customary international law of the sea. *Ocean Development and International Law, 45,* 239–259.
20. Beckman, R. (2010, January). *Submarine cables—A critically important but neglected area of the law of the sea.* 7th International Conference on Legal Regimes of Sea, Air, Space and Antarctica (ISIL Conference). New Delhi. https://cil.nus.edu.sg/wp/wp-content/uploads/2010/01/Beckman-PDF-ISIL-Submarine-Cables-rev-8-Jan-10.pdf. Accessed 7 January 2017.
21. Renault, L. 1882. *The Protection of Submarine Telegraphs and the Paris Conference* (Oct–Nov 1882), drawn from International Law Review.

22. Kaye, S. (2006–2007). International measures to protect oil platforms, pipelines, and submarine cables from attack. *Tulna Maritime Law Journal, 31*, 377–423.
23. Coffen-Smout, S., & Herbert, G. J. (2000). Submarine cables: A challenge for ocean management. *Marine Policy, 24*, 441–448.
24. UN Documents Concerning Development and Codification of International Law, Supplement to 41(4). *American Journal of International Law*, October 1947.
25. Tanaka, Y. (2012). *The international law of the sea*. Cambridge University Press.
26. Miller, H. (1930). The Hague codification conference. *Ameican Journal of International Law, 24*, 674–693.
27. Kraska, J. (2015). Submarine espionage in territorial waters. *Columbia Journal ofTransnational Law, 54*, 166–246.
28. Davenport, T. (2012). Submarine communications cables and law of the sea: Problems in law and practice. *Ocean Development and International Law, 43*, 201–242.
29. Takie, T. (2012). Law and policy for international submarines cables: An Asia-Pacific perspective. *Asian Journal of International Law, 2*, 205–233.
30. (High Seas Convention), 450 UNTS 11 (Article 26–30).
31. Article 30 of the Geneva Convention 1958. 29 Apr 1958, 499 UNTS (1964).
32. (Continental Shelf Convention 1958) Convention on the Continental Shelf, 29 Apr 1958, 499 UNTS (1964) at 312.
33. Mudric, M. (2010). Rights of states regarding underwater cables and pipelines. *Australian Resources and Energy Law Journal, 29*, 235–255.
34. UNCLOS 1982. The United Nations Convention on the Law of the Sea December 10, 1982, 1833 UNTS 3.
35. Mensah, T. A. (2015). Submarine cables and the international law of the sea. In L. del Castillo (Ed.),Law of the sea: From grotius to the international tribunal for the law of the sea: Liber amicorum Judge Hugo Caminos (pp. 725–749).
36. The Convention for the Protection of the Marine Environment of the North-East Atlantic or (OSPAR), 1992, 32 ILM 1069 (1992).
37. Davenport, T. (2013). Submarine communications cables and science: A New Frontier in Ocean Governance?. In H. N. Scheiber (Ed.), *Science technology, and new challenges to ocean law* (pp. 209–252). A Law of the Sea Institute Publication.
38. Burnett, D. (2013). Submarine cables on the continental shelf. In M. H. Nordquist (Ed.), *The regulation of continental shelf development* (pp. 53–70). Center for Oceans Law and Policy.
39. Nordquist M. H. (Ed.). (2014). *UN convention on the law of the sea commentary 1982 Online*. Center for Oceans Law and Policy, University of Virginia, Brill Publication.
40. A/CONF.62/WP.10 (ICNT, 1977), article 79, VIII Off. Rec.1, 17. Ibid., *at* 909 and 915.
41. A/CONF.62/WP.10 (ICNT, 1977), article 79, VIII Off. Rec.1, 20.
42. Treves, T. (2019). Due regard' obligations under the 1982 UN convention on the law of the sea: The laying of cables and activities in the area. *International Journal of Marine and Coastal Law, 34*, 167–194.
43. Kroon, D. (2018). Due regard in the high seas: The tension between submarine cables and deep seabed mining. *Australian International Law Journal, 24*, 35–57.
44. Raha, U. K. (2018). Legal analysis of the submarine cables regime with special reference to the exclusive economic zone: A grey area of the law of the sea. In A. Tiwari (Ed.), Legal audit—A compilation of recent socio-legal issues in India & abroad (pp. 42–48). Infinity Publication.
45. Beckman, R., & Davenport, T. (2012). *The EEZ regime: Reflections after 30 years, securing the ocean for the next generation*. LOSI Conference Papers, pp. 1–41. https://www.law.berkeley.edu/files/Beckman-Davenport-final.pdf. Accessed 22 May 2017.
46. Sun, Z. (2018). Protection of cable ships engaged in operations for submarine telecommunication cables. *Ocean Development and International Law, 49*, 118–133.
47. Friedman, A. (2017). Submarine telecommunication cables and a biodiversity agreement in ABNJ: Finding new routes for cooperation. *The International Journal of Marine and Coastal Law, 32*, 1–35.

48. Jayakar, K. (1998). Globalization and the legitimacy of international telecommunications standard-setting organizations. *Indiana Journal of Global Legal Studies, 15,* 711–738.
49. Schuster, D. B. (2015). International telecommunication union—150 years of history: Adaptation to change and the opportunity for reform. IEEE Communications Magazine—Communications Standards Supplement, pp. 10–15.
50. The ICPC. https://www.iscpc.org/about-the-icpc/. Accessed 16 March 2020.
51. Beckman, R. (2010). *1982 UNCLOS: A legal framework for cooperation between cable companies and coastal states*. International Cable Protection Committee (ICPC) Plenary Meeting, Mauritius, 2010.
52. Gady, F. S. (2011, May 25). Undersea cables: The achilles heel of our economies. *The Huffington Post*. https://www.huffingtonpost.com/franzstefan-gady/undersea-cables-the-achil_b_799808.html. Accessed 16 February 2018.
53. Cooper, H. F. (2018). *Undersea cables: The achilles heel of our economies*. http://highfrontier.org/january-8-2018-our-undersea-achilles-heel/. Accessed 16 February 2018.
54. Tsuruoka, D. (2018, January 6). Undersea cables the Achilles' heel in lead-up to new cold war. *Asia Times*. http://www.atimes.com/article/undersea-cables-achilles-heel-lead-new-cold-war/. Accessed 16 February 2018.
55. Davenport, T. (2018). The high seas freedom to lay submarine cables and the protection of the marine environment: Challenges in high seas governance. *Symposium on Governing High Seas Biodiversity, American Journal of International Law Unbound, 112,* 139–143.
56. Burnett, R., & Carter, L. (2017). International submarine cables and biodiversity of areas beyond national jurisdiction—The cloud beneath the sea. *Brill Research Perspectives in the Law of the Sea, 1,* 1–72.

Chapter 3
Challenges to the Laying and Protection of Submarine Cable in Selected Jurisdictions—A Legal and Comparative Analysis

3.1 Introduction

Submarine cable operators are to comply with the legal and regulatory standards across the marine jurisdictions. The laying of submarine cable, particularly within States' maritime jurisdiction, attracts relevant national laws such as the cable installation permit measures. A cable operator cannot lay cable in a coastal State's marine space unless there is consent from the latter. The submarine cable laying approval process is a part of the coastal States' law and executive standards concerning submarine cables. These laws include legal instruments and provisions on permits for cable route survey, laying, repair, maintenance, etc., and the protection of cables besides the law on the other maritime uses. These laws, other instruments, and measures together comprise the national legal framework on submarine cables. The national submarine cable regime has an essential role in the laying and protection of cable. Therefore, it is necessary to look into national laws and executive standards on submarine cable.

At the national level, many countries have adopted measures to regulate submarine cable operation at variance.[1] The submarine cable laws in many countries' in turn vary from country to country. Law on submarine cable in the UK and Australia differs from countries of the USA and South America, Asia, and Africa.[2] Many of these jurisdictions are yet to enact a dedicated law on cables except Australia and New Zealand.[3] As mentioned in an earlier chapter, many States who are yet to adopt comprehensive regulations on cables, particularly for the protection of cables, comprise a homogeneous group of jurisdictions, which will be regarded as '*other countries/ selected national jurisdictions*.'[4] *Other countries/selected national jurisdictions* indicate many States, including India, yet to adopt dedicated laws to ensure submarine cables' safety and reliability.

[1]Burnett et al. [1].

[2]AEP-Threats-to Undersea-Cable-Communications [2].

[3]Beckman [3].

[4]Chapter 4 of this study will deal with the comprehensive and dedicated national legislations on submarine cables of Australia and New Zealand.

U. K. Raha and Raju K. D., *Submarine Cables Protection and Regulations*,
https://doi.org/10.1007/978-981-16-3436-9_3

In the selected jurisdictions, there are several instruments in the form of regulations, orders, notifications, directives that regulate the laying and associated submarine cable activities therein. On many occasions, those instruments are the extensions of the national legislation on the sea and other marine uses that include fisheries, shipping, exploration, and exploitation of marine resources, etc. The national law of crimes also prescribes provisions for the protection of submarine cable and imposes a penalty for submarine cable damage. Besides, submarine cable operation in many jurisdictions requires meeting national maritime policy, environmental and other maritime and coastal habitat conservation measures. Therefore, laying the submarine cables is laying off the submarine cables to meet several national compliances and rely on multiple governmental departments comprising the national submarine cable governance framework.

This chapter deals with the selected jurisdictions and their national legal standards dealing with submarine cables. It analyses the submarine cable laws of these countries. Thus, submarine cable instruments from some of the jurisdictions from different continents are under consideration. This research relies on representative and advanced legal systems criteria for selecting submarine cable regimes of the selected jurisdictions across the continents.

This chapter aims to ascertain the submarine cable regimes' sources and identify the cable regimes' fundamental parameters, approaches, liability, and procedures in selected jurisdictions. It provides an overview of national submarine cables instruments' legal analysis and does not comprehensively deal with these cable instruments. It intends to outline principal submarine cable instruments that together encompass the legal frameworks of the States' within which cable operations are required to be operated as illustrations. This chapter intends to highlight with illustrations that many States are still negligent in adopting specific laws to ensure the cable system's safety and reliability. It specifically focuses on the identification of the significant features of the submarine cable-related instruments. It carries out a comparative analysis of the instruments' salient features' salient features' salient features to identify their commonalities and differences to drive essential guidance for developing a model legal framework for national instruments submarine cables.

3.2 The Basis for Identification of the Selected Jurisdictions

To begin with Asia, the marine spaces of several countries like India, Singapore, Malaysia, Indonesia, and China hold an essential place in the international submarine cable map.[5] Therefore, this research focuses on these countries' submarine cable regimes while dealing with the national submarine cable regimes in Asia.[6] In Europe, the UK and France are important countries contributing to developing the submarine

[5]Malecki and Wei [4].

[6]Sugadev [5].

cable regimes since the inception of the Cable Convention 1884.[7] Besides, the European Union (EU) regulations on submarine cables also apply to the EU countries, and therefore, those cable-related measures are under consideration. Both USA and Canada's submarine cable regimes are important as they have become the sources of major international submarine cable networks. Then, the discussion will continue with analyzing the relevant laws in some of the countries from South America and South Africa.

For this study, the researcher has accessed the International Cable Protection Committee (ICPC) website besides other sources.[8] The following parts of the chapter deal with analyzing the jurisdictions' submarine cable regimes selected from different continents, respectively.

3.3 Legal Analysis of the Law on Submarine Cables in Selected Jurisdictions—An Overview

3.3.1 Asia

3.3.1.1 India

The submarine cable operation within India's maritime zones attracts both of its legislations and secondary instruments. Those secondary instruments prescribe for procedural requirements concerning cables and are linked with governmental departments. All of those legal instruments mandate submarine cable operators to take approval from several governmental departments in India.[9]

According to the Territorial Waters, Continental Shelf, Exclusive Economic Zone, and Other Maritime Zones Act, 1976 (the MZI Act), the Indian government may not impede the laying or maintenance of cables in its EEZ and continental shelf.[10] Nevertheless, the said legislation authorizes Indian authorities to take any measures to protect India's interests. The term 'interests' may include many issues. Thereby, India may adopt many measures to regulate the freedom to lay, repair, and maintain submarine cables. Further, cable operators must take permission from the Indian authorities to delineate the course of the submarine cable.[11] The said requirement is

---

[7]Burnett et al. [1].

[8]The International Cable Protection Committee (ICPC) (restricted access).

[9]Other authorities: Ministry of Home Affairs (MOHA), Ministry of Defense (MOD), Directorate General of Shipping (DG Shipping), Indian Customs Department, Indian National Ship Owners' Association (INSA), Flag Officer, Offshore Defense Advisory Group (FODAG), Port Authorities. See Sugadev [5].

[10]India's Maritime Zones Act [6].

[11]Section 6 (7) of India's Maritime Zones Act [6].

arguably against UNCLOS provisions.[12] Moreover, Indian Oil and Gas Regulations also apply to cable operations.

India's sovereignty extends to its territorial waters (up to 12 nm). So, the Government of India is the authority to regulate submarine cable operations in these waters [Section 4 (3) of the MZI Act]. Section 6 (4) of the MZI Act provides that in the EEZ, any exploration and exploitation activities require the *terms of a license* or a letter of authority granted by the Central Government of India.[13] Arguably, this provision applies to deal with the operations related to the oil and gas in the EEZ and continental shelf and does not deal with the submarine cable operations.[14] Further, it is argued that the very basis of this permit requirement for cable is Section 6 (4) of the MZI Act, which does not include cables. Thereby, the same basis of a permit requirement for cable operation in India's EEZ is inaccurate and arguably against UNCLOS provision.[15]

As mentioned above, cable companies are required to take permission from various Indian authorities.[16] An explanation of regulations dealing with this permission process may be helpful to appreciate India's permit requirements. In pre-cable repair and post-repair operations, the cable repair ship is to visit an Indian port and comply with the regulations. Permission from respective Indian authorities comprises the three phases.[17] Before the commencement of repair, the permission process has two steps again. In the first phase, the cable ship personnel must take permission from the Indian Ministry of Home Affairs (MOHA) through the Department of Telecommunications (DOT). Since 2014, this permission process has been routed through the Indian Embassy. This permission lasts for one year. The MOD Guidelines 1996 and Directives 2006 seeks clearance from the Ministry of Defense (MOD) through the DOT.[18] Arguably these guidelines and directives apply to the exploration and exploitation of oil, gas and do not apply to submarine cables.[19]

The ship meets the Indian National Shipowners' Association (INSA) requirement determining whether any Indian cable ship can repair the cables; the process takes three to four days. It follows the DG Shipping Circular No. 2/2002. In practice,

[12] Article 79 (3), of UNCLOS [7].

[13] Section 6 (4) of India's Maritime Zones Act [6] provides 'No person (including a foreign government) shall, except under, and in accordance with the terms of a licence or a letter of authority granted by the Central Government, explore the continental shelf or exploit its resources or carry out any search or excavation or conduct any research within the continental shelf or drill therein or construct, maintain or operate any artificial island, off-shore terminal, installation or other structure or device therein for any purpose whatsoever.' A similar provision has also been provided and applied in the Continental Shelf, under Section 7 (5) of India's Maritime Zones Act 1976.

[14] The EEZ regime overlaps the Continental Shelf regime up to 200 nm. Sugadev [5], *at* 179.

[15] Sugadev [5] *at* 185.

[16] Burnett [8].

[17] Sugadev, Ibid.

[18] Burnett et al. [1], *at* 64.

[19] Sugadev, Ibid.

the Indian owner does not possess such a cable ship, and therefore, this requirement appears unrealistic.[20] Again, Shipping Development Circular 2013 requires to employ Indian crew in the foreign flagship working in the Indian coastal waters. This provision is also against exclusive flag States' authority [Art. 94(3) (b)]. The second phase of the permission process starts with the arrival of the ship at the port. At this stage, the ship needs to meet the customs duty and service tax liability, vessel conversion, Naval Inspection and Security Clearance (SNC), and the port clearance (inward). Indian Navy seals all the mobile platforms with a Very Small Aperture Terminal (VSAT) before the ship commences repair activities.[21] The last phase of permission starts at the end of the cable repair process when the ship returns to the port (Indian port), requiring compliance with the export formalities and port clearance (outward).[22] In precise, India's cable permit regime is expected to be streamlined under a lead agency in repose to its critical role in cable governance in South Asia.[23]

3.3.1.2 China

The State Council of China has issued Regulations on the Management of Laying Submarine Cables and Pipelines 1989 (the Regulations 1989). The Ministry of Land and Resources has also promulgated Regulations on the Protection of Submarine Cables and Pipelines 2004 (the Regulations 2004).[24] The 1989 Regulations provide detailed permit requirements for laying submarine cables in Chinese water. The Regulations 2004 prescribes preventive measures (report, protection zones, prohibition of certain activities there, the sacrifice of fishing gears, etc., that catch cables) and compensation against cable damage incidents. When the Regulations 1989 authorizes State Oceanic Administration (SOA), the Regulations 2004 empowers the Administration Department of the State Oceanographic Bureau to ensure those mandates' compliance. Further, submarine cable operation in Chinese marine space attracts its law on the administration of sea areas.[25]

Regulations on the Management of Laying Submarine Cables and Pipelines 1989 (The Regulations 1989)

Article 19 of the Regulations 1989 provides that 'the term 'cables,' as used in these provisions, refers to communications cables and electric cables.' The State Oceanographic Bureau of the People's Republic of China is the 'the competent authority

[20] Ibid.

[21] Sugadev [5], *at* 185.

[22] Ibid.

[23] Raha and Raju [9].

[24] Yincan et al. [10].

[25] China's Law [11].

under the Regulations 1989.[26] In 2002, the Law of the People's Republic of China on the Law on the Management of Sea Area Use had also connected the submarine cable laying with the State Council 'State Oceanic Administration's marine Administrative Department' (SOA). This Chinese lead agency (SOA) issues permits for laying submarine cables in China. The SOA requires foreign submarine cable owners to submit applications for the sea with necessary details should they wish to engage with the laying of submarine cables within Chinese maritime zones.[27] Thus, China approaches with lead agency for cables operation.

The Regulations 1989 require the cable operators to obtain approval from the competent authority for both local and foreign submarine cables conducting investigations and surveys of routes and other relevant activities concerning the laying submarine cables. Article 5 of the Regulation 1989 prescribes for an application for laying submarine cable with necessary details, and such an application must contain information on the name, nationality, and residence of the cable owner, detail about personnel laying cables, geographical area, time, items, methods, and equipment, etc. It also indicates 60 days' time period for processing of the application. Thus, the application must contain information about the cable operation and indicate the approval time frame.

Concerning the repair and maintenance of the submarine cables in China, the cable owners also require to apply to the competent authority before engaging with such cable operation. It also provides compensation in case the submarine cable operators cause damage to existing submarine cables.[28] The cable owners rely on the competent authority for any dispute relating to the submarine cable operation. This competent authority can supervise the submarine cable operation and impose a fine to implement the Regulations 1989. To sum up, the Regulations 1989 establishes a lead agency responsible for dealing with the submarine cable operation and implementation.

[26] Ministry of Commerce [12].

[27] Art. 4 of the China's Regulation 1989 provides 'when foreign companies, enterprises, and other foreign economic organizations or individuals have the necessity to lay submarine cables and pipelines and also to conduct investigations and survey of routes and other relevant activities for the aforesaid engineering projects in the inland seas and territorial seas of the People's Republic of China, they shall, in accordance with these provisions, apply to the competent authorities for approval; if they have the necessity to carry out the said activities on the continental shelves of the People's Republic of China, they shall notify the competent authorities in advance, but the routes they have selected and decided on for laying the cables and pipelines must have the consent of the competent authorities.'

[28] Article 13 of the China's Regulation 1989 provides 'Operators who are engaged in various activities at sea must protect the submarine cables and pipelines that have already been laid. Those who have caused damages to the said installations shall make compensations according to law.'

Regulations on the Protection of Submarine Cables and Pipelines 2004 (The Regulations 2004)

Regulations on the Protection of Submarine Cables and Pipelines 2004 (Regulations 2004) is an addition to the Regulations 1989. The Regulations 2004 provide provisions for the protection of submarine cable within the marine jurisdictions of China. It provides that the Administration Department of the State Oceanographic Bureau has authority for the supervision of submarine cable operation and the implementation of this regulation itself. First, this regulation requires the cable owners to submit a route chart and position chart of the submarine cables to the lead agency and inform about the activities relating to the submarine cable operators, the lead agency for publications.

The lead agency then reports to the public annually regarding the submarine cables' physical existence and their starting to terminal points. This lead agency is to declare the oceanic natural protection zones, ranging from 50 to 500 m of both sides of submarine cables. Article 8 is an essential provision of the regulations and states that-

> It's forbidden to dig sand, drill, drive a pile into the ground, lay in anchor, drag anchor, fish, net, breed or other sea operations that might damage the safety of submarine cables and pipelines within the protection zones of submarine cables and pipelines.

For the protection of submarine cables, the other sea operators are to take possible measures. Before engaging sea operation within the said protection zones, the operators agree with the existing cable owners on 'technical issues, protection procedures and claim of compensation, etc.'

An aggrieved party may submit a complaint against this regulation's violation to the State Oceanographic Bureau's Administration Department (lead agency). Articles 17–19 of the regulations prescribe liability to the breach of the regulations. A fine of 10,000 RMB for those cable owners 'who fail to put on record the route chart, position chart of submarine cables.'[29]

The non-compliances like unauthorized cable operation, failure to take adequate protection measures, damaging cables (Art 18) may attract liability, leading to the cessation of submarine cable operation or meet fine. The regulations also provide both civil and criminal liability if there is a discrepancy by the officials of this lead agency. *Lastly*, the lead agency is the forum for resolving any disputes arising from sea operators' and cable owners' activities.

Further, Chap. V of the Law of the People's Republic China on the Law on the Management of Sea Area Use 2001 provides for the royalties for using sea Aaeas.[30] The articles comprising Article 33 to Article 36 of this law contain provisions for royalties. For submarine cable operation, Article 33 provides for the imposition and collection of royalties to use the sea areas according to the State Council's rates for

---

[29] Article 17 of China's Regulation [13].

[30] China's Law [11].

the sea area use.[31] It prescribes that the submarine cable operators may require to pay royalty annually for the cable operation (Article 34) and avail concession in royalty as cable provides public services. In precise, China has prescribed several measures for cable operation.

The Chinese instruments' significant features on submarine cables are a lead agency, publication of cable chart, royalty for laying cables, the penalty for cable operators on damaging cables, a requirement for detailed information on laying cables. It also includes the cable protection zone, restricting certain marine activities, defining offense with civil and criminal liability, and resolving disputes. However, China imposes attendant costs for international submarine cable repairs beyond its territorial seas, and the approval process of such rearing is also time taking.[32]

3.3.1.3 Singapore

In Singapore, the Info-communications Media Development Authority (IDMA) deals with submarine cable operations.[33] The IDMA is Singapore's lead agency for laying submarine cables and its landing stations.[34] It prescribes guidance in both the landing and repair of submarine cables. The IDMA sets guidelines that facilitate in obtaining permits and processing of applications for the submarine cable operation. These guidelines are of two types—the Submarine Cable Deployment Guidelines and, secondly, the Submarine Cable Repair Guidelines. At the outset, it is to note that the IDMA has adopted these guidelines for guiding the cable operation; however, these instruments are not legal documents.

The Submarine Cable Deployment Guidelines 2010 (The Deployment Guidelines 2010)

The Deployment Guidelines 2010 facilitates cable companies who require to obtain necessary approvals and permits for cable laying into Singapore. These permit and approval procedures comprise the processing of five applications from several government authorities. Those authorities include the IDMA, marine port and urban development and environmental authorities, etc. These authorities consider various issues that may give rise to cable operation into Singapore. The priority of such

[31] Article 33 of China's Law [11] provides 'the State practices the system of using sea areas on the paid basis. Any entity or individual that uses a sea area shall pay royalties for the use according to the rates as provided by the State Council. The royalties for using sea areas shall, pursuant to the provisions of the State Council, be turned over to the State treasury. The concrete steps and measures for charging royalties for the use of sea areas by fishermen for breeding aquatics shall be separately formulated by the State Council.'

[32] Burnett [8].

[33] IMDA Deployment Guidelines [15].

[34] APEC [16].

considerations includes identifying cable route survey and cable corridors, Environmental Impact Assessment, other marine infrastructural assessment, land use, etc.

The Submarine Cable Repair Guidelines 2010 (The Repair Guidelines 2010)[35]

The Repair Guidelines 2010 suggest necessary support to the cable operators for conducting a quick cable repairing process into Singapore water. Therefore, the essential features of these guidelines are notable for the present research. An application for submarine cable repairing permission is to channel through the Marine Port Authority (MPA) of Singapore. Cable repair may be within the Singapore Port area or the Traffic Separation Scheme's vicinity (TSS). For cable repairs within ports, the cable companies apply to the Committee of Marine Projects (COMET) of the MPA. The cable operators are also required to submit an application to the MPA for repairing cables within the TSS. Such applications should include detailed operators, operations overview, repairing vessels, communication plan during repair, detailed repairing methodology, and involved personnel, etc.

Singapore has sought to facilitate cable operations with the lead agency. For laying cables, it prescribes information that relates to cable route survey and cable corridors, Environmental Impact Assessment, other marine infrastructural assessment, land use, etc. It also specifies authority that will facilitate the permission for the repairing of cables.

3.3.1.4 Indonesia—Regulation of Submarine Cables 1999 (The Minister of Transportation Decision No. 94/1999)

There is no lead agency in Indonesia that deals with the submarine cable operation; however, the Ministry of Transportation regulates permit measures for the submarine cable operation according to the minister of transportation decision no. 94/1999.[36] It has also not adopted a precise instrument dedicated to the laying and protection of submarine cables.[37]

Its submarine cable installation and repairing and maintenance system includes clearance from the Ministry of Defense and the Ministry of Transportation.[38] Further, a cable ship needs to obtain a Clearance Approval for Indonesian Territory from the governmental departments such as the Ministry of Foreign Affairs for

[35]IMDA Repairs Guidelines [14].

[36]Nugroho [17].

[37]Ibid., *at* 91.

[38]Ibid., *at* 92.

political clearance, the Indonesian National Armed Forces Headquarters for security clearance, and the Ministry for Transportation for technical clearance.[39]

Essential features of these Indonesian regulations include restricted areas, prohibited activities, and burying of cables for the protection of submarine cables, etc. This regulation suggests restricted areas for submarine cable, a surrounding area along the submarine cable route with a corridor of 3500 m. They prohibit activities like anchorage, dredging, mining, or other underwater activities except installing a new submarine cable. This regulation prescribes a distance of not less than 500 m between the new cable and the existing cable.

The protection of submarine cables explicitly provides for the burying of the cables with different depths, ranging from 2 to 0.5 m.[40] The Minister of Transportation may permit for armoring, anchoring, burial using concrete, or placing the cable inside a tunnel by drilling as other means of cable protection besides placing buoy; designation of restriction zone; and submitting of maps showing coordinates of the route to the Ministry of Transportation and other relevant agencies.[41]

The underwater environment safety analysis requirement is another crucial feature for Indonesia's submarine cable operation and marine environmental measures. According to Law No. 36/1999, disruption to telecommunication installations is now punishable with a maximum of six years of imprisonment or a maximum fine of Rp. 600,000,000.[42]

Government Regulation No. 20/2010 is another necessary regulation for Indonesia's submarine cable operation. It has prescribed that the underwater works included submarine cable activities. According to these provisions, only Indonesian vessels (Indonesian flag vessels) and people are eligible for the submarine cable activities within Indonesia's marine jurisdictions.

Indonesia's cable protection approach establishes a cable safety zone that restricts other marine activities and buries cables. It also has a concern for the marine environment and coastal employment too. There is scope to have an efficient cable regulatory system—a 'one door'/ 'one-stop shopping' policy for all permits and coordination among Indonesia's governmental authorities. A coordinated surveillance system using the Indonesian Navy, water police, or sea guards, or coast guards assisting in

---

[39] Ibid., *at* 93.

[40] Article 3 of this the Minister of Transportation Decision No. 94/1999 provides that the submarine cable communication system needs to be integrally protected and secure and suggest for Cable burial. And Article 5 provides

(a) From shore until 10 m depth, 2 m under the ocean floor;
(b) From 10 m until 15 m depth, 1 m under the ocean floor;
(c) From 10 m until 28 m depth, 0.5 m under the ocean floor; and
(d) beyond 28 m depths, the cable may be laid on the ocean floor provided that it can be assured to be in a stable condition.

[41] Nugroho [17], *at* 91.

[42] Ibid., *at* 87.

the cable systems' surveillance may help prevent interruption of telecommunication installations.[43]

3.3.1.5 Japan

Japan has been one of the signatories of the Cable Convention 1884. Japan's domestic law, i.e., the Telecommunications Business Law 1984, provides provisions for protecting submarine cables in Japan's marine space.[44] This law designates submarine cables as underwater cables, and Articles 140–143 deal with underwater cables' security.

It prescribes the cable operators are to submit a notification to the different authorities for laying underwater cables on Japan's seabed.[45] These Japanese authorities include minister and the relevant prefectural governors (including the Minister for Agriculture, Forestry, and Fisheries). The said notification must consist of the submarine cables' location submarine cables' locations, the time of the commencement

---

[43]Ibid., *at* 99–103.

[44]Japan's Law [18].

[45]Article 140 of Japan's Law [18] provides '(1) Any approved telecommunications carrier shall, before it lays an underwater cable to be used for its approved telecommunications business (hereinafter referred to as an 'underwater cable') under any waters used for public use (hereinafter referred to as 'waters'), submit a notification to the Minister and the relevant prefectural governor (including the Minister for Agriculture, Forestry and Fisheries, where the waters are fishing places over which the Minister exercises the power of the prefectural governor in accordance with the provisions of Article 136 of the Fisheries Law (Law No. 267 of 1949), the same shall apply to the following paragraph.) on the following matters:

(i) Locations of the underwater cable and areas for which an application of paragraph

(1) of the following article is to be filed (ii) Time of the commencement and completion of the installation work (iii) Outline of the installation work.

(2) When the relevant prefectural governor, upon receipt of a notification in accordance with the provisions of the preceding paragraph, deems it necessary to alter any of the matters pertaining to the notification in accordance with the provisions of the preceding paragraph after hearing the opinions of any person interested in the rights to fish (meaning fishery rights under the Fisheries Law; hereinafter the same shall apply.) or of any other person actually and duly engaged in fishing stipulated in the applicable cabinet order of paragraph (4) of the following article within the area of item (i) of the preceding paragraph or after taking into account the effect of the telecommunications cable laying on fishing, he or she may, after a necessary consultation with any other prefectural governor involved, if any, issue a notice to the Minister and said approved telecommunications carrier to that effect within thirty days from the day on which said notification was submitted to the governor.

(3) The provisions of Article 11 paragraph (6) of the Fisheries Law shall apply, mutatis mutandis, to the cases in accordance with the provisions of the preceding paragraph. In this case, 'the prefectural governor' in Article 11 paragraph (6) of the Fisheries Law shall be read as 'relevant prefectural governor who received the notification in accordance with the provisions of Article 140 paragraph (1) of the Telecommunications Business Law.'

(4) The approved telecommunications carrier shall, upon receiving the notice in accordance with the provisions of paragraph (2), change said matters. This shall not apply, however, to such matters that would seriously interfere with the carrying out of its business activities insofar as authorization has been obtained from the Minister not to make such changes with respect to said matters.'

and completion of the installation work, and an outline of the installation work. On receiving this notification, the said authority will consult with the interested persons in those area-like fishermen and may make a necessary alteration of the submarine cable operation and proposed route.

In continuation, the ministry may designate an area that may extend to 50–1000 m as the underwater cable protected area by a notice.[46] This provision prohibits certain activities like anchoring, fishing with a bottom dragnet, digging and gathering earth and sand or moor a boat, or rafting to the landmark in such a protected area.[47]

A prefectural governor may impose restrictions on fishing activities to protect submarine cables within the protected areas. This provision entitles the fishermen to compensate the cable owners if the latter's activities hamper the fishery rights.[48]

Japan's approach is also to adopt a cable safety zone and control certain marine activities to enhance cable protection. Additionally, it has intended to minimize interruptions to both cable operation and fishing activities.

3.3.1.6 *Vietnam—The Directive,* viz. *on Strengthening the Protection of Submarine Cables and Ensuring the Safety of International Telecommunications 2007*

In 2007, Vietnam has issued a directive for the protection of submarine cables on the backdrop of a severe disruption of national telecommunication due to submarine cable damage.[49] It has been appreciated that interruption in telecommunications infrastructure impacts the safety and security of national information and its image in the international community. It also considers that disturbances in the communication system negatively impact the countries' social and economic developments. Through the said directive, the Prime Minister of Vietnam urges the concerned ministers, heads

---

[46]Article 141 Article 140 of Japan's Law [18] provides '(1) When an application from an approved telecommunications carrier has been submitted, the Minister may, when it is deemed necessary for the protection of the underwater cable concerned with respect to which the laying procedures stipulated in the preceding article has been completed, designate an area not exceeding one thousand meters (or fifty meters with respect to a river to which the River Law (Law No.167 of 1964) shall apply, or shall apply, mutatis mutandis; hereinafter referred to as a 'river') from the underwater cable as a protected area...;

[47]Article 141 of Japan's Law [18] provides '(4) In a protected area of paragraph (1), no person shall anchor a boat or ship, engage in fishing with a bottom dragnet or in such manners as specified in the applicable cabinet order, dig and gather earth and sand or moor a boat or raft to the landmarks of the preceding paragraph....'

[48]Article 142 of Japan's Law [18] provides '(1) Any approved telecommunications carrier shall pay to any person holding a fishery right compensations for any loss caused by the revocation or changes of this person's fishery rights or by the suspension of the exercise thereof in accordance with the provisions of paragraph (5) of the preceding article.

(2) The provisions of Article 39 paragraphs (7) through (12) of the Fisheries Law shall apply, mutatis mutandis, to the compensations for loss in accordance with the provisions of the preceding paragraph. In this case, 'prefectures' in paragraphs (10) and (11) of the same article shall be read as 'approved telecommunications carriers.'

[49]ICPC (restricted access).

of ministerial agencies, heads of government agencies, Chairmen of the People's Committees at all levels to direct and take specific prohibitory measures. Such measures prohibit activities like digging, cutting, removing, transporting, storing and purchasing submarine cables in all forms. This directive urges the Ministry of Information and Communications to take the lead to collaborate with specific Ministries and authorities who may take measures for the promotion of educational activities and raise awareness and legal knowledge about the protection of telecommunication infrastructures, which includes submarine cables.

These authorities are the Ministry of Defense, the Ministry of Public Security, the Ministry of Agriculture and Rural Development, the Ministry of Natural Resources and Environment, and the People's Committees of coastal cities and provinces. The Ministry of Information and Communications is to take initiatives along with the Ministry of Defense and the Ministry of Public Security to facilitate cable operators by granting the latter the necessary license for laying and repairing submarine cables. The Ministry of Defense aims to strengthen monitoring vessels in submarine cables patrolling and safety and support submarine cable operations. The submarine cable protection initiatives need to get support from the Ministry of Public Security. The local administrations at the coastal levels promote awareness and knowledge to avoid submarine cable damage. This directive urges to support the international telecommunications operators in their initiatives to rerouting and restoring international telecommunication traffic. Vietnam has shown the utmost importance in promoting surveillance, awareness, and knowledge on cables' importance to minimize injury.

3.3.2 European Union

In the European Union (EU), the submarine cable operation must comply with a distinct cable regime. This cable regime comprises the individual national regimes of EU members and the international and EU legal frameworks.[50] The EU has adopted the environmental measures which apply to the cable laying operation within the region. It provides for Environmental Impact Assessment before cable laying. The measures also prescribe for zonal management like the Marine Protected Areas. It also prohibits activities relating to cable operation within the protected zones.[51]

---

50 Practice Note [19].

51 OSPER [20] issued Guidelines for Best Environmental Practices in Cable Laying and Operation, 2012.

3.3.2.1 Conventions and Guidelines and EU Regime

Two conventions, i.e., the Convention for the Protection of the Marine Environment of the North–East Atlantic 1992 (OSPAR Convention) and the Convention on Environmental Impact Assessment in a Transboundary Context (Espoo),[52] are relevant to the submarine cable operations in EU countries.

First, the OSPAR convention's objectives adopt an international marine environmental policy that includes preventing and eliminating marine pollution and sustainable marine use.[53] It applies to the North–East Atlantic marine areas, including several EU countries like France and the UK. Under the OSPAR Convention, the OSPAR Commission has agreed on OSPAR's Regulatory Regime for establishing Marine Protected Areas (MPAs) in Areas Beyond National Jurisdiction (ABNJ). Para 2.23 of this Regulatory Regime provides that its measures for MPA may apply to the cable laying.[54] *Secondly*, the Espoo Convention establishes obligations on the signatory States that include the EU countries to conduct an Environmental Impact Assessment (EIA) of a project that may cause significant adverse transboundary impacts. According to the Practice Note, the submarine cable operation itself may not result in a significant cross-border impact. Nevertheless, the EIA may apply to the submarine cable operation, which essentially becomes part of specific projects that have the potential to cause transboundary environmental harm.[55]

Next are the EU Regulations that have the potential to impact the submarine cable operation. In this connection, it is to be noted that there is uncertainty about applying those regulations in the UK due to Brexit. Nevertheless, those regulations do not become void automatically in the UK even after Brexit. And there is a reasonable assumption that those mandates will continue to apply to submarine cable operators in the UK.[56]

The noise or disturbance results from the submarine cable operation attract The Marine Strategy Framework Directive 2008 (MSFD) to preserve underwater noise and energy levels. The MSFD manages the economic and social use of marine waters to achieve 'Good Environmental Status' to encourage sustainable use and environmental protection. Therefore, this directive may lead to greater enforcement of environmental standards through EIA.[57]

With an objective, the Water Framework Directive 2003 ensures a reduction in the emission of hazardous chemicals or other substances into water resources to protect water resources and improve water quality. According to the Practice Note,

[52]See https://www.unece.org/environmental-policy/conventions/environmental-assessment/about-us/espoo-convention/enveiaeia/more.html. Accessed 02 Oct 2019. OSPER [20] and Espoo [21].

[53]MPAs in areas beyond national jurisdiction [22].

[54]Para 2.23 of the the OSPER [20] Regulatory Regime provides that 'In addition, there are also a number of human uses of the ocean, including in ABNJ, which may be subject to OSPAR regulation, for example measures relating to: scientific research, cable laying, dumping, construction of installations and artificial islands, and deep-sea tourism.

[55]Ibid. Practice Note *at* 16.

[56]Practice Note *at* 16.

[57]Ibid.

the submarine cable operation attracts this directive that requires 'Water Framework Directive Assessment.'[58] This assessment may assess the impact of submarine cable operation on water quality.

The Waste Framework Directive 2008 establishes a waste management regime known as the 'waste hierarchy.' It aims to regulate waste management to protect the environment and human health. This directive has the potential to apply to the submarine cable operation that may cause waste by submarine cable activities and abandoning dead cables on the seabed.[59]

The Birds Directive 2009 has come into force to support the bird's habitat. This directive may apply to the submarine cable operation should it cause disturbances to the bird's habitat in-between waters to landing stations, including beach manhole. Additionally, the Habitat Directive 1992 also focuses on the special area of conservation sites designated under this directive. The EU commission monitors the implementation of those conservation sites. Any submarine cable operation within those sites requires 'appropriate assessment' and authorization. 'Appropriate assessment' may need even if the submarine cable operation is beyond those conservation sites, provided that such activities have an impact on the conservation objectives in those sites. This assessment is known as the Habitats Regulations Assessment (HRA).[60]

The next important mandate is the Environment Impact Assessment Directive that assesses the effects of certain public and private projects on the environment, including the marine environment. The submarine cable operation itself does not fall under these directives. However, such regulation may apply to a project where submarine cable operation is a component, and therefore, EIA applies to the submarine cable operation. Interestingly, there are examples that the submarine cable operators are voluntarily undertaking the EIA to support the coastal authority in this purpose.[61]

3.3.2.2 UK

The submarine cable regime in the United Kingdom (UK) comprises international law, European law, and domestic instruments. The UK is the pioneer of the Cable Convention 1884. It has implemented the said Convention and adopted the Submarine Telegraph Act 1885.[62] Essential features of this legislation include the prescription for the liability against cable damage, the lights and signals by cable ships, and procedure for collection of evidence relating to the offenses under this legislation, etc. It is notable that the said legislation is applicable in the high sea on telegraph cable, which has rare application to the modern communication cable system. Besides this Cable Convention and its implementing legislation, UK is a party to the Geneva Convention on the high sea and UNCLOS. Therefore, the international submarine

---

[58] Ibid.

[59] Ibid.

[60] Practice note *at* 15.

[61] Ibid.

[62] [23] (c. 49).

cable beyond the 12 nm of the UK attracts this UNCLOS regime. The activities like the survey, laying, repair, and maintenance of the submarine cable meet legal and environmental imperatives. Therefore, the UK's submarine cable operators meet UK laws within the overriding European and international mandate and guidelines.

Marine and Coastal Access Act of 2009

The UK has adopted the Marine Policy Statement (MPS) and the Marine Plan to sustain its marine area.[63] Given the importance of the submarine cables, the MPS emphasis three issues.

The first issue is the submarine cable operation's potential impact and its response to other marine activities, including the marine environment. *Secondly,* the role of relevant marine authorities in marine activities' smooth functioning through the coordination among different stakeholders, including submarine cable operators. *Lastly,* it raises concerns about the potential damage of submarine cable due to primarily human activities. It highlights the role of relevant marine authorities to ensure the protection of these submarine cables.[64]

The Marine and Coastal Access Act 2009 (MCAA) (c 23) has provided the Marine Plan. Within the MCAA, the Marine Plan Authority designs the Marine Plan. Marine Plan is a guide to the marine users about the sustainable use of potential marine resources.[65] An application for laying submarine cable is to comply with the Marine Plan, which follows the MPS. As Mentioned above, the MCAA has also implemented the special area of conservation as designed under different EU Directives. Within MCAA, the conservation authorities issue guidance or directions that apply to submarine cable operations in England.[66]

A brief discussion of the UK's submarine cable licensing regime may provide necessary practical understanding about the regulatory requirements that cable operators are to meet before they could engage cable laying in England. Submarine cable operation in England is a licensable marine activity, and an authority deals with such licensing.[67]

The Marine Management Organization (MMO) is the authority that deals with submarine cable licensing in England as provided by the MCAA. UK licensing area consists of the seaward limits of the UK territorial sea, the EEZ, and the UK sector

---

[63]UK's Marine Policy Statement [25] provides umbrella framework that intends to embers all the marine use including the marine authorities and various marine activities including submarine cable operation. The paragraphs 3.7 of Chap. 3 of this Statement deals with the Telecommunications Cabling [24].

[64]UK Marine Policy Statement [25].

[65]Practice Note, *at* 18–21.

[66]Ibid.

[67]Section 66 of UK's Law [26] provides 'to carry out marine activities in or over the sea or on or under the seabed and to use a vehicle, vessel to deposit or remove any substance or object form the seabed, in the sea are subjected to the marine licensing regime.'

of the continental shelf.[68] The cable operators are to make an application to the MMO for a license to lay submarine cables. This application is to contain an array of information. Therefore, the cables applicants need to make a detailed consultation with and pre-submission advice from the MMO. Such negotiation between the MMO authority and the cable operators helps the latter to meet licensing terms.[69]

In this connection, it is notable that all submarine cable operator in the UK does not require a license.[70] A license is a must for the cable.

> constructed or used in connection with the exploration of the UK continental shelf; the exploitation of the natural resources of the UK continental shelf; the operations of artificial islands, installations and structures under UK jurisdiction; [and] the prevention, reduction or control of pollution from pipelines.[71]

A submarine cable that does not involve the above activities needs no license. Nevertheless, as mentioned above, the licensable activities that fall under the UK licensing area must meet licensing requirements,[72] such as the telecommunication cable operation. Therefore, submarine cable operation and the application of the submarine cable operating vehicles in the UK licensing area meet licensing requirements. Further, to initiate repairs and maintenance operation of submarine cable, the cable operator needs prior approval from the MMO.

Regarding the protection of submarine cables in the UK, a report is notable.[73] This report highlights the alarming security threat to the cable system by saying, 'due to threat from human aggression, the submarine cables' vulnerabilities being exploited is growing. It also notes that successful human aggression against Britain's undersea cable can lead to financial disaster on an unprecedented scale. It is a threat that is nothing short of existential. Lastly, the UK imposes a significant fee for fiber optic submarine telecommunications permits. It has prioritized offshore wind farms over submarine cable structures; however, it does not repair prior laid international cables or a safe separation between cables and other infrastructures.[74]

3.3.2.3 France

France is another EU country that has been one of the signatories of the Cable Convention 1884. It prescribes significant liability for the protection of submarine cables. Presently, the Code of Postal and Electronic Communications (the Code) is a France national law that defines breaking or injuring submarine cables. The Code comprises three primary sections, *firstly*, the Legislative part; *secondly*, the Regulatory part—Decrees in Council of State and *thirdly*, the Regulatory part—Simple

[68] Section 42(1) of UK's Law [26].

[69] Practice Note 2017, *at* 27.

[70] Ibid.

[71] Ibid.

[72] UK's Law [26].

[73] Sunak [27].

[74] Burnett [8], *at* 69.

Decrees, respectively.[75] The Legislative part and the Regulatory part—Decrees in Council of State are relevant as they contain the provisions applicable to submarine cables. Each of these said parts is further comprising of different books (different segments).[76] Book II of each of these parts deals with Electronic Communications that provides provisions for protecting submarine cables. Therefore, the provisions contain by Book II: Electronic Communications from each of these said parts are discussed in the following paragraphs.

First, Chapt. V of Book II: Electronic Communications of *the Legislative part* of the Code deals with protecting the submarine cables (Article L 72 to Article L 86). This chapter comprises both general provisions and penal provisions that apply in both territorial water and beyond.

It comprises the general provisions and the special provisions that impose pecuniary damages and imprisonment for causing cable damage. According to this provision, it is a liability for anyone to report to the local authority at the next port about the alleged involvement of causing submarine cable breaks. Art. L 72 prescribes general liability to report about any involvement of submarine cable damage without any mention about the place of cable damage and the following Art. L 73 to Art. L 76 deals with the prescription of the amount of penalty. It also provides that the accused are liable to judgments in civil proceedings. Art. L 75 imposes liability, and it provides that it is a crime not to declare about the said incident of cable damage, which may impose a fine and imprisonment as well. Then, the incident of several offenses of cable damage may invite a severe penalty as provided by Art. L 76. It is to note that Article X of the Convention for the Protection of Submarine Telegraph Cables provides the officers' preparation of the formal statements in charge relating to the submarine cable damage facts. Art. L 77 provides that any France nationals (France Flagship or its crew) who are accused of cable damage become subject of the France local jurisdictions, i.e., the State Prosecution Service.

Art. L 81 and Art. 82 impose a substantial penalty for deliberate damage of submarine cables within the territorial waters by any person (France national/ foreigner). Art. L 81 prescribes a hefty penalty of a fine of 3750 Euros and a term of imprisonment of five years for causing a deliberate breaking or causing any damage of submarine cables. This provision does not apply to the *force majeure* damaging of a submarine cable. This Code also provides provisions for the protection of officers in charge of collecting evidence of the cable damage. Those who cause interference against the duty of those said officers in charge are liable under the France Criminal Code. The Regulatory part of the Code is as follows.

Second, Chap. V of Book II: Electronic Communications of *the Regulatory part* of the Code deals with protecting the submarine cables (Article R 45–Article R 52). These provisions follow the relevant provisions' requirements provided with the Legislative part of the Code and divide into segments.

The first segment comprises with Art. R 45–Art. R 49 and apply to the non-territorial water. Art. R 45–Art. R 49 deals with issues that include cooperation with

[75]Frence Code of Communication [28, 29].

[76]Ibid.

the officer in charge, procedural measures to follow during cable operation; other marine activity and the protection of cable; and the liability against the offenses, etc. It imposes a fine if there is a refusal to produce documents and evidence to the officer in charge who is on board a ship under suspicion of cable damage's alleged involvement. Art. R 46 is a necessary provision with prescribed fines in cases the cable ship violates mandate that includes signaling requirements, failure to maintain a distance between cable ships and buoys. Then, failure to maintain distance from cable before anchorage and using fishing gear or nets and refusal to withdraw such fishing gears before the cable ship engages in cable repairing, etc. as well attract fine under Art. R 47.[77] Art. R 48 provides provisions against the manufacturing and use of tools and equipment that may apply to cable damage.

Second, Art. R 50–Art. R 52 apply to submarine cables within the territorial water. Art. R 50–Art. R 52 provide liability against cable damage in territorial water. According to these provisions, liabilities are such as provided by Art. R 45–Art. R 49. Art. 51 and Art. 52 prescribe hefty fines for those who have committed several incidents of breach of those provisions.

3.3.3 North America

3.3.3.1 United States of America

The United States of America (USA) holds some of the significant international submarine cables. Therefore, the US's current legal regime for submarine cable operation is notable. The USA is also one of the parties that have ratified the old cable convention. It is also noteworthy that this country is yet to become a party to UNCLOS 1982. In this connection, this part deals with the essential features of the US's submarine cable regime.[78]

The Submarine Cable Act, 29 February 1888, 47 US Code, implemented the Cable Convention 1884.[79] This US legislation provides provisions against damage to submarine cables and fishing within the exclusion zone. It defines deliberate or negligent submarine cable injuries as a federal offense that may attract fines, imprisonment, or both. § 21 of this act provides for intentional damage of cable and prescribes for both a monetary penalty of 5000 USD and/or imprisonment for up to two years. In comparison to wilful damage, this legislation provides for only three months imprisonment and/or 500 USD against negligent damage of submarine cable as provided with § 22 of this Act. § 25 provides for imprisonment of 10 days and/or 250 USD

[77]Ninety-Four Consortium Cable Owners v Eleven Named French Fishermen [30], Tribunal de Grande Instance de Boulogne Sur Mer (1st Chamber) 28 August 2009, (File No. 06/00229DG/LM). In this case the French Court found the fishermen guilty of interfering the cable repairing ship from cable operation within its territorial waters and imposed damages on fishermen.

[78]NOAA [31].

[79]47 U.S. Code [32].

against fishing within the exclusion zone. This law also empowers submarine cable owners to sue for damages in case their cables sustain injuries. However, such a small penalty for the violation of this law has little deterrence value.[80] According to a study, the US cable legislation has failed to establish minimum fishing distances from existing submarine cables to prevent it from harmful conduct likely to damage cables.

Additionally, there is no criminal charge record, much less a trial or conviction under this statute.[81] Further, the US Coast Guard and the US Attorney's office have less motivation and decline enforcement in case of violation due to the minor nature of liability.[82] Indeed, these small monetary fine amounts remain over 125 years, and this little penalty, therefore, does not serve as an effective deterrent to marine users to avoid cable damage.[83]

The subsequent development is the UNCLOS 1958 that imposes liability on the coastal State to restrict submarine cable operations unless there is a reasonable requirement. However, the US's cable law remains unchanged. Most importantly, UNCLOS 1982, as mentioned in Chap. 2, addresses the act of cable damage and activities likely to cause harm. Therefore, the coastal State may take preventive measures to control marine activities that working dangerously close to the cable.[84] However, the USA is yet to ratify UNCLOS 1982.[85] And US's submarine cable law is yet to update on the line of UNCLOS to take measures to prevent marine activities, which are likely to cause damage to a submarine cable. Therefore, the law on the protection of submarine cables on the US coast is no longer adequate.

Firstly, the US cable law 1885 continues with its outdated punishment regime against cable damage, and therefore, the US enforcement authority is less interested in its violation. Secondly, the USA is yet to ratify UNCLOS that provides measures for preventable human activities having the potential to cause cable damage. The US submarine cable law continues with its outdated provision in addressing modern-day threats to submarine cables, and this country needs to strengthen its domestic laws for laying and protecting cables.[86]

In the USA, a submarine cable operator may obtain a cable landing license from the Federal Communication Commission (FCC) following the Cable Landing License Act of 1921.[87] In turn, the FCC seeks approval of the US Department of State (acting through its Office of International Communications and Information Policy),

---

[80] Final Report 1 [33].

[81] Wagner [34].

[82] Ibid.

[83] AEP- Threats-to Undersea-Cable-Communications [35].

[84] Wagner [34], *at* 136.

[85] UNCLOS detabase [36].

[86] Coffen-Smout and Herbert [37].

[87] The Federal Communications Commission (FCC) [38] is an independent US government agency that regulates interstate and international communications facilitated by Submarine Cables etc.

coordinating with the US Department of Commerce's National Telecommunications and Information Administration and the US Department of Defense's Defense Information Systems Agency.

The FCC also confirms any cable landing plans to get approval from the Secretary of the Army.[88] Additionally, the submarine cable system in US water seeks other federal permits. The Rivers and Harbors Act of 1899 and the Clean Water Act apply to the cables that traverse through the US's coastal wetlands. Under these legislations, the US Army Corps of Engineers (Army Corps) grants submarine cables in the US's navigable waters.[89] This permission process also attracts the relevant provisions of the National Environmental Policy Act of 1969.[90] The State and local regulations on submarine cable operation primarily have a focus on environmental issues.[91] The Coastal Zone Management Act 1972 (CZMA) also applies to federal activities in the coastal areas.[92] The coastal activities like submarine cable operation in the US coast are, therefore, according to the CZMA, need to comply with State Coastal Zone Management Plans.[93]

3.3.3.2 Canada

Canadian marine space is an essential spot for the submarine cable map. Submarine cables connect Canada with the USA and EU across the Atlantic Ocean. Therefore, Canada's legal practice concerning submarine cable operation finds an important place in the national submarine cable regimes.[94]

The Navigable Waters Protection Act (NWPA) seeks approval from the Canadian Coast Guard for cable landing in Canada.[95] This approval includes an environmental assessment under the Canadian Environmental Assessment Act (CEAA).[96] The cable owners of those cables that do not land in Canada apply for licenses to the Federal Department of Industry Canada under the Telecommunications Act and NWPA, and CEAA. The submarine cable laying may also attract the Fisheries Act and the Canadian Environmental Protection Act to avoid conflict with the fishing habitat and

---

[88] Final Report 1 [33]. In practice several authorities including federal, State, and local government agencies issue licenses and permits for submarine cable operation in US. However, the primary regulator is the Federal Communications Commission (FCC) that is responsible for licensing all international submarine cable landing in the US. In this report, the FCC has examines the risks ot the submarine cable infrastructure and recommends for protection measures, best practices by submarine cable operators and by the US government.

[89] Final Report 1 [33], *at* 22.

[90] National Environmental Policy Act of 1969 (42 U.S.C. §4321 et seq. [39]).

[91] Final Report 1 [33], *at* 23.

[92] 16 U.S.C. 1451 et seq [40].

[93] Ibid., Final Report 1 [33], *at* 23.

[94] The country has ratified UNCLOS in 2003. Division for Ocean Affairs and the Law of the Sea, Oceans @ Law of the sea United Nations [41].

[95] R.S.C., [42], c. N-22.

[96] S.C. [43], c. 19, s. 52.

environmental measures.[97] Further, the environmental assessment process considers other social and economic aspects that include loss of fishers, etc.

Moreover, the submarine cable operation in Canadian water attracts integrated ocean management measures. The Oceans Act empowers the Federal Minister of Fisheries and Oceans for integrated and sustainable use of Canada's ocean spaces.[98] Considering the potential conflict between cable operators and other marine services, the Oceans Act prescribes integrated management plans for coastal and ocean areas.[99] The cable regulations in Canadian waters also prescribe environmental and fisheries measures.[100]

Liability for submarine cable damage attracts provisions for civil liability concerning private properties in Canada. Accordingly, a damaged cable's cable owner is to prove negligence on the vessel's interest under suspicion. In response, the defendant may rely on the principle of the due diligence principle as a defense.[101] Therefore, legal measures for the punishment against submarine cable damage and submarine cable protection are not clear. A study on *submarine cable and ocean management* also suggests strengthening Canada's national laws on submarine cables.[102]

The Case Before the Federal Court of Trial Division[103]

The submarine cable owners suffered losses due to cable cutting by a fishing vessel and file a lawsuit against the latter before the Canadian court for compensation.[104] The *Le Groupe QuébecTel Inc.* (the plaintiff Telus) laid two submarine cables across the St. Lawrence River, Canada (the river). Mr. Vallée, the master of a fishing vessel *Realice*, owned by Peracomo Inc., laid fishing gears and anchors on the river bottom. One of these anchors got hooked onto the plaintiff Telus submarine cable. Mr. Vallée hauled the anchor attached with the cable out of the water, cut the cable with an electric saw, and freed the anchor. A few days later, he repeated the same and cut another cable of the plaintiff Telus. The plaintiffs brought an action *in personam* against Peracomo and Mr. Vallée (the defendant) and *in rem* against the ship. The defendant also sued the insurance company, the underwriters, and third parties to the case.[105]

---

97 Coffen-Smout and Herbert [37], *at* 445.

98 Oceans Act (S.C. [44], c. 31).

99 Ibid., Coffen-Smout and Herbert [37], *at* 445.

100 The International Submarine Cable Regulations of the Telecommunications Act, [45].

101 Ibid. Coffen-Smout and Herbert [37].

102 Coffen-Smout and Herbert [37].

103 Société Telus Communication v. Peracomo Inc., [46] FC 494 (CanLII) (ICPC, restricted access).

104 Ibid.

105 Ibid.

The court had to determine several issues, *firstly* the liability of the defendants and plaintiffs; *secondly*, the quantum of damages and cost of action. T*hirdly*, the defendant's entitlement to limit his liability and insurance claim.[106]

This case attracts Canadian maritime law for liability that includes the English common law that provides that the defendant owed a duty of care to anyone who is so near and directly affected by the plaintiff's action,[107] a subject of both national and international law on maritime liability.

In this case, the defendant deliberately cut the cable in two with an electric saw twice in quick succession. The cable's existence was in public notice due to the wide publication of applicable marine chats about which the defendant was not aware and considered the cables were abandoned.[108]

It is a civil wrong akin to a battery. The loss resulted from the intentional act of the cable cut even though the consequential loss was not intended. The defendant intentionally cut the cables, and the consequent result of his action is a loss. In this case, the plaintiff was to prove that the defendant had the intent to cause loss or reckless and with the knowledge that such failure would probably result as provided by Article 4 of the *Convention on Limitation of Liability for Maritime Claims, 1976, as amended by the 1996 Protocol* (the 1996 Convention)[109] as implemented by the Marine Liability Act[110] in Canada.

The court found that both the cable cut and such loss were intentional as the defendant did not make himself aware of the cable. The defendant had a duty to know about the existence of the submarine cable, which is a 'navigational hazard' according to the *Charts and Nautical Publications Regulations, 1995* (SOR/95-149). Again the 'loss' in the 1976 Convention certainly includes physical damage.[111]

The court again held that:

> the cause of the loss was not lacked notice on Telus' part. The cause of loss was not the fact that the cable was not buried. The cause of loss was not that the cable was hooked by a snow crab anchor. The loss was caused because Mr. Vallée intentionally and deliberately cut the cable in two with an electric saw.[112]

The loss was the diminution in the cable's value, and that did not extend to the cost of cable repair and disrupt telecommunication service. Thus, the defendant was liable.[113]

Under the maritime liability regime, if his act does not result in loss of life or personal injury, the erring party is entitled to limit liability except in certain circumstances. The resultant failure in the present case does not result in death or personal injury that still arose from an intentional act.

---

106 Ibid.

107 *Donoghue v Stevenson*, [47] AC 562.

108 *Peracomo Inc. v. Société Telus Communications* [48], *Supra* note 99.

109 1456 UNTS 221 [49].

110 S.C. 2001, c. 6 [50].

111 *Peracomo Inc. v. Société Telus Communications* [51].

112 Peracomo Inc. v. Société Telus Communications [52], *Para* 47.

113 Ibid.

> Section 29 of the Marine Liability Act limits their liability to the principal amount of $500,000. However, that right to limit is lost in accordance with article 4 of the Convention on Limitation of Liability for Maritime Claims, 1976, as amended by the 1996 Protocol, Schedule I to the said Maritime Liability Act.[114]

The Maritime Liability Act provides for liability to the principal amount of $500,000. However, according to the 1976 Convention and Maritime Liability Act, the defendant is barred from the limited liability entitlement if he intends and knowledge about the probable loss of his act or omission.[115] The defendant's acts of cable cut and loss were intentional, as provided above.[116]

Regarding the contributory negligence on the part of the plaintiff, the court relies on observing the marine expert, who found no flaw in cable installation. The cables were laid on the bottom of the river bed, too soft to support cable burial. The cable burial, considering the use of the river and its bed, was no viable alternative. The said cable installation, therefore, did not cause contributory negligence on the cable owner's part. Further, the fishing vessel whose fishing gears should try to disengage by normal methods if hooked a cable should try to disengage. Failure of that, he must abandon the said fishing gears without cutting the cable. The cable owners indemnify such sacrifice. The point is the vessel operators must know about the existence of the submarine cable routes.[117]

The Case Before the Federal Court of Appeal Canada

The defendant moved before the Federal Court of Appeal.[118] The court negated the appeal by saying:

> Despite the valiant efforts of counsel for the appellants and our panel's sympathy for Mr. Vallée's plight, we would dismiss the appeal with costs in favor of the respondents and Third-party."[119]

The Case Before the Supreme Court of Canada[120]

In the Supreme Court, the majority of the Judges, four concurring (McLachlin C.J. and Rothstein, Cromwell and Karakatsanis J. J.) and one dissenting (Wagner J.), found that the plaintiff's action was not to cause intended loss within the meaning of the Art. 4 of the 1976 Convention. Still, according to the majority of the Judges,

---

114Peracomo Inc. v. Société Telus Communications [54], Para 9.

115Section 26 of S.C. [53], c. 6.

116Ibid., Peracomo Inc. v. Société Telus Communications [54], Para 9.

117Ibid.

118Peracomo Inc. v. Société Telus Communications, [55] FCA 199 (CanLII).

119Peracomo Inc. v. Société Telus Communications, [55] FCA 199 (CanLII), Para 81.

120Peracomo Inc. v. TELUS Communications Co., [56] SCC 29 (CanLII).

it was willful misconduct.Therefore, the Supreme Court held that the defendant is entitled to limit his liability at $500,000; however, he lost his insurance coverage.[121]

This case breaks new ground on national and international maritime law on submarine cables relating to the cable faults issues. It highlights the remedy in response to the intentional conduct of submarine cable damage that interferes with telecommunication. Nevertheless, the submarine cable cut incident happened within Canadian waters; still, it involves the Canadian common law, which bears English common law influences, and international law on liability for maritime claims, which has been enforced at the domestic level.[122] Therefore, this case has implications on domestic submarine cable governance in other jurisdictions also.

3.3.4 South America

The countries such as Columbia have established security areas along the lines of submarine cables within their waters.[123] Uruguay[124] and Argentina prohibit fishing in the areas where submarine cables or facilities exist and those methods of fishing that could cause damage to the cables.[125]

3.3.4.1 Argentina

The Law of Navigation 20.094 and the Penal Code of Argentina provide provision for the protection of submarine cables.[126] It prohibits fishing in places where submarine cables or facilities exist. It also bans fishing methods that threaten cable injuries. In violation of these provisions, the captain or patron or fishing captain meets a fine of Sixteen to three hundred and twenty-three Argentine Pesso. Further, the enforcing authority under this provision has the power to prohibit even navigation to any ship violating this provision. Argentina's penal provisions prescribe arrangements to support submarine cable operation. Art 194 provides that unless there is a situation of common danger, people may meet imprisonment, extending from three months to two years if they prevent, hinder, or obstruct the regular operation of public communication services. The submarine cable provides public communication services; therefore, interferences with the submarine cable operation may lead to imprisonment. Article 196 imposes a jail term for six months to two years for the submarine cable shipwreck by imprudence or negligence or inexperience. This provision also prescribes a higher jail term that may reach up to four years if such a

[121]Ibid., Para 6, 35 and 71.

[122]ICPC (restricted access).

[123]General maritime direction—Resolution Number 204 of [57].

[124]Maritime Provision No. 128 [58].

[125]The Law of Navigation 20.094 [59].

[126]ICPC (restricted access).

shipwreck led to damage to a person's death. Article 198 provides provisions against the intentional act of depredation or violence against ships or people or things in the sea or navigable rivers. Such violent activities are punishable with imprisonment for three years to fifteen years.[127]

3.3.4.2 Chili

Chili's General Law of Telecommunications, Article 13B (b) provides that any malicious interferences with, intercepts, or interrupts with the telecommunications services may attract confinement in military prison and the seizure of the equipment and facilities. General Regulations of Order, Security and Discipline of Ships, and the Coast of the Republic under Section DS 1340 Article 327 and penal provision also provide provision for criminal damage of submarine cables in Chili.[128]

3.3.4.3 Columbia

Colombia has issued General Maritime Direction 2012 under which, as provided by the direction, there should be security areas along the lines of submarine cables in Colombian waters. This direction comprises the safety zones' provisions, adjusting of conflicting marine activities, including submarine cable operation, prohibiting anchoring, enforcing authority, and a prescription for civil and criminal penalties against submarine cable damage.

Article 1 of this direction establishes safety zones that comprise the authorized laying of submarine cable communications areas. Such safety areas cover and include the parallel extending 500 m on either side of the submarine cables within the areas of the national maritime jurisdiction of Columbia. It prohibits anchoring any kind of ship and trawling and, according to this provision, and performing a maritime activity that wholly or partly maintains contact with the seabed (Art. 2). Such restriction may not apply to the rough weather or innocent passage under the notice of the Maritime Authority of Colombia. Article 3 empowers the Maritime Authority of Colombia to take preventive measures necessary to avoid damage to the submarine communication cable. The respective Port Captain has the authority to control the Colombian flag vessel movement to restrict potential injury to the cables in safety zones. The next necessary provision relates to the accommodation of conflicting marine activities. Thusm Article 5 prescribes that the other marine users and infrastructures must respect the submarine cable operators' rights. Most importantly, Article 6 of this direction empowers the Maritime Authority of Colombia to punish any submarine communication cable's damage.

[127] ICPC (Restricted access).

[128] Ibid.

3.3.4.4 Uruguay

Provisions under Uruguay Penal Code prescribe for crimes against public security under Chap. IV. Article 217 provides that any attempt to disrupt the continuity of wire or wireless telecommunications is punishable with imprisonment that may extend to three months to three years. Within this provision, the removal, damage, or destruction of telecommunication facilities are aggravated forms of this crime. This provision prescribes a higher penalty to any submarine telecommunications infrastructure damage that includes submarine cables irrespective of an effective interruption of the telecommunication services. A potential risk of disruption may also attract a hefty penalty.[129]

Uruguay also provides provisions imposing restrictions on fishing gears in the specified area that comprises one nm of each side of submarine communications cables.[130] This instrument is mentioned explicitly for submarine cables within Uruguay's Exclusive Economic Zone. It prohibits the fishing activities that have partial contact with the seabed and anchors within these specified areas. Article 148 also provides a submarine cable zone that comprises one nautical mile on each side of the submarine cables within Uruguay's maritime jurisdiction. It prescribes hefty fines against anchoring or engaging in any activity, including fishing within the submarine cable zone.[131]

Telefónica International Wholesale Services America (Tiws) and Others Versus Tamika S A. and Other

The plaintiff, in this case, approached before the First Court of Appeals.[132] He claimed the redressal for damages suffered by him against the defendant, the keepers of the fishing vessels Santa Sofía and her fishing gears, which had allegedly broken the plaintiff's submarine communication cable within the Exclusive Economic Zone of Uruguay. The court found indications about the alleged involvement of the said fishing vessel in the plaintiff's cable breakage without direct evidence. The court considered the facts, *firstly*, the proximity of the vessel's location and the cable breakage time. *Secondly*, the vessel's application of fishing gears, and thirdly, the vessel was trying to locate and retrieve fishing gear in that vicinity and, lastly, the officer's testimony on board of the vessel along with the vessel's logbook. On a consistent and relevant set of secondary facts, the court concluded that the alleged ships had the highest possibility to break the plaintiff's submarine cable. The court

---

[129]ICPC (restricted access).

[130]Republica Oriental Del Uruguay, National Navy, National Naval Prefecture, Maritime Provision No. 128, Montevideo, 22 February 2011 [60].

[131]ICPC (restricted access).

[132]The Supreme Court is the apex court of Uruguay. Bebellow the Supreme Court there are Court of Appeals.

finally held the defendant liable for the plaintiff's cable breakage and awarded for damages.[133]

3.3.5 *Africa*

3.3.5.1 Ghana

Ghana Shipping (Protection of Offshore Operations and Assets) Regulations 2012 (The Regulations 2012)[134]

The Regulations 2012 came into force to protect submarine communications cables and pipelines, and offshore installations within Ghana's national maritime jurisdictions. The point is that this Regulations 2012 prescribes the establishment of the protection and safety zones where it either prohibits or restricts certain marine activities. It also prescribes offenses and the penalties against its violation besides the permitting requirements for submarine cable operation.[135] The following paragraph deals with the salient features of this Regulations 2012.

This Regulations 2012 comprises thirteen provisions dealing with several submarine cable-related issues that include the protection measures by providing safety zones, protection mechanisms, protection areas, permits for drilling and safety permit, and enforcement.

Regulation 6 is the most important regulation that deals with the protection of subsea cables.[136] It prescribes that the minister has the authority to give gazette notification about establishing a submarine cable protection area. According to this provision, the subsea cable protection area will be around a subsea cable or any length of the cable to ensure the protection of the subsea cables. The notification will define the protected area, which may not extend beyond fifty meters on either side of the specified cable centreline. The next necessary regulation is Regulation 7 that prohibits certain activities within the protected areas.[137]

---

[133] Telefónica International Wholesale Services America (Tiws) and Others versus Tamika S A. And Other, First Court of Appeals in Civil Matters, Official Notice 0003-000193/2015 [61].

[134] Ghana Maritime Authority [62].

[135] ICPC (restricted access).

[136] Section 6 of the Ghana's Regulations [64] provides that (1) The Minister may, by notice published in the Gazette, establish a protection area around a subsea cable or any length of the cable to protect any subsea cable.

(2) The protection area established under sub regulation (1) shall be defined in the Gazette and shall extend not more than fifty metres on either side of the centre line of the specified cable which has the coordinates of latitude and longitude specified in the Gazette.

[137] Regulation 7 of the Ghana's Regulations 2012 provides that the following operations are prohibited in the protection area notified in the Gazette in accordance with regulations 5 and 6:

(a) fishing operations conducted from a ship in the protection area; and
(b) anchoring in the protection area, except where the anchoring is necessary for the purpose of saving life or a ship.

It explicitly prohibits fishing operations with fishing vessels and anchoring within the subsea cable protection area. According to Regulation 10 (d), submarine cable operators take safety permits from the Ghana Maritime Authority. This Regulation 2012 has provided that safety permits if granted, remain valid for one year from the date of its issuance, and it is renewable. Then regulations 8 and 9 apply to the mobile offshore drilling units. It is a fact that the submarine cable operation generally does not come under the offshore drilling operation, which involves the offshore exploration and exploitation of marine resources. Still, the submarine cable operation in certain circumstances engages with the burial of cables that may attract these regulations. In present case, the mobile offshore drilling units, the submarine cable ships, and equipment are to obtain safety operating permits from the Ghana Maritime Authority and can engage in operation within Ghana's maritime zones with due notice to the maritime authority. In this connection, it should be noted that the Safety Permit B provided by the Second Schedule of these regulations, as mentioned in Regulation 10, apply to the submarine cable operators besides other marine operators.[138]

However, the First Schedule of the regulations provides a Safety Permit Form that applies to the offshore drill units. The Miscellaneous Provisions of this Regulations 2012 deals with the enforcement of these regulations. For the present purpose, ship operators are liable if they carry out an operation prohibited in the subsea protection area. Such an offender is liable on summary conviction.

This provision also prescribes the quantum of the penalty for individuals and a body corporate with varying degrees. The individual offender who commits an offense under this regulation is liable to a fine, which may extend from fifty penalty units to seven thousand five hundred penalty units or fifteen years of imprisonment or both the fine and the imprisonment.

A body corporate commits such an offense may meet a fine of five hundred penalty units, extending to ten thousand penalty units.[139] Further, a submarine cable operator is liable on summary conviction to a fine of thousand penalty units or five years imprisonment or both the fine and the imprisonment if he fails to register with the Ghana Maritime Authority or obtain a safety permit from the latter.[140] Regulation 12 also provides the defense to the above offenses, and the basis of the defense is the situation beyond human control and to avoid life threats of the assets and persons.

---

[138] SAFETY PERMIT B, SECOND SCHEDULE (Regulation 10 (2) of the Regulations, [63]. Form for Safety Permit for cables, pipelines, devices, structures or equipment located in an area within Ghana's maritime jurisdiction.

[139] Regulation 11(b), 11(c) and 11(d) of Ghana's Law 2012.

[140] Regulation 11(d) of Ghana's Law 2012.

3.4 Comparative and Legal Analysis on Legal Instruments and Other Arrangements Across the Selected Jurisdictions and Comparative Chart on Instruments on Submarine Cables in the Selected Jurisdictions

As mentioned above, several legal, regulatory instruments and arrangements represent the submarine cable regimes across the selected jurisdictions.[141] This section will highlight and arrange the essential commonalities and divergences that underpin the existing cable regimes thematically. It will help distinguish the scope and administration pattern concerning the laying and protection of cables across the jurisdictions.

In many jurisdictions, the submarine cable measures have been linked with significant national legislation such as the Law of the Sea, Telecommunication Law, and Shipping Laws. These legislations authorize relevant government departments to issue instruments for submarine cable operations. These instruments include several notifications, orders, directives, etc.

Countries like China, Japan, Indonesia, Singapore, and Vietnam adopted regulations, a directive to support submarine cable operation, and submarine cable protection. According to India's MZI Act, Indian authorities require the submarine cable companies to take prior permission to delineate the submarine cable course and cable operation within India's EEZ. The State Council of China and the Ministry of Land and Resources have promulgated Regulation 1989 and Regulation 2004.

A lead agency has a significant role in laying and protecting cables. The State Oceanic Administration (SOA) is the lead agency for issuing permits for laying submarine cables in China's maritime zones.[142] The Chinese regulation requires cable companies to make an application for a permit for cable laying. Such an application must contain the name, nationality, and residence of the cable owner, detail about personnel laying cables, geographical area, time, items, methods, equipment, etc.[143]

---

[141] Burnett et al. [1], *at* 90.

[142] Article 3 of China's Regulations 1989 provides 'The competent authorities for the administration of the laying of submarine cables and pipelines in such areas as the said inland seas, territorial seas and continental shelves, and also for the investigations and survey of routes and other relevant activities for the aforesaid ngineering projects, shall be the State Oceanographic Bureau of the People's Republic of China (hereinafter referred to as "the competent authorities").' see also p. 67 of this chapter.

[143] Article 5 of China's Regulations 1989 provides 'The owners of the submarine cables and pipelines (hereinafter referred to as "the owners") shall file a written application with the competent authorities 60 days before they start the investigations and survey of routes for laying the submarine cables and pipelines. The written application shall contain the following:

1. The name, nationality, and residence of the owner;
2. The name, nationality, and residence as well as the chief person-in-charge of the unit which will conduct the investigations and survey of the routes for laying the submarine cables and pipelines;
3. The precise geographical areas in which the investigations and survey are to be conducted for laying the submarine cables and pipelines;

The SOA suggests 60 days period for issuing a permit. The cable operators are also to make applications to the SOA for permission to engage in cable repairing. The SOA is the competent authority to resolve any dispute relating to cable operation. And the Administration Department of the State Oceanographic Bureau is responsible for the implementation of provisions for the protection of submarine cables. In Singapore, the Info-communications Development Authority is a led agency.[144] It issues permits for cable laying and repairing. Vietnam has come up with a directive that prescribes the Ministry of Information and Communication as the lead agency that, with other authorities, will facilitate the approval process for laying submarine cable.[145] The Marine Management Organization (MMO) of England is the appropriate cable that considers and issues permits for laying submarine cable in the UK.[146] It also extends consultation to the cable operators to facilitate the latter in submitting a complete application for a license with necessary detailed specifications. The cable operators also need to take approval from MMO for repairing and maintenance of cables. The Federal Communication Commission (FCC) issues permit for cable operation in US water.[147] Canadian Federal Department Industry issues permit submarine cable operation in Canada for those cables not landing in Canada. However, Canadian

4. The time, the items, methods and equipment—including the ship to be used: its name, nationality, tonnage, and major pieces of equipment and their functions—for conducting the investigations and survey of routes for laying the submarine cables and pipelines. The competent authorities shall make a reply within 30 days as of the date of receipt of the application.

[144]1.1 of the Guidelines of Deployments 2010 provides 'The Info-communications Development Authority of Singapore (IDA) is the lead agency for facilitating the deployment of submarine cable systems into Singapore. IDA provides guidance to interested parties and facilitates the process for applying for the necessary permits from various authorities.'

[145]Paragraph 2 of the DIRECTIVE On Strengthening the Protection of Submarine Cables and Ensuring the Safety of International Telecommunications provides 'The Ministry of Information and Communications:

(a) To collaborate with the Ministry of Defense, the Ministry of Public Security, the Ministry of Agriculture and Rural Development, the Ministry of Natural Resources and Environment and People's Committees of coastal cities and provinces to promote educational activities and raise awareness and legal knowledge about protecting telecommunication infrastructures in general and submarine cables in particular;

(b) To take primary responsibility and collaborate with the Ministry of Public Security and other relevant agencies on the basis of the Ordinance on the Protection of Important Facilities related to National Security, to draft and submit to the Prime Minister for approval the list of important telecommunications facilities related to national security;

(c) To take primary responsibility and promptly collaborate with the Ministry of Defense and the Ministry of Public Security to license foreign vessels to enter Viet Nam's maritime zones to lay and repair submarine cables in accordance with the law; supervise and guide telecommunications enterprises to take measures to protect their submarine cables and ensure the safety of national and international information.

[146]See relevant portion of this Chapter.

[147]See relevant portion of this Chapter.

Coast Guard accepts applications for laying cables landing in Canada. The Maritime Authority of Colombia is the competent authority to implement submarine cable laws. The Ghana Maritime Authority is the appropriate authority that issue permits for submarine cable operation there.[148] It also issues safety permits for engaging cable operation in the sea.

Conversely, in India, there is no lead agency for cable operation. However, submarine cable operation in Indian waters needs as many as seven permits.[149] In case of repair of a damaged cable, the cable operators meet this extremely onerous permit requirement.[150] This permit process is one of the lengthiest approval processes. In 2011, one of such permit process takes 90–94 days and costs between USD 45,000 and USD 70,000 every day.[151] India's permit process has developed in response to several concerns such as national security, immigration, customs, economy and safety, and the environment. However, the best practices on repair vessel permit highlights on pre-approval process. Such a pre-approval process may complete a few steps of India's permit process in advance.[152]

India's cable repair approval process is, therefore, complicated and lengthy. Indonesia is yet to establish a lead agency; however, the Ministry of Transport supports the submarine cable operation therein. There is no led agency for submarine cable operation in Japan, where several authorities permit cable laying.

In many jurisdictions, cable safety zones have been an essential approach for the protection of submarine cables. Article 13 of Regulation 1989 of China provides that the cable operators incur liability for causing damage to an existing cable and awards compensation.[153] Regulation 1989 of China prescribes wide publication and makes awareness among public and marine users about the cables' existence. It also prescribes for mutual arrangements between sea users and cable operators to avoid cable damage. Indonesia's regulation prescribes for the restricted areas and cable corridor comprising 3500 m to protect submarine cables. It prescribes maintaining a distance of more than 500 m between cables.[154] It also suggests cable burying and the use of navigational buoys to trace cables by the mariners. Japan's law on

---

[148] Paragraph 10 of Ghana's Law [64] provides 'A person who intends to (a) operate a vessel, (b) site an installation, (c) site a storage facility, or (d) lay a pipeline, a cable, an equipment or any other structure or device on the seabed in an area within Ghana's maritime jurisdiction shall obtain a permit from the Ghana Maritime Authority.

[149] Rapp et al. [65].

[150] Burnett et al. eds., [8], *at* 174.

[151] Ibid., *at* 175.

[152] Ibid., Rapp et al. [65], *at* 382.

[153] Article 13 of China's Regulation 1989 provides 'Operators who are engaged in various activities at sea must protect the submarine cables and pipelines that have already been laid. Those who have caused damages to the said installations shall make compensations according to law.

In the event that disputes arise over the exploitation of the seas and oceans and the normal functioning of submarine cables and pipelines, the disputes shall be mediated and handled by the competent authorities.

[154] Article 1 of Indonesia's KM. No. 94 Tahun [66] states 'Containing the definition of telecommunication submarine cable, protection and restricted area. The meaning of restricted area is the surrounding area along the submarine cable route with corridor 3500 m which is forbidden to

submarine cable prescribes 50–1000 m as the underwater cable protected area. The directive for the protection of submarine cables in Vietnam urges the concerned authorities to protect submarine cables that include the promotion of awareness and legal education about the safety and security of national telecommunications infrastructures. It also encourages controlling the movement of vessels patrolling, having the potential to cause injury to the submarine cables. Law on submarine cable in France provides detailed provision for the protection of cables. National law provides provisions for the protection of submarine cables in Argentina. Law establishes security areas extending 500 m along the lines of submarine cables in Colombian waters. Uruguay designs the specified area for submarine cables that comprise 1 nm of each side of submarine communications cables. Ghana has adopted a law to establish a submarine cable protection area comprising 50 m on either side of the specified cable centreline.[155] Indeed, the submarine cable protection zones include wide marine spaces; however, cable corridors focus on the narrow space comprising both sides of the cable route channels.[156]

Controlling certain marine activities having the potential to cause cable injury also remains vital for cable protection strategy. The control of activities may have various dimensions. The Chinese regulation prohibits activities that include digging sand, drilling, driving a pile into the ground, laying in anchor, dragging anchor, fishing, breeding, or other sea operation potential to cause cable injury within the oceanic natural protection zones.[157] The regulation in Indonesia prohibits activities like anchorage, dredging, mining, or other underwater activities within the cable corridors. Then Japan's law on submarine cable prohibits activities like anchoring, engaging in fishing with a bottom dragnet, or digging and gathering earth and sand or moor a boat or rafting to the landmark in the underwater cable protected area. Vietnam's directive on submarine cable prescribes certain activities like digging, cutting, removing, transporting, storing. It also prohibits the purchasing of submarine cables in all forms. Argentina has adopted a law that prohibits fishing and fishing methods potential causing submarine cable damage. It also prohibits navigation of a ship that causes cable damage. Submarine cable measures in Colombia prohibit anchoring any vessel and trawling and, according to this provision, and performance of a maritime activity that wholly or partly maintains contacts with the

---

conduct anchorage, dredging, mining or other underwater activities, except for new submarine cable installation. The distance between new cable and existing cable not less than 500 m is required.'

[155]Paragraph 6 of Ghalan's Law, 2012 provides '(1) The Minister may, by notice published in the *Gazette,* establish a protection area around a subsea cable or any length of the cable to protect any subsea cable.

(2) The protection area established under subregulation (1) shall be defined in the *Gazette* and shall extend not more than fifty metres on either side of the centre line of the specified cable which has the coordinates of latitude and longitude specified in the *Gazette.*'

[156]Davenport [67].

[157]Article 8 of China's Regulations [68] provides 'It's forbidden to dig sand, drill, drive a pile into the ground, lay in anchor, drag anchor, fish, net, breed or other sea operations that might damage the safety of submarine cables and pipelines within the protection zones of submarine cables and pipelines.'

seabed. The Colombian authority is empowered to take preventive measures to avoid submarine cable damage therein. Uruguay restricts fishing in the cable area. Ghana prohibits fishing operations with fishing vessels and anchoring within the subsea cable protection area.[158] However, countries like India have yet to adopt measures to control marine activities near submarine cable lines within Indian maritime zones and submarine cables' risks.[159]

The cable protection scheme also includes compensating the other marine users for the losses incurred in saving cables. The fishers in releasing fishing gears, etc.came in contact with cables break the cable. Fishers are indemnified against the sacrifice of those gears to avoid cable breaking. Both China and Japan provide provisions for compensation to the fishermen and other marine users to protect submarine cables and the smooth functioning of cable operation.

Several countries have an emphasis on the publication and awareness and reporting about the cables. The Chinese regulation provides that the failure to submit the cable root chart by cable owner to the Chinese lead agency for cable may attract the former a fine of 10,000 RMB.[160]

Many jurisdictions have prescribed for civil and/ criminal liability against breach of their submarine cable-related measures. These measures are related to the protection of cables, publications, awareness, reporting, etc. The Chinese law prescribes that the cable operators' unauthorized use of the sea and their failure to take measures to protect cable attract liability. France law imposes liability to report about the alleged involvement with the cable damage. It provides for civil liability. Failure to inform about the cable damage may attract criminal penalties that may impose fines and

[158]Paragraph 7 of Ghana's Law, 2012 provides The following operations are prohibited in the protection area notified in the *Gazette* in accordance with regulations 5 and 6:

(a) fishing operations conducted from a ship in the protection area; and

(b) anchoring in the protection area, except where the anchoring is necessary for the purpose of saving life or a ship.

[159]'it is essential that its maritime strategy also include the new priority for the protection and care of undersea cables.' See Rapp et al. [65], at 383.

[160]Article 17 of China's Regulations [68] provides 'In any of the following circumstances for the owner(s) of submarine cables and pipelines, the Administration Departments of the local people's government above the county level under the State Oceanographic Bureau shall order the party to correct the situation within a specified period; in the event of a failure to correct the situation with the time limit, a fine of not more than RMB 10,000 shall be imposed:

1. the registration information of the precious route chart and position chart of the submarine cables and pipelines, etc. has not been filed;
2. results of regular checking and inspection of the submarine cables and pipelines and other protection measures have not been reported;
3. results of the investigations and surveying activities for identifying the routes for laying submarine cables and pipelines, the laying, maintenance, alteration, dismantling and abandonment of submarine cables and pipelines have not been reported to the public in time;
4. results of entrusting the relative entities.

imprisonment. Causing deliberate breaking or causing any damage to a cable may attract a hefty penalty that may impose a fine of 3750 Euros or imprisonment for fivne years or both.[161]

In the USA, causing submarine cable damage is a federal offense that attracts fines and imprisonment. It imposes a monetary penalty of 5000 USD or/and imprisonment for two years for intentional cable damage, while negligent cable damage attracts liability for only three months imprisonment and/or 500 USD. Fishing in the exclusion zone may impose imprisonment for ten days and/or 250 USD.[162] The incident of cable damage follows civil liability concerning private property in Canada. Fishing and using the fishing method that may cause cable damage may impose a fine of Sixteen to three hundred and twenty-three Argentine Pesso in Argentina. It also provides imprisonment for three months to two years for interfering with public communication services. This law imposes imprisonment for six months to two years for submarine cable shipwrecking. It also prescribes for imprisonment term that may extend from three years to fifteen years for any deliberate act of depredation or violence to the vessel, including cable ships or things in the sea. The confinement in military prison and the seizure of the equipment and facilities are the punishment against any malicious interferences with, intercepts, or interrupts with the telecommunications services in Chili. Uruguay's law prescribes imprisonment of three months to three years for any attempt to disrupt the continuity of wire or wireless telecommunications. It also imposes heavy punishment for removal, damage, or the destruction of submarine cable facilities. Ghana prescribes a penalty against engaging in prohibited activities in specified areas and imposes a penalty from fifty penalty units to 7500 penalty units or fifteen years of imprisonment or both the fine and the jail. And from fifty penalty units to 7500 penalty units or fifteen years of imprisonment or both the fine. A body corporate may meet 10,000 penalty units for such a violation.[163]

National laws also have suggested procedural provisions. The France law imposes liability for not assisting the investigating officer on board a vessel in suspicion. It also provides provisions imposing penalties in failure to maintain signals, the distance between cable ships and buoys, and fishing vessels and fishing gears. The fishing vessels may bear liability if they refuse to withdrawal fishing nets and gears.

---

[161] See relevant paragraphs of this Chapter.

[162] See relevant paragraphs of this Chapter.

[163] Paragraph 11(5) of Ghana's Law 2012 provides 'A person who

(a) operates a vessel,
(b) sites an installation,
(c) sites a storage facility, or
(d) lays a pipe, cable, equipment or any other structure or device on the seabed or in an area within Ghana's maritime jurisdiction. Without registering with the-Ghana Maritime Authority or obtaining a safety, permit from the Ghana Maritime Authority commits an offence and is liable on summary conviction to a fine of not more than five thousand penalty units or to a term of imprisonment of not more than five years or to both the fine and the imprisonment.

National conservation measures also attract submarine cable operations in many jurisdictions. Indonesia's regulation on submarine cable operation suggests underwater environmental safety measures. EU offers marine habitats, conservation measures, EIA and MPA, and acceptable environmental standards for the submarine cable operation.[164] The US's environmental and coastal management measures apply to the submarine cable operation. Environmental assessment is also a requirement for submarine cable operation in Canadian water and coastal management measures.

In many countries, the national submarine cable law is yet to take appropriate measures addressing vulnerability to the submarine cable from the human aggressions like theft and terrorism in the submarine cable choke points.[165] Threats to the submarine cable damage are always there. Indeed, the legal provision dealing with maritime piracy at the national level may not be enough to deal with the incident of submarine cable theft.[166]

To sum up this analysis, it represents that States' practices on submarine cable governance vary across jurisdictions. Submarine cable regulations in England, the USA, China, Colombia, Ghana rely on regulatory authority to deal with cable installation permits. Countries such as France have prescribed significant deterrence on cable damage to discourage potential threats to cables. Many States chose to adopt a spatial ocean management approach to strengthen submarine cable protection by establishing a cable protection zone and imposing control on identified marine activities concerning such protection zones. These protection measures and control set varying standards across the jurisdictions. Existing cable protection zone areas vary from 50 to 3500 m. Besides other cable standards, few countries like Vietnam and Singapore urge building cooperation and promoting awareness among the stakeholders concerning the submarine cable system.

The submarine cable operators must also meet essential marine environmental conservation standards, especially in EU jurisdictions. The MPA, EIA, marine policy statements, pollution standards, waste management, conservation directives on water, waste management, habitat, a special area of conservations, etc., apply to cable operation. According to Canada, an integrated ocean management approach in dealing with submarine cable becomes useful, which has also prescribed liability on cable damage based on the principle of due diligence.

Regarding the regulatory aspect of submarine cable, many countries offer onerous permit requirements for cables that involves multiple governmental departments presenting complex cable governance system. Many countries such as India, Indonesia, Japan, Canada, and Argentina are neglecting to adopt a dedicated submarine cable regulatory authority. A submarine cable installation permit system involving several local authorities poses a significant challenge to the cable operators. Many countries, including the USA, still rely on outdated laws to protect the cable. These laws prescribe the little penalty, which was adopted in the context of the 1884 Cable Convention and is no longer adequate to deter potential cable damage. Indeed,

---

[164] OSPAR Convention [69].

[165] Wrathall [70].

[166] Beckman [3], *at* 15–16.

this study reveals that these jurisdictions have been neglecting to update or adopting effective submarine cable law. Complexities, inconsistencies stress the existing legal and regulatory regime on cable. They are significantly lagging in ensuring the security and reliability of the submarine cable system across the jurisdictions.

The analysis indicates general States' practices and their approaches and interests toward cable governance. It gives clues to the sources of instruments their authority. It also suggests the sources of national instruments on cable and their essential features. These essential features include the lead agency, declaration of submarine cable protection zone or corridors, imposing control on certain marine activities, prescribing liabilities on violations, promoting awareness program, and cooperative mechanism among the marine users *inter se* and coastal authorities. These parameters supply the basis to a model legal framework on cables.

Further, the parameters also represent diversity in their scope and enforcement procedures. Such diversity could become helpful in determining the scope of the proposed parameters of the legal framework. Further, proposed guidelines should also focus on addressing States' vital interests, including national security, immigration, customs, economics, safety, and environmental concerns, pre-approval, and lead the agency.[167]

In this connection, the following relevant studies also emphasize on strengthening of national submarine cable regulatory regimes.

3.5 Final Report—Protection of Submarine Cables Through Spatial Separation

The Final Report highlights a model for cable protection.[168] According to this report, a submarine cable protection model follows a spatial separation. It aims to minimize interactions between submarine cable activities and among cables and other marine activities. It aims to reduce direct and indirect risks to the submarine cable damage and cable outage time. Its emphasis on the recommendations and standards for separation developed by the cable industry and coordination and agreement mechanisms between cable operators *inter se* and other marine actors like fishing organizations, etc. It appreciates formal spatial-separation schemes under the national legal and regulatory schemes. This suggestive model of cable protection comprises the following measures.

Firstly, submarine cable industries engage and agreed on a set of standards and awareness initiatives to accommodate competing marine activities for cable protection. Laying cables away from other marine infrastructures and wide publication and awareness about cable's existence among all the marine users remain essential tools to cable operators to reduce cable damage. Importantly, ICPC, a regional organization like the North American Submarine Cable Association (NASCA) and Subsea

[167] Rapp et al. [65], *at* 378.

[168] Final Report 1, 2017 *at* 46–55.

Cables UK, etc., at the national level set standards for cable operation and its interaction with other marine activities. The ICPC has come with a basic set of standards that guide different submarine cable operation phases and accommodation of other marine activities like pipeline operation and other offshore civil infrastructure to reduce the threat to cable damage. Those sets of guidelines are mutually coordinated among the shared seabed users to minimize the cable operation's risk and protection.

Secondly, the measure is to establish a minimum distance between and among other marine activities. Most importantly, the third and fourth measures deal with the imposition of restrictions and prohibitions on certain marine activities on or near the submarine cable routes widely known as cable protection zones and cable corridors and prescription of liability for cable damage, respectively. The fifth step indicates planned marine activities, widely known as marine spatial planning. This planning focuses on the specific marine area and plans to accommodate existing and potential marine activities and protect the marine environment. The last step focuses on the coordination and cooperation among the cable operators and other marine users, including fishers, pipelines, offshore infrastructures, etc. The cable operator negotiates with the regional fisheries organization on identifying issues like fishing and non-fishing areas and the mode of several activities for sharing seabeds peacefully. Another study also recommended measures to promote the reliability of the submarine cable system.[169]

3.6 Reliability of Global Undersea Communications Cable Infrastructure (ROGUCCI)

A recent report recommends several measures to enhance the reliability of the submarine cable communication system. These recommendations include avoiding clustering of cable routes, preparedness for quick cable repairs and hostile cable cut, cooperation among stakeholders, stringent cable regime and governance, communication and trade interests, stakeholders due diligence, the lead agency, awareness about the critical cable, reserve plan to address cable outage.[170]

This report to reduce cable hostilities at several submarine cable choke points recommendss a minimum concentration of international submarine cable routes. Submarine cable outage is a time-sensitive issue and highly dependent on the approval process of the coastal States' permit process. Therefore, these reports highlight the reduction of approval time to minimize cable outage time.

There is a regional cable ship station that remains standing by to rush immediately for cable repair. This report also emphasizes the readiness of stakeholders to prevent and address the intentional threats of cable damage. This report strongly recommends practicing confidence and cooperation, coordination, preparedness among cable industries and dedicated submarine cable authorities at different levels to

[169] Rauscher [71], *at* 98–137.

[170] Ibid.

enhance the submarine cable systems reliability. It also recommends enriched submarine cable governance driven by the cable industry. This report also highlights the role of financial sectors that rely on cable communication in developing measures to enhance submarine cable system resiliency. It also highlights the need for due diligence of stakeholders relies on submarine cable communication. Therefore, it suggests proactive participation among the cable industry and other users like financial industries. This report's next important recommendation rightly highlights the need to adopt stringent legal and policy measures to protect submarine cable infrastructure at the State levels. Lack of awareness about the role and vulnerabilities of cables and challenges to the cable operators in the absence of clear legal and policy measures continuously hamper cable operation and protection efforts. Therefore, this report strongly recommends adequate knowledge and awareness about the cable system among the users and government authorities. The report's following recommendation deals with the cables' capacity development to carry more traffic load. Lastly, this report suggests a backup plan against the tremendous damage to the submarine cable system (Table 3.1).

3.7 Summary

The current survey of the instruments on cable in the selected jurisdictions reveals that many jurisdictions do not deal with the submarine cables with the specific laws and authorities. States have responded with varying degrees of compliances to their international obligations concerning the laying and protection of cables. Many jurisdictions offer numerous secondary instruments empowering several domestic authorities to prescribe various approval requirements for laying cables and related other activities. In many jurisdictions, such permit requirements and procedural measures are not readily available. Thus, the cable operators meet difficulties in identifying the legal requirements and the following procedure to consent from the domestic authority to lay, repair, and maintain cables therein. Arguably, submarine cable regimes are, in many cases, suffered from both excessiveness and inadequacies. Such complexities are also linked with the absence of the dedicated cable authorities. Conversely, this analysis reveals that many jurisdictions have shown negligence approaches toward adopting adequate legal measures to protect cables. The submarine cable regime in most of the jurisdictions remains silent on the security of the cables.

It also reveals that some jurisdictions have been approaching a dedicated agency for cables and promoting awareness and reporting to facilitate cable systems. It finds that many States have adopted a few measures prescribing penalty against the breaking or damaging cables and cable safety zones or corridors. This analysis underscores that except for the few jurisdictions, in many States, breaking or injuring cables is either not illegal or rise trifle liabilities, which offer little incentives to the enforcement agencies.

Nevertheless, it helps to distinguish specific approaches and parameters, having a potential role in cable governance. These parameters are:

Table 3.1 Legal instruments and other arrangements on submarine cables in selected jurisdictions—comparative chart

Selected jurisdictions	Name of the instruments	Jurisdictions	Lead agency	SC protection/restricted areas	Prohibited/restricted activities in protection zones	Offenses and penalty and liability	Permit measures for the installation of new cables	Procedure for the enforcement	Fees, indemnity/compensation and promotion of awareness on cable system and miscellaneous
China	Regulations on the Management of Laying Submarine Cables and Pipelines 1989 (Regulations 1989) Regulations on the Protection of Submarine Cables and Pipelines 2004 (Regulations 2004)	Communication and Electric cables in Inland seas and TW	Administration Department of the State Oceanographic Bureau	Oceanic Protection zones, natural protection zones which range from 50 to 500 m of either side of submarine cables	Dig sand, drill, drive a pile into the ground, lay in anchor, drag anchor, fish, net, breed or other sea operations	10,000 RMB on failure to put cable chart civil and criminal liability	Lead agency grants the permit for laying cables within the Chinese maritime spaces. 60 days' time period for processing of the application	An aggrieved party may complain to the Administration Department of the State Oceanographic Bureau	Royalty imposes for laying cables liability which may extend to the stop of submarine cable operation or fine publication of the cable chart
Indonesia	The Minister of Transportation Decision No. 94/1999 (Regulation of Submarine Cables 1999) Government Regulation No. 20/2010		No lead agency. the Ministry of Transportation issues important measures for the submarine cable operation	Cable corridor 3500 m, distance between cables 500 m burying cables-2 to 0.5 m organizing navigational buoys, requirement for Indonesian cable ships and crew	Anchorage, dredging, mining or other underwater activities	NIL	Multiple authorities	NIL	Penalty- for deliberate cable damage without mentioning further detail

(continued)

Table 3.1 (continued)

Selected jurisdictions	Name of the instruments	Jurisdictions	Lead agency	SC protection/restricted areas	Prohibited/restricted activities in protection zones	Offenses and penalty and liability	Permit measures for the installation of new cables	Procedure for the enforcement	Fees, indemnity/compensation and promotion of awareness on cable system and miscellaneous
Japan	Telecommunications Business Law of Japan (Law No. 86 of December 25, 1984)	Underwater cables—cover cables both in sea and river	No lead agency, Minister and the relevant prefectural governor deals with laying cables	50–1000 m underwater cable protected area	Anchoring, engaging in fishing with a bottom dragnet or digging and gathering earth and sand or moor a boat or rafting to the landmark	Authority may impose a restriction on the suspension of fishing in PZ and award compensation for the loss of catch, authorities include Minister and the relevant prefectural governors (including the Minister for Agriculture, Forestry and Fisheries)	Multiple authority, include Minister and the relevant prefectural governors (including the Minister for Agriculture, Forestry and Fisheries)	NIL	Fishermen may claim compensation if their fishery rights are interfered
India	No specific instrument on SC Territorial Waters, Continental Shelf, Exclusive Economic Zone, and Other Maritime Zones Act, 1976 (ACT No. 80 of 1976) and resources related instruments apply to cables	NIL	No lead agency	NIL	NIL	NIL	No nodal agency onerous approval requirement, seven authority involves and takes 48 days approx. for approval	NIL	NIL

(continued)

Table 3.1 (continued)

Selected jurisdictions	Name of the instruments	Jurisdictions	Lead agency	SC protection/restricted areas	Prohibited/restricted activities in protection zones	Offenses and penalty and liability	Permit measures for the installation of new cables	Procedure for the enforcement	Fees, indemnity/compensation and promotion of awareness on cable system and miscellaneous
Singapore	The Submarine Cable Deployment Guidelines 2010 and The Submarine Cable Repair Guidelines 2010	Singapore water	Info Communication Media Development Authority (IDMA)	Cable corridors, silent about the area	NIL	NIL	obtaining permits from IDMA, five applications from several authorities in Singapore, Maritime Port Authority- for approval for cable repair applications	NIL	NIL

(continued)

Table 3.1 (continued)

Selected jurisdictions	Name of the instruments	Jurisdictions	Lead agency	SC protection/restricted areas	Prohibited/restricted activities in protection zones	Offenses and penalty and liability	Permit measures for the installation of new cables	Procedure for the enforcement	Fees, indemnity/compensation and promotion of awareness on cable system and miscellaneous
Vietnam	Directive, viz. On Strengthening the Protection of Submarine Cables and Ensuring the Safety of International Telecommunications 2007		Ministry of Information and Communications and the Ministry of Defense and the Ministry of Public Security	NIL	Acts of digging, cutting, removing, transporting, storing, and purchasing submarine cables in all forms	NIL	Permits involve several authorities	The Ministry of Defense is to take initiatives to strengthen monitoring vessels in the vicinity of submarine cables patrolling and safety and to support submarine cable operations. The submarine cable protection initiatives are to be supported by the Ministry of Public Security	Promotion of awareness, education, legal knowledge about the protection of SC

(continued)

Table 3.1 (continued)

Selected jurisdictions	Name of the instruments	Jurisdictions	Lead agency	SC protection/restricted areas	Prohibited/restricted activities in protection zones	Offenses and penalty and liability	Permit measures for the installation of new cables	Procedure for the enforcement	Fees, indemnity/compensation and promotion of awareness on cable system and miscellaneous
European Union	Convention for the Protection of the Marine Environment of the North–East Atlantic (OSPAR) Convention on Environmental Impact Assessment in a Transboundary Context (ESPOO) Marine Strategy Framework Directive Water Framework Directive Waste Framework Directive Birds Directive Habitats Directive Environmental Impact Assessment Directive				No list of prohibited activities Restricted activities include Marine Protected Areas (MPAs) in Areas Beyond National Jurisdiction (ABNJ) Environmental Impact Assessment (EIA) 'Appropriate assessment' for Conservation sites				

(continued)

Table 3.1 (continued)

Selected jurisdictions	Name of the instruments	Jurisdictions	Lead agency	SC protection/restricted areas	Prohibited/restricted activities in protection zones	Offenses and penalty and liability	Permit measures for the installation of new cables	Procedure for the enforcement	Fees, indemnity/compensation and promotion of awareness on cable system and miscellaneous
United Kingdom	The Submarine Telegraph Act, 1885 (c. 49) The Marine and Coastal Access Act 2009 (MCAA) (c 23) Marine Plan Marine Policy Statement (MPS)		The Marine Management Organization (MMO)				Detailed permit measures approved by MMO		Follow signaling and minimum distance mandate

(continued)

Table 3.1 (continued)

Selected jurisdictions	Name of the instruments	Jurisdictions	Lead agency	SC protection/restricted areas	Prohibited/restricted activities in protection zones	Offenses and penalty and liability	Permit measures for the installation of new cables	Procedure for the enforcement	Fees, indemnity/compensation and promotion of awareness on cable system and miscellaneous
France	The Code of Postal and Electronic Communications The Book II: Electronic Communications				Anchorage and using fishing gear or nets and refusal to withdraw such fishing gears	Civil/criminal proceedings civil/criminal proceedings impose a fine and imprisonment a heavy penalty of a fine of 3750 Euros and term of imprisonment of five years for deliberate cable breaking fines in cases that include the vessel that engaged with cable operation violate signaling mandate, failure to maintain distance cable ships and buoys and refusal to withdrawal fishing gears and vessels and refuse to show documents to the officers			Liability to report of involving cable damage and produce documents to the enforcing officer, follow signaling and minimum distance mandate

(continued)

Table 3.1 (continued)

Selected jurisdictions	Name of the instruments	Jurisdictions	Lead agency	SC protection/restricted areas	Prohibited/restricted activities in protection zones	Offenses and penalty and liability	Permit measures for the installation of new cables	Procedure for the enforcement	Fees, indemnity/compensation and promotion of awareness on cable system and miscellaneous
USA	47 US Code The Coastal Zone Management Act (CZMA) National Environmental Policy Act of 1969 State Coastal Zone Management Plans		The Federal Communications Commission (FCC)		Authorities are empowered to take preventive measures	monetary fine of 5000 US dollar and/or imprisonment up to 2 years for intentional breakage of cable only 3 months imprisonment and/or 500 US dollar for negligent cable damage imprisonment of 10 days and/or 250 US dollar against fishing within the exclusion zone	Permit measures involved with several authorities under FCC		Not ratified UNCLOS
Canada	Canadian Environmental Assessment Act, 2012 (S.C. 2012, c. 19, s. 52) Canadian Navigable Waters Act [42], c N-22) The Oceans Act *Maritime Liability Act*		The Federal Department Industry Canada Canadian Coast Guard			Civil liability, proof of negligence defense—due diligence			Integrated ocean management approach

(continued)

Table 3.1 (continued)

Selected jurisdictions	Name of the instruments	Jurisdictions	Lead agency	SC protection/restricted areas	Prohibited/restricted activities in protection zones	Offenses and penalty and liability	Permit measures for the installation of new cables	Procedure for the enforcement	Fees, indemnity/compensation and promotion of awareness on cable system and miscellaneous
Argentina	The Law of Navigation 20.094, and the Penal Code of Argentina				Prohibits fishing in the places where submarine cables or facilities exist prohibits those methods of fishing that can cause damage	Fine of Sixteen to three hundred and twenty-three Argentine Pesso six months to two years of imprisonment for submarine cable shipwreck			
Chili	General Law of Telecommunications					Any malicious interferences with, intercepts or interrupts with the telecommunications services may attract confinement in military prison and the seizure of the equipment and facilities the penal provision also provides provision for criminal damage			

(continued)

Table 3.1 (continued)

Selected jurisdictions	Name of the instruments	Jurisdictions	Lead agency	SC protection/restricted areas	Prohibited/restricted activities in protection zones	Offenses and penalty and liability	Permit measures for the installation of new cables	Procedure for the enforcement	Fees, indemnity/compensation and promotion of awareness on cable system and miscellaneous
Columbia	General Maritime Direction 2012		Maritime authority of Colombia	Security areas are established along the lines of submarine cables safety zones extending 500 m on either side of the submarine cables	Anchoring of any kind of ship and trawling and according to this provision any performance of maritime activity that wholly or partly maintains contacts with the seabed is also barred	Maritime Authority of Colombia to punish any damage to the submarine communication cable			
Uruguay	Uruguay Penal Code			A specified area that comprises one nm of each side of submarine communications cables	Restriction on the use of the fishing gear fishing activities that have even partial contact with the seabed and the use of anchors within this specified area	Aggravated form of this crime—removal, damage or the destruction of facilities related to the telecommunication higher penalty for submarine cables damage the heavy fine against anchoring or engaging any kind of activity including fishing within the submarine cable zone			

(continued)

Table 3.1 (continued)

Selected jurisdictions	Name of the instruments	Jurisdictions	Lead agency	SC protection/restricted areas	Prohibited/restricted activities in protection zones	Offenses and penalty and liability	Permit measures for the installation of new cables	Procedure for the enforcement	Fees, indemnity/compensation and promotion of awareness on cable system and miscellaneous
Ghana	Ghana Shipping (Protection of Offshore Operations and Assets) Regulations		Ghana Maritime Authority	Submarine cable protection area fifty meters on either side of the centerline of the specified cable	Fishing operations with fishing vessels and anchoring within the subsea cable protection area	Ship operators for operation prohibited in the subsea protection area fine for fifty penalty units to seven thousand five hundred penalty units or fifteen years of imprisonment or to both the fine and the imprisonment A body corporate—fine of five hundred penalty units which may extend to ten thousand penalty units Failure to register cable operation or obtain safety permit—thousand penalty units or five years imprisonment or to both the fine and the imprisonment	Safety permit for cable operators		The situation beyond human control and to avoid life threats of the assets and persons

- submarine cable protection zone and corridor;
- prohibited, restrictive, and preventive activities in specified submarine cable areas;
- an arrangement among submarine cable operators, other marine users, and coastal authorities;
- national law on submarine cable damage both imposing civil liability and criminal sanction;
- establishment of the lead agency at the national levels;
- awareness program on submarine cable operation and its protection.

These arrangements in the current form in existing submarine cables-related instruments are suffering from substantial limitations too. Such as random prescriptions of cable protection areas, prohibited and preventive activities, and liabilities without further clarity about the enforcing agencies. Still, the potentials of these measures may be derived through appropriate actions.

The reports developed by submarine cable operators and academic institutions have highlighted the necessity of a model standard for the laying and protecting submarine cables. These reports suggest several parameters such as spatial marine planning, controlling other marine activities, publication, awareness about cables among other marine users, coordination and cooperation among marine users, and stringent legal and policy measures for cables. All of these parameters are the essential basis in the quest for a model standard for cables.

The dedicated legislation on submarine cables in Australia and New Zealand may clarify the essential parameters of a specific instrument on cables. Therefore, the cable regimes in Australia and New Zealand become the subject matter of the following chapter.

References

1. Burnett, R., et al. (2013). *Submarine cables: The handbook of law and policy* (pp. 6–90). Martinus Nijhoff Publicataion.
2. AEP-Threats-to Undersea-Cable-Communications 2017. https://www.dni.gov/files/PE/Documents/1---2017-AEP-Threats-to-Undersea-Cable-Communications.pdf. Accessed January 21 2019.
3. Beckman, R. (2010). Submarine cables—A critically important but neglected area ofthe law of the sea. In *7th International conference on legal regimes of sea, air, space and Antarctica (ISIL Conference)*. https://cil.nus.edu.sg/wp/wp-content/uploads/2010/01/Beckman-PDF-ISIL-Submarine-Cables-rev-8-Jan-10.pdf. Accessed January 7, 2017.
4. Malecki, E. J., & Wei, H. (2009). A wired world: The evolving geography ofsubmarine cables and the shift to Asia. *Annals of the Association of American Geographers, 99*, 360–382.
5. Sugadev, A. (2016). India's critical position in the global submarine cable network: An analysis of Indian law and practice on cable repairs. *Indian Journal of International Law, 56*, 173–200.
6. (Indian Maritime Zones Act 1976) The Territorial Waters, Continental Shelf, Exclusive Economic Zone and other Maritime Zones Act, 1976, (ACT No. 80 of 1976).
7. (UNCLOS 1982) The United Nations Convention on the Law of the Sea 1982, 1833 UNTS 3.
8. Burnett, D. (2013b). Submarine cables on the continental shelf. In M. H. Nordquist (Ed.), *The regulation of continental shelf development*. Center for Oceans Law and Policy (Vol. 17, pp. 53–70).

9. Raha, U. K., & Raju, K. D. (2018). Critical telecommunication infrastructure in South Asia: An opportunity. *Sri Lanka Journal of International Law, 26*, 79–102.
10. Yincan, Y., Xinmin, J., Guofu, & Wei, J. (2018). *Submarine optical cable engineering* (p. 203). Elsevier Publication.
11. (China's Law 2001) Law of the People's Republic of China on the Administration of Sea Areas 2001 (No. 61). http://www.fdi.gov.cn/1800000121_39_2329_0_7.html. Accessed November 08, 2019.
12. Ministry of Commerce. http://english.mofcom.gov.cn/aarticle/lawsdata/chineselaw/200211/20021100050627.html. Accessed November 08, 2019.
13. China's Regulations 2004.https://cil.nus.edu.sg/wp-content/uploads/2010/10/TaraDavenport-Rhodes-ICPC-Article-on-Submarine-Cables.pdf. Accessed November 08, 2019.
14. IMDA Repairs Guidelines 2010. The Infocomm Media Development Authority (IMDA). https://www.imda.gov.sg/search-results?keyword=The%20Submarine%20Cable%20Deployment%20Guidelines%202010%20&category=all&support=undefined&orgType=&industry=&persona=&page=1. Accessed November 09, 2019.
15. IMDA Deployment Guidelines 2010. See https://www.imda.gov.sg/-/media/imda/files/regulation-licensing-and-consultations/codes-of-practice-and-guidelines/subcablelanding.pdf?la=en. Accessed November 09, 2019.
16. APEC 2011. Report on *Submarine Cable Information Sharing Project: Legislative Practices and Points of Contact,* Asia Pacific Economic Cooperation (APEC, 2011) at Attachment A.
17. Nugroho, H. B. (2012). Law of the sea aspects of Indonesian national legislation on submarine telecommunications cable, in maritime border diplomacy. *Center for Oceans Law and Policy, 16*, 79–105.
18. Japan's Law 1984. Telecommunications Business Law of Japan (Law No. 86 of December 25, 1984).
19. Practice Note 2017. Practice Note on '*The Laying and Maintenance of Subsea Cables—The Planning and Environmental Regulatory Consenting Process*' Friday, Feb. 03, 2017. https://www.escaeu.org/news/?newsid=58. Accessed September 02, 2019.
20. OSPER 1992. The Oslo and Paris Convention for Protection of the Marine Environment of the North-East Atlantic 1992 (OSPER) issued Guidelines for Best Environmental Practices in Cable Laying and Operation, 2012.
21. Espoo 1989. Convention on Environmental Impact Assessment in a Transboundary Context (Espoo) 1989 UNTS 309, 30 ILM 800 (1991). See https://www.unece.org/environmental-policy/conventions/environmental-assessment/about-us/espoo-convention/enveiaeia/more.html. Accessed October 02, 2019.
22. MPAs in areas beyond national jurisdiction. https://www.ospar.org/work-areas/bdc/marine-protected-areas/mpas-in-areas-beyond-national-jurisdiction. Accessed October 02, 2019.
23. 1885 (c. 49). See http://www.legislation.gov.uk/ukpga/Vict/48-49/49/contents. Accessed September 02, 2019.
24. Telecommunications Cabling. https://www.gov.uk/government/publications/uk-marine-policy-statement. Accessed October 05, 2019.
25. UK Marine Policy Statement. https://assets.publishing.service.gov.uk/government/uploads/system/uploads/attachment_data/file/69322/pb3654-marine-policy-statement-110316.pdf. Accessed October 05, 2019.
26. UK's Law 2009. Marine and Coastal Access Act 2009.
27. Sunak, R. (2017). *Undersea cables-indispensable, insecure* (Policy Exchange, London). https://policyexchange.org.uk/publication/undersea-cables-indispensable-insecure/. Accessed November 14, 2019.
28. Frence Code of Communication. https://archives.arcep.fr/index.php?id=8&L=1. Accessed October 08, 2019.
29. Frence Code of Communication. See https://www.legifrance.gouv.fr/affichCode.do;jsessionid=8E8801234004D0F85E9A4EFDC89717B4.tplgfr27s_1?cidTexte=LEGITEXT000006070987&dateTexte=20140114. Accessed October 08, 2019.

30. Ninety-Four Consortium Cable Owners case .Ninety-Four Consortium Cable Owners v Eleven Named French Fishermen, Tribunal de Grande Instance de Boulogne Sur Mer (1st Chamber) 28 August 2009 (File No 06/00229DG/LM).
31. NOAA. National Oceanic and Atmospheric Administration (NOAA) Seaward Limit of Laws. https://www.gc.noaa.gov/gcil_seaward.html#submarine. Accessed October 20, 2019.
32. U.S. Code. Submarine Cables Act, 29 February 1888, 47 U.S. Code (came into force, May 1, 1888), see https://uscode.house.gov/view.xhtml?path=/prelim@title47/chapter2&edition=prelim. Accessed October 21, 2019. See also https://www.gc.noaa.gov/gcil_seaward.html#submarine. Accessed October 20, 2019.
33. Final Report 1. Final Report 1: Separation, the Communications Security, Reliability and Interoperability Council IV, Working Group 8 ("WG8"), Dec 2014. https://www.fcc.gov/about-fcc/advisory-committees/communications-security-reliability-and-interoperability-0. Accessed October 22, 2019.
34. Wagner, E. (1995). Submarine cables and protections provided by the law of the sea. *Marine Policy, 19*, 127–136.
35. AEP- Threats-to Undersea-Cable-Communications Sep. 28, 2017. See https://www.dni.gov/files/PE/Documents/1---2017-AEP-Threats-to-Undersea-Cable-Communications.pdf. Accessed October 21, 2019.
36. UNCLOS database. See https://www.unclosdebate.org/argument/287/us-should-ratify-un-convention-law-sea-unclos. Accessed January 22, 2021.
37. Coffen-Smout, S., & Herbert, G. J. (2000). Submarine cables: A challenge for ocean management. *Marine Policy, 24*, 441–448.
38. FCC. See https://www.fcc.gov/research-reports/guides/submarine-cable-landing-licenses#targetText=The%20Cable%20Landing%20License%20Act%20states%20that%20no%20person%20shall,President%20of%20the%20United%20States.%22. Accessed October 21, 2019.
39. U.S.C. §4321 et seq. National Environmental Policy Act of 1969 (42 U.S.C. §4321 et seq.).
40. U.S.C. 1451 et seq. The Coastal Zone Management Act 1972 (CZMA) (16 U.S.C. 1451 et seq.).
41. Division for Ocean Affairs and the Law of the Sea, Oceans @ Law of the sea United Nations. See https://www.un.org/Depts/los/reference_files/chronological_lists_of_ratifications.htm. Accessed October 23, 2019.
42. R.S.C., 1985, c. N-22. Canadian Navigable Waters Act (R.S.C., 1985, c. N-22).
43. S.C. 2012, c. 19, s. 52. Canadian Environmental Assessment Act, 2012 (S.C. 2012, c. 19, s. 52).
44. Oceans Act (S.C. 1996, c. 31).
45. The International Submarine Cable Regulations of the Telecommunications Act, 1993.
46. Société Telus Communication v. Peracomo Inc., 2011 FC 494 (CanLII) (ICPC, restricted access).
47. Donoghue v Stevenson, [1932] AC 562.
48. Peracomo Inc. v. Société Telus Communications 2011, *Supra* note 99.
49. Convention on Limitation of Liability for Maritime Claims, 1976 (1456 UNTS 221).
50. S.C. 2001, c. 6. Maritime Liability Act (S.C. 2001, c. 6).
51. Peracomo Inc. v. Société Telus Communications 2011.
52. Peracomo Inc. v. Société Telus Communications 2011,
53. Section 26 of the Marine Liability Act (S.C. 2001, c. 6).
54. Peracomo Inc. v. Société Telus Communications 2011, Para 9.
55. Peracomo Inc. v. Société Telus Communications, 2012 FCA 199 (CanLII), See http://canlii.ca/t/frx79. Accessed October 31, 2019.
56. Peracomo Inc. v. TELUS Communications Co., 2014 SCC 29 (CanLII), See http://canlii.ca/t/g6ldv. Accessed October 31, 2019.
57. General maritime direction—Resolution Number 204 of 2012.
58. Maritime Provision No. 128.
59. The Law of Navigation 20.094.

60. Republica Oriental Del Uruguay, National Navy, National Naval Prefecture, Maritime Provision No. 128, Montevideo, 22 February 2011.
61. Telefónica International Wholesale Services America (Tiws) and Others vs. Tamika S A. and Other, First Court of Appeals in Civil Matters, Official Notice 0003–000193/2015.
62. Ghana Maritime Authority, See https://www.ghanamaritime.org/uploads/Ghana%20Shipping%20(Protection%20of%20Offshore%20Operations%20and%20Assets)%20Regulations%202012%20LI%202010.pdf/. Accessed November 05, 2019.
63. Safety Permit B. Safety Permit B, Second Schedule (Regulation 10 (2) of the Regulations, 2012).
64. Ghana's Regulation. (2012). Ghana Shipping (Protection OF OFFSHORE OPERATIONS AND ASSETS) REGULATIONS, 2012.
65. Rapp, R. J., et al. (2012). India's critical role in the reliance of the global undersea communications cable infrastructure. *Strategic Analysis, 36*, 375–383.
66. Indonesia's KM. No. 94 Tahun 1999. KM. No. 94 Tahun 1999 of Indonesia.
67. Davenport, T. (2012). Submarine communications cables and law of the sea: Problems in law and practice. *Ocean Development & International Law, 43*, 201–242.
68. China's Regulation. (2004). Regulations of the Protection of Submarine Cables and Pipelines 2004.
69. OSPAR Convention 1992.
70. Wrathall, L. R. (2011). The vulnerability of subsea infrastructure to underwater attack: Legal shortcomings and the way forward. 12, 224–257.
71. Rauscher, K. F. (2010). *Reliability of global undersea communications cable infrastructure (ROGUCCI)*. The Report, Issue I, (2010). www.ieee-rogucci.org. Accessed March 21, 2017.

Chapter 4
An Integrated Approach toward Submarine Cables in Australia and New Zealand—A Way Forward

4.1 Introduction

Clear and specific national legislation and regulatory mechanism on submarine cable are rare except for a few. It is only Australia and New Zealand that have adopted dedicated legislations for submarine cables.[1] The legislations are the Telecommunications Act 1997 of Australia and the Protection of Submarine Cables and Pipelines Act 1996 of New Zealand. These legislations intend to seek recourse to the appropriate legal provisions and regulatory mechanism to lay and protect submarine cables.

Submarine cable regimes of Australia and New Zealand deal with several essential measures, including an institutional arrangement for laying cables and other related activities, cable protection zones to address cables' vulnerabilities, enforcement mechanisms for implementing these laws, etc.[2] An analysis of these legislations and their relevant provisions could help explain the scope and basis of its stakeholders' rights and liabilities, penalties, regulatory and enforcement procedures, etc. It will also help identify the fundamental principles, parameters, ocean governance approaches, and the basic structure of these cable regimes. A comparison among these laws may help in ascertaining their merits and weaknesses. Thus, this chapter undertakes a comparative study on the submarine cable regimes of Australia and New Zealand. It intends to answer whether these cable regimes facilitate cable operation and its protection in Australia and New Zealand waters.

The fundamental principles, approaches, essential parameters, and legislative schemes of Australia and New Zealand's cable regimes could be significantly meaningful in identifying the primary basis for a model framework for a national instrument on submarine cables.

[1]Takie [1].

[2]Raha and Raju [2].

U. K. Raha and Raju K. D., *Submarine Cables Protection and Regulations*,
https://doi.org/10.1007/978-981-16-3436-9_4

4.2 Australia and New Zealand—Dedicated Legal Regimes on Submarine Cable

Australia's submarine cable regime comprises the Submarine Cables and Pipeline Protection Act 1963, the Schedule 3A of the Telecommunications Act 1997 (the 1997 Act of Australia), and the Australian Communication and Media Authority Act 2005 (the ACMA Act).[3] For New Zealand, it is the Protection of Submarine Cables and Pipelines Act 1996 (the 1996 Act of New Zealand).[4] These are the dedicated submarine cable regimes that have sought to comprehensively address the issues and challenges of laying and protecting the submarine cable. The schemes of these cable regimes are reflective of their integrated approaches. This legislation establishes submarine cable protection zones or protected areas and prohibits and prevents activities in those protected areas for cables' security. They prescribe liability for acts of breaking or injuring cables or such attempts as well within and beyond the submarine cable protection zones. These cable safety areas are within and beyond States' territorial waters (TW) within the national marine spaces. These laws also provide provisions dealing with enforcement and institutional setup and precise procedural mechanisms. They offer a regulatory structure for cable installation permits, etc.

The integrated approach of submarine cable governance relates to the broader ocean management issue that speaks about the accommodation of competing for marine activities and not just 'fishing versus cable.'[5] It is accommodating of all activities and measures affecting coastal and marine ecosystems. As it provided under the Ocean Act of Canada that provides for

> the integrated management and sustainable development of Canada's oceans and their resources, the application of both an ecosystem and precautionary approach to the conservation, management and use of marine resources, and the use of inclusive, collaborative approaches for planning and decision-making.[6]

It is part of 'ocean management that is about balance decision making regarding ocean space use.'[7] Integrated ocean management includes a partnership among the fishing industry, submarine cable industry, and all other users and interests from the Canadian perspective. That also highlights the significance of area-based management and zonation such as 'corridor for all submarine cables.' In particular, an integrated approach toward the submarine cable governance eyes on

> the development of a transparent and stable interdepartmental process for the coordinated planning, management, and regulation of submarine cables, inclusive of all interested and involved parties.[8]

---

[3] Act No. 61 [3, 4, 5].

[4] [6] No. 22.

[5] Coffen-Smout and Herbert [7].

[6] Ibid.

[7] Ibid.

[8] Coffen-Smout and Herbert [7].

Both Australia and New Zealand also sought to respond to all stakeholders interested in marine space dealing with the submarine cable regulations. The following sections deal with analyzing the essential provisions of Australia and New Zealand's cable regimes, respectively.

4.3 Australia

4.3.1 Background of Schedule 3A

Australia's submarine cable regime has been enriched through several developing phases. In the 1960s, it has enacted the Submarine Cables and Pipeline Protection Act of 1963 law to deal with submarine cables and pipelines.[9] Regarding submarine cables, this legislation is on the Cable Convention 1884 and has adopted provisions to protect cable.[10] It applies to the submarine cables on high seas, which includes the EEZ of Australia.[11] Along with other issues, this legislation prescribes a penalty for breaking or injuring submarine cable.[12] It also specifies cable owners' liability for damaging

---

[9] Act No. 61 of [3].

[10] "*...Australian nationals and ships are also subject to the provisions of the Submarine Cables and Pipelines Protection Act 1963 which reflects Australia's obligations under UNCLOS and the Convention for the Protection of Submarine Telegraph Cables of 1884, and these obligations apply to Australian nationals and ships in all waters globally.*" See also [8]. See Australian Government, Federal List of Legislation.

[11] Section 5 of the Act No. 61 of [3] of Australia provides.

"the Act applies only to cables and pipelines beneath the high seas (1) This Act applies only to a submarine cable or pipeline, or that part of a submarine cable or pipeline: (a) that is beneath the high seas or in the exclusive economic zone; and (b) that is not a submarine cable (within the meaning of Schedule 3A to the Telecommunications Act 1997) in a protection zone (within the meaning of that Schedule)".

[12] Section 7 of the Act No. 61 of [3] of Australia States.

"Persons not to break or injure submarine cables or pipelines (1) A person commits an offence if the person engages in conduct and the conduct results in a ship registered in Australia or in a Territory breaking or injuring: (a) a submarine telegraph or a telephone cable in such a manner as might interrupt or obstruct telegraphic or telephonic communications; or (b) a submarine pipeline; or (c) a submarine high-voltage cable. Penalty: Imprisonment for 12 months or 20 penalty units. (1A) A person commits an offence if the person engages in conduct and the person is negligent as to whether the conduct will result in a ship registered in Australia or in a Territory breaking or injuring:

(a) a submarine telegraph or a telephone cable in such a manner as might interrupt or obstruct telegraphic or telephonic communications; or (b) a submarine pipeline; or (c) a submarine high-voltage cable. Penalty: Imprisonment for 3 months or 10 penalty units. (2) Where: (a) a breakage of, or an injury to, a cablecosts to users have not been or pipeline is caused by persons acting with the sole object of saving their lives or their ships; and (b) those persons took all necessary precautions to avoid breaking or injuring the cable or pipeline, the last preceding subsection does not apply in relation to the break or injury. (3) In this section: engage in conduct means: (a) do an act; or (b) omit to perform an act".

cable during cable operation.[13] Another relevant provision of the legislation deals with indemnity against fishing gears' sacrifice to minimize cable damage.

Regarding the implementation procedure of any offense under it, the legislation prescribes summary proceedings. Later on, this 1960s legislation has been modified substantially by an updated cable regime in the 1990s. However, the 1960s legislation is still in force and applied to the cables that are not covered by the 1990s law.

In the 1990s, the Australian Information Economy Advisory Council had conducted a National Bandwidth Inquiry.[14] This inquiry raised concern for the protection of submarine cables in Australian waters. It identified the inadequacy of Australia's submarine cable regulatory framework. It recommended adopting provisions for the submarine cables, particularly the cables that were significant to Australia for its global communication networks.[15] The inquiry also recommended and emphasized a robust submarine cable regularity regime for submarine cables of national importance within Australian waters.[16] It stressed the establishment of an integrated submarine cable management system. According to these recommendations, such a cable management system would function under a designated authority to be established for this purpose.[17] The inquiry's recommendations also pleaded for enhanced deterrence against cable damage to limit the breaking or injuring of submarine cables so that the security and reliability of Australia's telecommunication networks are improved.[18] In response, the government of Australia initiated the necessary legislative process to accommodate those recommendations.[19]

In this regard, Explanatory Memorandum that deals with the key issues relating to proposed legislation is notable.[20] It categorically pointed out that the Government of Australia had recognized the importance of the submarine cable networks.[21] It also raised concerns about cable breakings and lack of security for submarine fiber optic telecommunications cables. It recognized the vulnerability of the submarine cable infrastructure-exposed to damage from various activities, fishing, anchoring of vessels, dredging, intentional human aggression in terrorist activities, etc.[22] It raised concern over an enormous loss that results from cable damage in the process of cable

---

[13]Section 8 of the Act No. 61 of [3] of Australia provides "Liability for breaking or injuring a cable or pipeline If a person, in the course of laying or repairing a submarine cable or pipeline of which he or she is the owner, causes a break in or injury to another cable or pipeline, he or she is liable to bear the cost of repairing the break or injury".

[14]National Bandwidth Inquiry [9]. See the Explanatory Memorandum to Bill [10].

[15]The Explanatory Memorandum to Bill [10].

[16]Ibid.

[17]National Bandwidth Inquiry [9].

[18]National Bandwidth Inquiry [9].

[19]Explanatory Memorandum to Bill [10].

[20]Ibid.

[21]Ibid.

[22]Ibid., *at* 1.

breaks, repairing of submarine cable, and, most importantly, severance of communication.[23] Finally, it concluded that both the Submarine Cables and Pipelines Protection Act 1963 and the Telecommunications Act 1997 were not adequate to address the existing and emerging challenges to the submarine cables within Australian waters.[24] Thus, the recommendations suggest robust arrangements that will ensure, among others, sufficient deterrence for breaking cables, enhanced compensation, an institutional setup to support submarine cable operation, etc.

Therefore, there are two amendments.[25] By the Telecommunications and Other Legislation Amendment (Protection of Submarine Cables and other Measures) Bill 2005, the Telecommunication Act 1997 has been amended to adopt specific laws on submarine cables.[26] At present, the Telecommunications Act 1997 is enriched with both an additional *Section* and *Schedule*.[27] It inserts Part 24 A and Section 484A to Part 24 and Section 484 of the 1997 Act of Australia.[28] This Section 484A of the 1997 Act of Australia contains Schedule 3A—a dedicated scheme for laying and protecting submarine cables.[29] The Schedule 3A (the Schedule), among others, approves declarations of protection zones over submarine cables of Australia's national significance with the regulatory support by an authority.

The Australian Communication and Media Authority Act 2005 (the ACMA Act) establishes the Australian Communication and Media Authority.[30] The Schedule empowers the ACMA to make a declaration of cable protection zones, grants permission to install a submarine cable in Australian waters, and imposes control on specific activities to set significant penalties for non-compliance 2005 Act.[31] In this connection, it is notable that the penalties for cable damage under the 1963 Act would not

[23]Cable owners estimate the direct cost to them of repairing a cable break at between $1.2 million and $3.3 million. The flow-on costs to users have not been estimated the Explanatory Memorandum to the Bill, [10], *at* 1.

[24]The Explanatory Memorandum to the Bill [10].

[25]The Amendment Bill [11].

[26]Ibid.

[27]Schedule 3A, Act 1997 (No. 47, 1997) [12].

[28]Section 484 under Part 24 of the No. 47, 1997 deals with the Carriers' Powers and Immunities.

[29]"*Schedule 3A outlines a regime for establishing, enforcing and reviewing protection zones over submarine cables that are considered to be of 'national significance (i.e., cables that link Australia to global networks and are vital to the national interest)*". See also the Explanatory Memorandum to Bill [10], *at* 41.

[30]Act [13] (No. 45, 2005).

[31]The explanatory memorandum to Bill [10], to the legislations indicates that its main objectives were *first* to provide security and reliability for the submarine cable component of Australia's national information infrastructure *secondly* to clarify the liability for compensation and lastly to provide increased consistency and clarity in the Commonwealth telecommunications regulatory regime. To achieve, it prescribes the following measures. *Firstly*, establishing a scheme for declaring protection zones over submarine cables of national significance. Secondly, prohibiting or restricting activities likely to damage submarine cables inside protection zones. Thirdly, creating offenses for damaging a submarine cable within a protection zone, punishable by fine or imprisonment lastly establishing permit regime for the installation of submarine cables in Australian waters inside and outside of protection zones and the execution of the measures are rested upon the Australian Federal Police.

apply within the Submarine Cable Protection Zones.[32] Thus, the 1963 Act remained in force to the cables beyond the submarine cable protection zones established under the Schedule.

The Schedule sets three overreaching objectives and focuses on ensuring the submarine cables' security and reliability with enhanced deterrence and clarity and consistency in the regulatory regime.[33] These objectives, according to ACMA Review Report 2010, have four pillars.[34] *Firstly*, establishing a scheme for a declaration of protection zones; *secondly*, prohibiting or restricting activities threatening to cable damage; *thirdly*, prescribing penalties and its implementation; and *lastly*, cooperation between cable operators and local administrations with monitoring police force.[35]

The ACMA Review Report 2010 also suggests several recommendations. Such recommendations include consultation between the ACMA and the Commonwealth Attorney-General in certain issues, ACMA's enhanced authority on protection zone and its standards, removing potential inconsistency between Schedule 3A and UNCLOS, an extension of the Schedule to the domestic submarine cables, etc. These recommendations were the basis of the Telecommunications Legislation Amendment (Submarine Cable Protection) Bill 2013.[36] It led to the present form of the Schedule 3A that set out a regulatory regime for the protection of submarine telecommunications cables in Australian waters covering both the international and domestic submarine cables.[37] The outer limit of a protection zone will extend up to the limit of Australia's exclusive economic zone or to the edge of the continental shelf, whichever is the further. The following analysis will reveal the notable features of Australia's legislative and regulatory arrangements for submarine cables. It deals with the analysis of both the 2005 Act and Schedule 3A of the 1997 Act of Australia.[38]

---

[32]The amendment made changes to the Schedule 3 to No. 47, 1997, and the Submarine Cable and Pipeline Protection Act 1963. The amendment limits the application of 1963 Act to the submarine cable of national significance that will be governed by the proposed Schedule 3A, and 1963 Act will remain applicable to the all other submarine cables and pipeline beneath the high seas or in the exclusive economic zone. The 1963 Act applies to oil and gas pipelines and high-voltage cables as well as to telecommunications cables and applies only in Australia's Exclusive Economic Zone and under the high seas, not within Australia's territorial waters. This legislation provides little incentives to the protection of the submarine cables and the pipelines as well.

[33]The objectives of Government action relating to submarine telecommunications cables are to provide security and reliability for the submarine cable component of Australia's national information infrastructure; clarify the liability for compensation, and provide increased consistency and clarity in the Commonwealth telecommunications regulatory regime. Explanatory Memorandum to the Bill 2005.

[34]ACMA Review Report [14]. It was a statutory review report under clause 89 of the Schedule 3A to be prepared by the ACMA to review the operation of Schedule 3A within five years after this Schedule commenced. The ACMA required to publish it and report to the Minister Communications. This report made several recommendations for further evaluation of the Schedule 3A.

[35]ACMA Review Report [14].

[36]Australian Government, Federal List of Legislation [15], See <https://www.legislation.gov.au/Details/C2013B00200/Download> (last updated March 30, 2020).

[37]Act 1997 (No. 47, [12]).

[38]Schedule 3A. Act [12] (No. 47, 1997). The arrangement of the Schedule maintains the following scheme. The schedule is divided into five parts. The first and the fifth parts deal with the preliminary and the miscellaneous respectively.

4.3.2 Definition and Scope of the Schedule

The Schedule has defined submarine cables as part of a line link that lies beneath Australian waters and has been laid for purposes that include connecting Australia with a place outside Australia. The submarine cables cover the domestic cable laid for purposes that involve connecting the areas in Australia.[39] Also, Clause 2 of the Schedule 3A *submarine cable* means:

(a) "a domestic submarine cable; or
(b) An international submarine cable".[40]

The Schedule 3A will cover international cables entering Australia's TW and connecting its territory and the domestic submarine cables (cables that enter Australia's TW and connect to Australia from another place in Australia). Thus, a cable transiting through Australia's water only does not attract Schedule 3A.[41]

Part 1 deals with the preliminary. **Part 2** is the most important segment of this scheme. This part has been again divided into five divisions which have been further divided into subdivisions. Division 2, 3 and 4 are the most important. Division 2 of this Part deals with the declarations and the prerequisites to a declaration of a protection zone. Then Division 3 deals with the varying or revoking a declaration with its prerequisites of a protection zone. It follows the Division 4 which deals with the offenses about a protection zone. It has been subdivided into three subdivisions when the first one deal with the damaging of submarine cables and the next is dedicated to the engaging in prohibited or restricted activities, the last one deals with the breach by a foreign nationals and foreign ships. Division 5 provides for the claims for damages and Indemnity for loss of anchor etc.

Part 3 relates to the Installation permits of submarine cables. It suggest separate arrangements for installation permits on international and domestic submarine cable. It also consists of five divisions. Starting with simple outline of the part in first division, Division 2 deals with protection zone permits. Division 3 on non-protection zone permit. Division 4 imposes conditions for installation. Division 5 defines offences relating to installation of cables.

Part 4 deals with the compensation and **Part 5** with Miscellaneous.

[39]Clause 2 of the Schedule 3A. Act [12] (No. 47, 1997). See also Explanatory Memorandum to the Bill [8], *at* 28.

[40]Clause 2(5) of the Schedule 3A. Act [12] (No. 47, 1997) provides "submarine Cable also includes the part of the submarine cable. Clause 2(5) a reference in this Schedule to a *submarine cable* includes a reference to a part of a submarine cable, and submarine cable means that part of a line link (within the meaning of Section 30) (a) that is aid on or beneath the seabed that lies beneath Australian waters. And (b) that is laid for the purpose that include connecting a place in Australia with a place outside of Australia (whether or not the cable is laid via another place in Australia); and includes any device attached to that part of the line link, if the device is used in or in connection with the line link". See ACMA Report 2010, p. 5.

[41]Clause 2 of the Schedule 3A. Act [12] (No. 47, 1997). defines "Australian Waters it means:

(a) the waters of the territorial sea of Australia; and

(b) the waters of the exclusive economic zone of Australia; and

(c) the sea above that part of the continental shelf of Australia that is beyond the limits of the exclusive economic zone".

4.3.3 *Schedule 3A and the ACMA Act on Protection Zone Related to Submarine Cables*

Australian Communications and Media Authority Act 2005 (the ACMA Act) provides for the Australian Communications and Media Authority (ACMA/the authority) in place of the old institutions in this regard. Both the ACA and the Australian Broadcasting Authority merge into ACMA.[42] The ACMA is the nodal regulatory authority to the 1997 Act of Australia. The Schedule 3A empowers the ACMA to make a declaration of a submarine cable protection zone and suggests several procedural steps.[43] Clause 2 of the Schedule states that the protection zone means a protection zone declared by the ACMA under Clause 4 of the Schedule. The ACMA may issue a proposal of a protection zone for a cable, which in its opinion, is a submarine cable of national significance.[44] It performs specific responsibilities, and in declaring a cable, the procreation zone follows certain procedural standards established by the Schedule.

The ACMA develops and publishes a protection zone proposal seeking public submission, consults with the Environmental Secretary, and considers the proposed marine area's environment and heritage standards. Its consultation and submission include the cable operators' response, other stakeholders such as other marine users, etc. Any such declaration must provide detail on an area of the zone and its restrictions.[45] ACMA also reserves its discretion to declare a requested protection zone. If it publishes the proposal of a declaration of the protection zone, it must specify the nominal location of the cable/s area of the zone. Clause 9 of the Schedule prescribes that for one submarine cable, the area consists of the area within 1852 m on either side of the cable. For more than one cable, they consist of a site within 1852 m from each of the two outermost cables. The declaration also considers activities relating to marine and energy infrastructure that may cause cable damage. Such activities may range from installation, construction, civil engineering work, exploring, or exploiting resources to conducting research activities and maintaining those structures, etc. ACMA has a responsibility to publish a summary of the proposal of a protection

---

[42]Section 3 of the ACMA Act [13]. No. 45, 2005 provides that ACMA means the Australian Communications and Media Authority.

[43]Clause 4 of the Schedule 3A. Act [12] (No. 47, 1997) provides "ACMA may declare a protection zone-

(1) The ACMA may, by legislative instrument, declare a protection zone in relation to one or more submarine cables, or one or more submarine cables that are proposed to be installed, in Australian waters.

(1A) The ACMA must not declare a protection zone in relation to one or more domestic submarine cables, or one or more domestic submarine cables that are proposed to be installed, unless: (a) the cable or cables are specified in the regulations; or (b) the route or routes of the proposed cable or cables are specified in the regulations.

(2) Before the ACMA declares a protection zone, the ACMA must comply with Subdivision B. Also and Section 8 of the ACMA Act 2005 provides the functions of the ACMA includes Functions conferred on the ACMA by the Telecommunication Act 1997 (No. 47, 1997). Act 2005 (No. 45, 2005)".

[44]The Division 2 and 3 of Part 2 of the Schedule 3A. Act [12] (No. 47, 1997).

[45]Ibid.

zone. If the protection zone is beyond Australia's TW, the summary publication also includes foreign circulations. It is to note that the declaration of a protection zone is a legislative instrument, and the ACMA is responsible for ensuring it to be tabled before Parliament.

ACMA has authority for the renewal or revocation of the submarine cable protection zone too. It again follows procedural steps starting with developing a proposal for proposed alterations, publication, and consultation for modifying or revoking a declaration of a protection zone.

In 2007, the ACMS declared two submarine cable protection zones located off the Sydney coasts.[46] The Submarine Cable (Northern Sydney Protection Zone) Declaration 2007 establishes the Northern Sydney Protection Zone extending from Narrabeen Beach to 40 nautical miles offshore.[47] And by Submarine Cable (Southern Sydney Protection Zone) Declaration 2007, the Southern Sydney Protection Zone has come into existence that extends from Tamarama and Clovelly Beach to 30 nautical miles offshore.[48] This Sydney cable protection zones cover the Southern Cross cable that connects Australia with New Zealand, Fiji, and the USA, and the Australia–Japan cable connects it with Guam, Japan, and Asia. Besides, Gondwana-1 cables that link with New Caledonia and the PPC-1 cable connecting Guam and Endeavor cable to connect Hawaii.[49] By the Submarine Cable (Perth Protection Zone) Declaration 2007, the third zone is located off the Perth coast. The SEA-ME-WE3 cable connects Australia with South East Asia, the Middle East, and Western Europe, and it falls under the Perth cable protection zone. It extends from City Beach to 51 nautical miles offshore and covers an area of up to one nautical mile on either side of the cable.[50] The ACMA and the said Declarations authorize prescribing modifications to the list of prohibitory and restricted activities concerning the protection zone.

4.3.4 *Schedule 3A and the ACMA Act on Protection Zone Related Prohibited and Restricted Activities*

The Telecommunications Act 1997 and its Schedule 3A empower the ACMA to protect the submarine cables of national significance to Australia. Among others, the ACMA, in this regard, has adopted measures to control marine activities, which have the potential to cause cable injury. Its Protection Zone Declaration statement provides for marine activities to be prohibited and restricted. In this declaration statement, the ACMA prescribes a list that covers various marine activities that are prohibited or restricted and specifies the extent to which it exercises control on such activities. Such controlling measures are two types. *Firstly*, it prohibits some marine activities

46For detail about thses cable protection zones, see Australia Communications Media Authority (C).

47Sydney Protection Zone A [17].

48Sydney Protection Zone B.

49Ibid.

50ACMA [16].

that pose a potential threat to submarine cables.[51] Then, some of the marine activities, though they are dangerous to cables, still are permitted with certain restrictions.[52]

---

[51]Clause 10 of the Schedule 3A. Act [12] (No. 47, 1997) provides "the list of Prohibited activities-

(1) A declaration of a protection zone may specify activities that are prohibited in the protection zone.
(2) If a declaration of a protection zone does not specify activities that are prohibited in the protection zone, the activities specified in sub-clause (4) are prohibited.
(3) An activity which is specified in a declaration of a protection zone must be an activity that is covered by sub-clause (4).
(4) This sub clause covers the following activities:

  (a) the use of:
    (i) trawl gear that is designed to work on or near the seabed (for example, a demersal trawl); or
    (ii) a net anchored to the seabed and kept upright by floats (for example, a demersal gillnet); or
    (iii) a fishing line that is designed to catch fish at or near the seabed (for example, a demersal line); or
    (iv) a dredge; or
    (v) a pot or trap; or
    (vi) a squid jig; or
    (vii) a seine; or
    (viii) a structure moored to the seabed with the primary function of attracting fish for capture (for example, a fish aggregating device);
  (b) towing, operating, or suspending from a ship:
    (i) any item mentioned in paragraph (a); or
    (ii) a net, line, rope, chain or any other thing used in connection with fishing operations;
  (c) lowering, raising or suspending an anchor from a ship;
  (d) sand mining;
  (e) exploring for or exploiting resources (other than marine species);
  (f) mining or the use of mining techniques;
  (g) any activity that involves a serious risk that an object will connect with the seabed, if a connection between the object and a submarine cable would be capable of damaging the cable;
  (h) an activity specified in the regulations, being an activity that, if done near a submarine cable, would involve a serious risk of damaging the cable.

(5) However, sub-clause (4) does not cover an activity if:

  (a) the activity is carried on by, or on behalf of, a person who owns or operates a submarine cable in the protection zone; and
  (b) The activity consists of the maintenance or repair of the submarine cable.
  11 Restricted activities.

(1) A declaration of a protection zone may specify restrictions that are imposed in the protection zone on activities in the protection zone.
(2) An activity on which restrictions are imposed must be an activity that is covered by subclause (3).
(3) This subclause covers the following activities:

  (a) the use of:

The ACMA exercises discretion in specifying the activities and included in the declaration. Such prohibitory activities, among others, include towing, trawl gear, anchoring, dredge, mining, etc. Similarly, the restrictive activities, among others, involve anchoring in a protection zone, lowering, raising, or suspending a hotline from a ship, demersal fishing using J-hooks, use of or towing, operating or suspending from a ship a net anchored to the seabed or a grapnel. Further, activities like the use of an explosive or explosive device are also restricted in the protection zone. Clause 10(5) of the Schedule exempts the repairing and maintenance activities from the list of

---

(i) a net that is above the seabed at all times; or
(ii) lures or baits attached to a line towed behind a ship;
(b) towing, operating, or suspending from a ship:
(i) any item mentioned in paragraph (a); or
(ii) a net, line, rope, chain or any other thing used in connection with fishing operations;
(c) fishing using a line;
(d) installing, maintaining or removing an electricity cable, an oil or gas pipeline, any like cables or pipelines, and any associated equipment;
(e) constructing, maintaining or removing an installation for the use of ships;
(f) constructing or maintaining navigational aids;
(g) any activity that involves a risk that an object will connect with the seabed, if a connection between the object and a submarine cable would be capable of damaging the cable;
(h) an activity specified in the regulations, being an activity that, if done near a submarine cable, could involve a risk of damaging the cable.

(4) However, subclause (3) does not cover an activity if:

(a) the activity is carried on by, or on behalf of, a person who owns or operates a submarine cable in the protection zone; and
(b) the activity consists of the maintenance or repair of the submarine cable".

[52]Clause 11 of the Schedule 3A. Act [12] (No. 47, 1997) deals with the "Restricted activities-

(1) A declaration of a protection zone may specify restrictions that are imposed in the protection zone on activities in the protection zone.
(2) An activity on which restrictions are imposed must be an activity that is covered by subclause (3).
(3) This subclause covers the following activities: (a) the use of: (i) a net that is above the seabed at all times; or (ii) lures or baits attached to a line towed behind a ship; (b) towing, operating, or suspending from a ship: (i) any item mentioned in paragraph (a); or (ii) a net, line, rope, chain or any other thing used in connection with fishing operations; (c) fishing using a line; (d) installing, maintaining or removing an electricity cable, an oil or gas pipeline, any like cables or pipelines and any associated equipment; (e) constructing, maintaining or removing an installation for the use of ships; (f) constructing or maintaining navigational aids; (g) any activity that involves a risk that an object will connect with the seabed, if a connection between the object and a submarine cable would be capable of damaging the cable; (h) an activity specified in the regulations, being an activity that, if done near a submarine cable, could involve a risk of damaging the cable.
(4) However, subclause (3) does not cover an activity if: (a) the activity is carried on by, or on behalf of, a person who owns or operates a submarine cable in the protection zone; and (b) the activity consists of the maintenance or repair of the submarine cable".

prohibited activities. And, Clause 11(4) also exempts the repairing and maintenance activities from the list of restricted activities instead of the prohibited activities.

4.3.5 Schedule 3A and the ACMA Act on Submarine Cables Installation Permits

The next important feature of the legislation is an installation permit for laying submarine cables. Schedule 3A of the Telecommunications Act 1997 intends to establish a streamlined process for applying submarine cable installation permits. It covers both international and domestic cables in the protection and non-protection zones installation permits as well. Both procedures for obtaining protection zone installation permits on submarine cables of national significance and non-protection zone installation permits are similar to a broad extent.

A protection zone installation permit process starts with submitting an application to the ACMA and relevant information on proposed cable routes, carriers, charges, etc.[53] On receiving such an application, the ACMA consults with the Attorney-General's Department (AGD) and the Home Affairs Secretary and other persons it considers relevant. Before granting a protection zone installation permit beyond Australia's TW, ACMA needs to get approval from AGD to consider such application in compliance with the UNCLOS provisions and national security interests and consult with the Secretary, Home Affairs.[54] This application process, to some extent, exempts several State and Territorial Laws such as laws on environment and natural and cultural heritage. The ACMA processes the application expeditiously (between 25 and 35 working days) and grants a permit with certain conditions unless rejected on security ground. Such conditions include the carriers to install cable within route specified by ACMA, compliance of Commonwealth regulatory approval, security parameters, and other conditions fixed by ACMA. A protection zone installation permit remains valid for 18 months. It may be suspended or canceled on breaching its conditions or Code of Practice. Before such cancellation, the carrier gets 30 days' notice and an opportunity of being heard. The non-protection zone installation permit process follows an almost similar process. It applies to submarine cables other than cables of national significance. It takes 60–90 working days to complete.[55] Both permit processes refer to the domestic submarine cables as well.

Further, the Schedule prescribes certain conditions applicable to the installation of submarine cables. Such conditions require the carriers to comply with Australia's obligations under international agreements such as UNCLOS. It also requires the installation process should produce minimum inconvenience to the environment,

[53]Clause 51 & 52 of the Schedule 3A. Act [12] (No. 47, 1997). Section 60 of the ACMA Act, [13] (No. 45, 2005) Act deals with Charges relating to ACMA's expenses and provides that the ACMA may, by written instrument, make determinations fixing charges…).

[54]Clause 55A of the Schedule 3A. Act [12] (No. 47, 1997).

[55]Clause 64–76 of the Schedule 3A. Act [12] (No. 47, 1997).

persons, property, etc.[56] The Schedule also empowers ACMA to take necessary measures for streamlining the installation permit process.

4.3.6 *Offenses and Penalties Under Schedule 3A and ACMA Act*

Schedule 3A prescribes both civil and criminal liabilities for its breaches such as damaging cables, prohibited or restricted activities in the protection zone, installing cables without permits, breach of conditions for permits and installation of cables, etc.

Division 4 of Part 2 of the Schedule deals with the offenses in relation to a submarine cable protection zone. It prescribes significant penalties for damaging cables and engaging with prohibited or restricted activities within cable protection zones.

Clause 36 of the Schedule defines an offense of cable damage and states that a person engaging in conduct that results in damage to a submarine cable commits an offense of cable damage. It also prescribes penalties imprisonment for ten years or 600 penalty units or both.[57] According to Clause 37, a negligent act of cable damage is also an offense punishable with imprisonment for three years or 180 penalty units or both.[58] In both cases, the liability is strict except for the incidents that save a life or ship; prevent pollution; reasonable steps were taken to avoid cable damage, and the

---

[56]Clause 79–82 of the Schedule 3A. Act [12] (No. 47, 1997).

[57]Clause 36 of the Schedule 3A. Act [12] (No. 47, 1997) deals with "the damaging a submarine cable-

(1) A person commits an offence if:

- (a) the person engages in conduct; and
- (b) the conduct results in damage to a submarine cable; and
- (c) the cable is in a protection zone.

  Penalty: Imprisonment for 10 years or 600 penalty units, or both.

(2) Strict liability applies to paragraph (1)(c)".

[58]37 of the Schedule 3A. Act [12] (No. 47, 1997) "Negligently damaging a submarine cable-

(1) A person commits an offence if:

- (a) the person engages in conduct; and
- (b) the conduct results in damage to a submarine cable; and
- (c) the person is negligent as to the fact that the conduct results in that damage; and
- (d) the cable is in a protection zone.

  Penalty: Imprisonment for 3 years or 180 penalty units, or both.

(2) (2) Strict liability applies to paragraph (1)(d)".

defendant is the owner of the damaged cable.[59] These defenses are also applicable to the liabilities that arise from engaging with prohibited or restrictive activities.

Clause 40 defines the offense of a person who engages in prohibited or restricted activities in the protection zone. Such engagement may attract imprisonment for five years or 300 penalty units.[60] The accused may meet with an even more significant penalty, which may extend to 7 years' imprisonment or 420 penalty units or both such conduct or engagement in view of making a commercial gain.[61]

An accused of an offense concerning the prohibited or restricted activities within protection zones, as stated above, may be the master or owner of a ship and other persons who commit such offense on the permission of the former. The owner or master of a ship is also liable for his recklessness because the ship is used in the commission of the offense. Accordingly, these offenses are punishable under Clauses 40 and 41 of the Schedule, respectively. Further, Clause 44A provides that Division 4 does not apply to the foreign nationals for their alleged act or omission beyond Australia's TW. Such alleged foreign national may not involve a ship or may involve a foreign ship.

---

[59]Clause 38 of the Schedule 3A. Act [12] (No. 47, 1997) deals with the "defence to offences of damaging a submarine cable.

Subclauses 36(1) and 37(1) do not apply if: (a) the conduct that resulted in damage to the submarine cable was necessary to save a life or a ship; or

(b) the conduct that resulted in damage to the submarine cable was necessary to prevent pollution; or (c) the defendant took all reasonable steps to avoid causing damage to the submarine cable; or (d) the defendant is the carrier who owns or operates the submarine cable; or (e) when the conduct occurred, the defendant was acting on behalf of the carrier who owns or operates the submarine cable".

[60]Clause 40 of the Schedule 3A. Act [12] (No. 47, 1997) deals with "the engaging in prohibited or restricted activities-

A person commits an offence if: (a) the person engages in conduct; and (b) the conduct occurs in a protection zone; and (c) the conduct: (i) is prohibited in the protection zone; or

(ii) contravenes a restriction imposed on an activity in the protection zone; and (d) the conduct is not engaged in by the carrier who owns or operates the cable, or a person acting on behalf of such a carrier, for the purpose of maintaining or repairing a submarine cable for which the carrier is responsible; and (e) the conduct is not engaged in by a carrier who holds a protection zone installation permit, or a person acting on such a carrier's behalf, in, or in the course of, the installation of a submarine cable in accordance with the permit.

Penalty: Imprisonment for 5 years or 300 penalty units, or both".

[61]Clause 41 of the Schedule 3A. Act [12] (No. 47, 1997) deals with "aggravated offence of engaging in prohibited or restricted activities-

A person commits an offence if: (a) the person engages in conduct; and (b) the conduct occurs in a protection zone; and (c) the conduct: (i) is prohibited in the protection zone; or (ii) contravenes a restriction imposed on an activity in the protection zone; and (d) the person engages in the conduct with the intention of making a commercial gain; and (e) the conduct is not engaged in by the carrier who owns or operates the cable, or a person acting on behalf of such a carrier, for the purpose of maintaining or repairing a submarine cable for which the carrier is responsible; and (f) the conduct is not engaged in by a carrier who holds a protection zone installation permit, or a person acting on such a carrier's behalf, in, or in the course of, the installation of a submarine cable in accordance with the permit".

Penalty: Imprisonment for 7 years or 420 penalty units, or both".

The next phase of penalty is concerning the installation permits, as provided by Division 5 of Part 3 of the Schedule. Clause 84 of the Schedule states that installing an international submarine cable without a permit within Australian waters, be it in a protection or non-protection zone, is an offense punishable with 200 penalty units. Installation of a domestic submarine cable in the protection zone is also punishable with 200 penalty units. Clause 84 of the Schedule prescribes a fine, extending to 100 penalty units for violating conditions of an installation permits fixed by this Part 3 as discussed above. However, if a foreign national involves such contravening act or omission beyond Australian TW relating to such permit conditions, it may not be accused without the Attorney-General's written permission.[62] Clause 86 also imposes liability on failure to remove an unlawfully installed submarine cable, and such an act is punishable with 200 penalty units.

4.3.7 Claims, Indemnity, and Compensation

The relevant provisions of Division 5 of Part 2 prescribe for damages and indemnity, and Part 4 of the Schedule is dedicated to the compensation to loss or acquisition of property. Clause 45 provides that a claim for damages against loss or damage in relation to the protection zone may occur due to cable damage or contravening with prohibited or restricted activities.[63] It also states that such claims may be mutually agreed upon or determined by the court. Clause 46 provides that marine users, especially fishermen, may sacrifice their fishing gears to avoid cable damage and claim

---

[62]Clause 85 of the Schedule 3A. Act [12] (No. 47, 1997) deals with "violation of installation permit condition-

(1) A carrier commits an offence if: (a) the carrier holds a permit under this Part authorising the installation of a submarine cable; and (b) the carrier, or a person acting on behalf of the carrier, engages in conduct; and (c) the conduct breaches a condition of the permit.

Penalty: 100 penalty units.

(2) A proceeding for an offence committed by a person against subclause (1) must not be commenced without the written consent of the Attorney-General if: (a) the person is a foreign national; and (b) the offence involved an act or omission outside Australia;".

[63]Clause 45 of the Schedule 3A. Act [12] (No. 47, 1997) related with the "claims of damages-

(1) A person who suffers, directly or indirectly, loss or damage: (a) because a submarine cable in a protection zone is damaged by conduct of another person; or (b) because another person engages in conduct that is prohibited in a protection zone; or (c) because another person engages in conduct that contravenes a restriction imposed on an activity in a protection zone; may recover the amount of the loss or damage: (d) against that other person; or (e) against any person involved in the contravention (whether or not a person is convicted of an offence in respect of the contravention)".

indemnity against such sacrifice from the carriers.[64] It is to note that indemnity is for the loss of equipment, and it does not include the catches.

Clause 87 of Part 4 of the Schedule provides that a person who has suffered financial loss or damage to his property due to a carrier's act is entitled to get compensation from the latter. Such compensation may be mutually agreed on between such an aggrieved person and the carrier or determined by the competent court. The carrier is also liable for the acquisition of property concerning his actions and the existence of rights conferred on him by this Schedule (Clause 88). These provisions also provide that in the cases for damages, indemnity, and compensation, the claimant may initiate the recovery process before the Federal Court of Australia.

4.3.8 Liability and Enforcement

The legislation adopts a principle of strict liability on violation of its provisions, in particular, concerning the protection of cables. Criminal Code 1995 of Australia deals with strict liability.[65] Several offenses under this Schedule concerning protection zones start with the cable damage, infringement of prohibited or restricted activities, and cable installation without a permit to attract strict liability.Thus, the prosecution is not necessarily required to prove a mental element of these crimes (intention, knowledge, recklessness, or negligence); however, the persecution needs to establish

---

[64]Clause 46 of the Schedule 3A. Act [12] (No. 47, 1997) provides "indemnity for loss of anchor etc.-

(1) If: (a) after all reasonable precautionary measures have been taken, an anchor, a net or any other fishing gear belonging to a ship is sacrificed in order to avoid damaging a submarine cable in a protection zone; and (b) at the time the sacrifice is made, no person on board the ship is engaging in conduct: (i) that is prohibited in the protection zone; or (ii) that contravenes a restriction imposed on an activity in the protection zone; the owner of the ship is entitled to be indemnified for that loss by the carrier responsible for the submarine cable.

(2) Jurisdiction is conferred on the Federal Court in any matter arising under this clause in respect of which a civil proceeding is instituted under this clause".

[65]**Section 6.1** of Australia's Criminal Code [18] **provides-**

"Strict liability.

(1) If a law that creates an offense provides that the offense is an offense of strict liability:

   (a) there are no fault elements for any of the physical elements of the offense; and
   (b) the defense of mistake of fact under Section 9.2 is available.

(2) If a law that creates an offense provides that strict liability applies to a particular physical element of the offense:

   (a) there are no fault elements for that physical element; and
   (b) the defense of mistake of fact under Section 9.2 is available about that physical element.

(3) The existence of strict liability does not make any other defense unavailable".

that the offense's relevant physical element did occur. The accused bears the evidential burden thereof under the same Code.[66] He may advance a plea of the mistake of fact as his defense. An accused of any of the said offenses in the submarine cable protection zone may take the plea of ignorance of the place of occurrence, i.e., a submarine cable protection zone position.[67]

As mentioned above, the Federal Court of Australia is an appropriate forum for any of the disputes to Schedule 3A. The Australian Federal Police (AFP) is the enforcement agency of the offenses under this Schedule. According to the Crime Act, 1914 of Australia, a range of enforcement jurisdictions relevant to Schedule 3A.[68] Additionally, the ACMA has the authority to enforce breaches relating to carrier license conditions.[69]

4.4 New Zealand

The Protection of Submarine Cables and Pipelines Act 1996 of New Zealand is another example of a dedicated national law (1996 Act of New Zealand).[70] It has dealt with submarine cables and pipelines; however, this analysis focuses only on the submarine cable. Before that, New Zealand had adopted the Submarine Cables and Pipelines Protection Act, 1966 (the 1996 Act).[71] Since then, it has also brought changes in its cable regime to address present-day challenges in laying and protecting cables. Thus, the 1996 Act of New Zealand has come into operation.

In compliance with New Zealand's obligation under international law, the 1996 Act of New Zealand aims to consolidate and repeal the 1966 Act of New Zealand to extend better submarine cable protection. This legislation's scheme suggests is legislation's scheme suggests its fundamental principles and approach represents an array of provisions that intend to define liability and offenses to the cable damage. It establishes a submarine cable *protected area* and prescribes penalties for its violation. The enforcement authority assignment and suggesting proceedings of the offenses and maritime surveillance also remain essential parts of the legislation. The 1996 Act of New Zealand also provides promulgation of order for navigations, fishing, submarine cable operation, etc.

66 Division 13.3 of Section 3 of Australia's Criminal Code [18].

67 Explanatory Memorandum to Bill [10], *at* 72.

68 Explanatory Memorandum to the Bill [8], *at* 37.

69 Explanatory Memorandum to Bill [10], *at* 46.

70 Public Act [19] No. 22).

71 [20] No. 5.

4.4.1 Scope of the 1996 Act of New Zealand

Section 2 of the 1996 Act of New Zealand defines the submarine cable as a cable that lies beneath the high seas or the territorial sea of New Zealand or the internal waters of New Zealand.[72] It applies to an act by New Zealand's subjects or anyone within its TW and an ordinary citizen or person ordinarily resident or the person from the New Zealand Ship.[73]

Part II of the Act 1996 [19] of New Zealand is the most crucial segment of this legislation. It deals with the protection of cables and its enforcement mechanisms as well. It provides both substantive and procedural measures and includes measures that define liability, indemnity for loss of equipment, the offense, prohibition of certain activities, the protected areas, enforcement officers and their powers, procedures for the collection of evidence, seizer, and forfeiture of property and maritime surveillance equipment.

4.4.2 Protected Area for Submarine Cables

The 1996 Act of New Zealand prescribes the identification of a *protected area* for submarine cables and regulations of specific activities to such areas. According to Section 12 of the legislation, the Governor-General, on the recommendation of the Minister, may declare an area as protected areas within the internal water, TW, and EEZ of New Zealand.[74] The Minister may recommend the protected areas if he is

---

[72]Section 2 of the Public Act [19] No. 22. It also defines cables as Cable includes works within the meaning of Section 2 of the Electricity Act 1992 and a line within the meaning of Section 2 of the Telecommunicating Act 1987.

[73]Section 4 of the Public Act [19] No. 22.

[74]Section 12 of the Public Act [19] No. 22 deals with "the protected areas-

(1) The Governor-General may from time to time, by Order in Council made on the recommendation of the Minister, declare any of the following areas to be a protected area for the purposes of this Act: (a) an area within the internal waters of New Zealand: (b) an area within the territorial sea of New Zealand: (c) an area within the exclusive economic zone of New Zealand (as de- scribed in Section 9 of the Territorial Sea, Contiguous Zone, and Exclusive Economic Zone Act 1977). (2) The Minister shall not make a recommendation under subsection (1) unless—(a) the Minister has first consulted with such persons or organisations representing such persons as the Minister considers would be affected by the order; and (b) those persons or organisations have a reasonable opportunity to make submissions to the Minister; and (c) the Minister has regard to those submissions. (3) A failure to comply with subsection (2) does not affect the validity of any Order in Council made under subsection (1). (4) An Order in Council under subsection (1) may—(a) apply

(i) generally in respect of an area to which it relates: (ii) differently in respect of specified areas or classes of areas within the general area specified in the Order in Council: (iii) generally in respect of all ships: (iv) differently in respect of specified ships or classes of ships: (v) generally in respect of all methods of fishing: (vi) differently in respect of specified methods of fishing: (b) impose requirements in respect of specified ships or classes of ships that must be met before a ship or class of ships qualifies for exclusion from the application of the order. (5) The Minister shall publish a notice of the making of an Order in Council under subsection (1) in—(a) each of satisfied with the outcome of a detailed consultation process conducted between him and interested stakeholders for this purpose. 'Catch Fish—Not Cables' phrase is evolved to save submarine cables. Specific activities in the declared *protected area* have been regulated to ensure the protection of submarine cable damage. The protected area standards prescribe several marine activities such as fishing operations from a ship, anchoring, are prohibited, and use of fishing equipment or anchoring, which are yet to be deployed fully, also deemed as contravening activities.[75]

4.4.3 Protection and Enforcement Officer and Seizure and Forfeiture of Property and Enforcement

The 1996 Act of New Zealand prescribes both protection officers[76] and enforcement officers[77] to implement this law. For this law, the enforcement officer is deemed to be a protection officer. About the enforcement, currently, the New Zealand Police and Royal New Zealand Navy are empowered to enforce the offense. Its personnel of these security forces is designated as the enforcement officers.

The legislation provides significant authority to the enforcement officer essential to the implementation of its provisions. First, the protection officer may ask a vessel that, in his opinion, is contravening with the protected area standards.[78] Second, he has the authority to seize fishing equipment concerning violation of protected area

---

the metropolitan daily newspapers published in Auckland, Wellington, Christchurch, and Dunedin, respectively; and (b) the Gazette. (6) The Minister may, by notice in the Gazette, declare that an Order in Council under this section does not apply in respect of a specified ship or class of ships, and may in like manner vary or revoke any such notice. (7) A declaration under subsection (6) may be made unconditionally or upon or subject to such conditions that are specified in the notice. (8) Notwithstanding the provisions of an Order in Council under this section, any such notice has effect according to its tenor. (9) Subsections (2), (3), and (5) apply, with such modifications as may be necessary, to the making of a declaration under subsection (6)".

[75] Section 13 of the Public Act [19] No. 22 provides-

"(1) ..... (a) fishing operations are conducted from a ship in an area declared to be a protected area in respect of that ship under Section 12(1); or (b) a ship is anchored in any such area,....and

Section 13 (4) .... (a) a net, line, rope, chain, or any other thing used in connection with fishing operations being towed by, or operated or suspended from, a ship; or (b) an anchor being lowered or suspended from, or raised by, a ship,...".

[76] Protection officer means a protection officer appointed under Section 16

"Protection officers (1) The Minister may from time to time, by notice in the Gazette, appoint a person to be a protection officer. (2) For the purposes of this Act, an enforcement officer is deemed to be a protection officer".

[77] Section 2 of the Public Act [19] No. 22 provides "enforcement officer means—

(a) a constable:

(b) an officer in command of a ship of the New Zealand Naval Forces:

(c) an officer of the New Zealand Naval Forces of the rank of Midshipman or above".

[78] Section 17 of the Public Act [19] No. 22 provides "a Ship may be ordered from protected area-

(1) If a protection officer believes on reasonable grounds that a ship or equipment belonging to a ship is being used in a protected area in the commission of an offence against Section 13, the

standards.[79] Then, he may ask the master of a vessel to extend his (master) assistance in identifying a ship in suspicion of its alleged violation.[80] The enforcement officer under this law is empowered to obtain documents and information in relation to the alleged infringement.[81]

Furthermore, the legislation prescribes the procedure for obtaining evidence to be submitted before the court and seizure of the alleged property. In this connection, the protection officer is empowered to seize equipment or the vessels in question.[82] This property comes under the custody of the crown. After the seizure, the protection officer is required to notify the local police, and the equipment may be returned to

---

protection officer may, by any means of communication, order the master of the ship to remove the ship from that area".

[79]Section 18 of the Public Act [19] No. 22 provides "for Seizure of fishing equipment in protected area-

(1) A protection officer who finds fishing equipment may seize the equipment if he or she believes on reasonable grounds that—(a) the area in which he or she finds the equipment is declared to be a protected area by an Order in Council under Section 12(1); and (b) the equipment has been left there by a ship to which the order applies".

[80]Section 19 of the Public Act [19] No. 22, provides "the Master to identify ship-

(1) If,—(a) a protection officer believes on reasonable grounds that a ship or equipment belonging to a ship is being used in the commission of an offence against Section 13; and (b) a request for identification is made to the ship by the protection officer,—the master of the ship must advise the protection officer of the master's name, owner's name, ship's name, place of registry, register number, and such further information as may be relevant to the identity of the master and owner and the identity of the ship that may be requested by the protection officer".

[81]Section 20 of the Public Act [19] No. 22 provides "Power to obtain documents and information-

(1) If an enforcement officer has reasonable cause to believe that an offence is being or has been committed against this Act by or from or in relation to a ship, the enforcement officer may, for the purposes of enforcing the provisions of this Act,—(a) require the owner or the master or a member of the crew of the ship to produce a certificate, official logbook, or other document in the possession or under the control of the owner, master, or crew member that relates to the ship: (b) require the master to produce a certificate of registration, charter, or other document, or to provide other information relating to the owner of the ship:

(c) require the master of the ship, or any other person on board the ship, to produce a document, or to give an explanation or information, as may be necessary to assist in identifying the location, conduct, and movements of the ship, or the actions of any person on board the ship at the time relevant to the suspected commission of an offence against this Act: (d) take or make copies of a document produced under this section, if the document is relevant to the suspected commission of an offence against this Act. (2) An enforcement officer may—(a) take possession of and remove any such document from the place where it is kept for such period of time as is reasonable in the circumstances; and (b) require a person to reproduce, or assist the enforcement officer to reproduce, in usable form any information recorded or stored on a document electronically or by other means. (3) Nothing in paragraph (b) or paragraph (c) of subsection (1) requires a person to answer a question if to do so would tend to incriminate that person. (4) For the purposes of this section document means a document in any form; and includes—(a) any writing on or in any material; and (b) information recorded or stored by means of a tape recorder, computer, or other device; and material subsequently derived from information so recorded or stored; and (c) a record, book, graph, or drawing; and (d) a photograph, film, negative, tape, disk, or other device in which 1 or more visual images are embodied or stored so as to be capable (with or without the aid of equipment) of being reproduced".

[82]Section 21 of the Public Act [19] No. 22 provides "the Power of seizure-

its owner, who is willing to bear the cost for the same. The protection officer is also empowered to seek information about a ship's identity and other relevant documents from persons related to it. This procedure suggests that the Minister or court may order forfeiture or release of such property (Sections 31–34). Further, while exercising his authority under this law, the enforcement officer may seek the assistance of a person available in the area of operation and is obliged to assist the enforcement officer accordingly.[83] The enforcement officer, however, before exercising his authority, must produce his identity (Section 22).

The 1996 Act of New Zealand prescribes that the District Court or the High Court of New Zealand has jurisdictions to adjudicate any dispute under this law. However, the prosecution of a case that involves a foreign national or foreign ship for their alleged offense committed beyond New Zeeland's TW needs prior consent from the Attorney-General (Section 27). The legislation also approves applying maritime surveillance equipment for monitoring or alleged threat to the submarine cables.[84] Its procedure follows the Criminal Procedure Act 2011 of New Zealand.[85]

4.4.4 Compensation and Indemnity and Liability and Offense

Section 7 of the 1996 Act of New Zealand defines a person's liability if he causes cable injury while laying or repairing submarine cables.[86] The claimant may claim indemnity for a loss he incurs due to fishing equipment's sacrifice (Section 8).

The 1996 Act of New Zealand has prescribed liabilities and defined offenses concerning the cable damage, protected area, protection, enforcement officer, or maritime surveillance. Most importantly, Section 11 establishes the offense for willful or negligence incidents of cable damage and prescribes hefty fines in case of

---

(1) An enforcement officer may seize a ship or other property if the officer believes on reasonable grounds that the ship or other property is being used in the commission of an offence against Section 13".

[83]Section 22 of the Public Act [19] No. 22 provides for "Persons assisting enforcement officer-

"An enforcement officer exercising a power conferred on the officer by this Act may call upon a person in the vicinity for assistance, and every person so called upon is authorised to render such assistance".

[84]Section 35 of the Public Act [19] No. 22 has approved "maritime surveillance equipment-

"The Minister may from time to time, by notice in the Gazette, approve equipment of any kind to be approved maritime surveillance equipment for the purposes of this Act".

[85]New Zealand's [21] No. 81.

[86]Section 7 of the the Public Act [19] No. 22 deals with "the Liability in respect of damage to cable or pipeline-

"A person who, in the course of laying or repairing a submarine cable or sub- marine pipeline of which the person is the owner, damages another submarine cable or submarine pipeline, is liable for the cost of repairing that damage, and such liability—(a) is in addition to any other liability to which the person may be subject; and (b) applies whether or not—(i) the damage to the submarine cable or submarine pipeline was caused by that person's negligence; or (ii) the person has been convicted of an offence relating to that damage".

cable damage.[87] He may be liable if he facilitates the cable damage by permitting his ship or equipment to be used to damaged submarine cables. The master or owner, if found guilty under this provision, may meet the fine, which may not exceed 250,000 dollars. All the ships may not come under this liability, and the Minister may by an order absolve individual ships from liability.

Both the owner and the master of a ship are liable for anchoring in the protected areas.[88] Section 13 defines offense concerning the protected area where fishing or anchoring is an offense. It suggests liability, even if the fishing equipment or anchor was not deployed fully. If done because of obtaining a commercial gain, such an offense may incur liabilities, which may not exceed 100,000 dollars. Else, such liability may not exceed 20,000 dollars. Both Sections 11 and 13 may exempt cable damage by saving a life or reasonable precaution. Thus, such a contravening activity is no offense if it results from saving of life or ship or happened when all reasonable precautions have been taken to avoid the damage.

---

[87]Section 11 of the the Public Act [19] No. 22 defines "Offence to damage submarine cable or pipeline-

(1) Every person commits an offence and is liable on conviction to a fine not exceeding $250,000 who

(a) wilfully or negligently either damages, or causes or permits a ship or equipment belonging to a ship to damage, a submarine cable or submarine pipeline; or (b) is the owner or master of a ship that is used in the commission of an offence against paragraph (a). (2) An owner or master of a ship who is convicted of an offence against paragraph (a) of subsection (1) is not liable for an offence against paragraph (b) of that subsection arising out of the same course of conduct. (3) It is a defence to a prosecution for an offence against this section if the defendant proves that the damage which is alleged to constitute the offence was caused by persons acting with the sole object of saving life or a ship after having taken all reasonable precautions to avoid the damage. (4) For the purposes of this section, a person who causes an event by an act or omission which he or she knows would probably cause it, being reckless whether that event happens or not, is deemed to have caused it wilfully".

[88]Section 13 of the the Public Act [19] No. 22 define "Offences in respect of protected areas-

(1) Subject to subsection (3), if—(a) fishing operations are conducted from a ship in an area declared to be a protected area in respect of that ship under Section 12(1); or (b) a ship is anchored in any such area—the owner and the master of the ship each commits an offence and is each liable on conviction to the appropriate penalty under Sect. 15. (2) Subject to subsection (3), every person who fails to comply with, or acts in contravention of, an Order in Council under Section 12(1) commits an offence and is liable on conviction to the appropriate penalty under Section 15.

(3) A person is not liable for an offence against this section involving a ship to which a notice under Section 12(6) applies.

(4) Where in proceedings for an offence against this section, an enforcement officer or a protection officer gives evidence that he or she observed—(a) a net, line, rope, chain, or any other thing used in connection with fishing operations being towed by, or operated or suspended from, a ship; or (b) an anchor being lowered or suspended from, or raised by, a ship,—it shall be presumed that, in the absence of evidence to the contrary, fishing operations were being conducted from the ship or the ship was anchored, as the case may be.

(5) Where in proceedings for an offence against this section, evidence is given of an image made by approved maritime surveillance equipment, being an image showing—(a) a net, line, rope, chain, or any other thing used in connection with fishing operations being towed by, or operated or suspended from, a ship; or (b) an anchor being lowered or suspended from, or raised by, a ship,—it shall be presumed that, in the absence of evidence to the contrary, fishing operations were being conducted from the ship or the ship was anchored, as the case may be".

A breach of a provision relating to enforcement and protection officer is also an offense under this legislation. Disobedience to an order of a protection officer asking the alleged ship to leave the protected area is an offense, and it may meet a fine not exceeding 10,000 dollars.[89] The protection officer may also ask the master for assistance in identifying a vessel in suspicion concerning the protected area and failure, which may also incur him a fine that must not exceed 5000 dollars.[90] Section 20 obliges the master or owner of a ship to produce documents to the enforcement officer, and failure to which may incur him a fine, which may not exceed 5000 dollars. Again the master or owner of a vessel in suspicion must not resist or obstruct an enforcement officer engaged in seizure of property under Section 21 of this law may attract a fine not exceed 10,000 dollars.[91] This law prescribes a violation relating to marine surveillance equipment that may invite a fine not exceed 5000 dollars.[92] It also specifies liability for failure to remove a cable that ceased to be used (Sections 9 and10), and it may meet the accused a fine not exceeding 5000 dollars.

---

[89] Section 17 of the the Public Act [19] No. 22 states "a Ship may be ordered from protected area-

(1) If a protection officer believes on reasonable grounds that a ship or equipment belonging to a ship is being used in a protected area in the commission of an offence against Section 13, the protection officer may, by any means of communication, order the master of the ship to remove the ship from that area. (2) Without derogating from any other provision of this Act, a master who, without reasonable cause, fails within a reasonable period of time to comply with an order given under this section, commits an offence and is liable on conviction to a fine not exceeding $10,000".

[90] Section 19 of the the Public Act [19] No. 22 provides "Master to identify ship-

(1) If,—(a) a protection officer believes on reasonable grounds that a ship or equipment belonging to a ship is being used in the commission of an offence against Section 13; and (b) a request for identification is made to the ship by the protection officer,—the master of the ship must advise the protection officer of the master's name, owner's name, ship's name, place of registry, register number, and such further information as may be relevant to the identity of the master and owner and the identity of the ship that may be requested by the protection officer. (2) A master who, without reasonable cause, fails within a reasonable period of time to comply with subsection (1) commits an offence and is liable on conviction to a fine not exceeding $5,000".

[91] Section 21 (2) of the the Public Act [19] No. 22 states that

"Every person commits an offence and is liable on conviction to a fine not exceeding $10,000 who

(a) resists or obstructs an enforcement officer exercising the power of seizure under this section; or

(b) fails without reasonable cause to comply with the requirements of an enforcement officer exercising the power of seizure under this section".

[92] Section 29 of the the Public Act [19] No. 22 deals with the "Offence to tamper or interfere with approved maritime surveillance equipment-

"Every person commits an offence and is liable on conviction to a fine not exceeding $5,000 who—(a) tampers with approved maritime surveillance equipment; or (b) interferes with—(i) approved maritime surveillance equipment; or (ii) the operation of approved maritime surveillance equipment".

4.5 Comparative Analysis Between Submarine Cable Regimes of Australia and New Zealand

For a long, submarine cable operation and its protection get a priority in both Australia and New Zealand. In the 1960s, these governments adopted dedicated legislations on submarine cables together with the pipelines. Later, they have also responded to the submarine cable issues and intended to strengthen their submarine cable regimes by adopting appropriate legal and regulatory regimes. Thus, both Schedule 3A of the 1997 Act of Australia and the 1996 Act of New Zealand have come into force. Both of these submarine cable regimes bear common features in relation to their fundamental principles, approaches, liabilities, procedures, etc.; still, they are distinct in certain respects.

Regarding the scope and application, these laws apply to the Australian waters and up to EEZ of New Zealand, respectively. The Schedule applies to both international and domestic cables. It affirms an establishment of a protection zone within Australia's EEZ and its sea above that becomes part of Australia's continental shelf and is beyond the limits of its exclusive economic zone.[93] The 1996 Act covers all cables and does not specify an international or domestic cable etc. Compared to the 1996 Act of New Zealand, the 1997 Act of Australia prescribes more comprehensive application. It includes cables and other devices attached to the cables. Importantly, in spirit, both of the laws have focused on the telecommunication line. It is doubtful whether submarine cables under these legislations include another cable like submarine power cables.

Both laws have affirmed an establishment of a submarine cable safety zone within marine spaces. Notably, the EEZ regime coexists with the international High Sea regime. In this international water, these countries have specific and limited rights and jurisdictions, as dealt with in the second chapter of this study. It appears as an extension of the national authority to the international water, i.e., the EEZ. These laws are prescribing extended jurisdictions.

Schedule 3A, with regulatory support from the ACMA, intends to strengthen the security of submarine cables and extend support to the carriers concerning cable operation. Both the Schedule and the ACMA declare a *protection zone*-a a legislative instrument. These legislations state that a detailed list of activities within this protection zone is either prohibited or restricted. Given extending support to the carriers in cable operation, these laws press on a streamlined installation permit process. Thus, the ACMA process an application for protection zone installation permits expeditiously (25–35 working days), and such process also exempts specific State and Territorial laws. A non-protection permit application takes 60–90 working days. The ACMA Act also prescribes certain permit conditions for installation permits and installation conditions.

The 1996 Act of New Zealand also prescribes a *protected area* for cables. However, unlike Schedule 3A, which affirms regulatory support from a dedicated

[93]Clause 2 of the Schedule 3A of No. 47, [19] Act.

regulatory body to the declaration of a protection zone, the 1996 Act of New Zealand suggests that the Minister is responsible for recommending a protected area for cables. The 1996 Act of New Zealand does not imply a regulatory authority in dealing with the declaration of cables protected area in detail. Its prohibited activities concerning such protected areas include fishing equipment and anchors. A presence of a vessel with fishing equipment and anchor which may not be deployed fully is deemed to be an infringement of this law. Nevertheless, the 1997 Act of Australia suggests a comprehensive list of activities relating to the protection zone.

Schedule 3A suggests an area within 1852 m, either side of the cable is the length of the protection zone. This 1852 m on either side from the two outmost cables and the area between cables is the total area of protection zone in case of multiple cables in Australian waters. The length of a protected area under the 1996 Act of New Zealand rests on the discretions of the Minister.

Both legislations have made it compulsory to make a consultation before declaring protection areas. The ACMA must consult with the AGD concerning protection zone and installation permits about the marine spaces beyond Australia's TW. The Minister also consults with various stakeholders before making recommendations for a protected area. It reflects that both States are concerned about their extraterritorial prescriptions on protection zones—a potential area of contraventions with international law (Table 4.1).

Schedule 3A defines several offenses and prescribes penalties on violation of its provisions. It prescribes punishment for imprisonment or fine or both for certain contravening activities. The significant offenses are concerning the breaking of cables, interfering with the prohibited and restricted activities. This Schedule specifies monetary fines only in certain violations, such as installing cables without installation permits, breach of a permit, and installation conditions.

It prescribes for both civil, criminal liabilities on violation of its law. It imposes a penalty of imprisonment, extending to ten years or 600 penalty units or both for intentional submarine cable damage. It provides a lesser punishment for negligent damage to submarine cables that may extend to three years of imprisonment or a fine with 180 penalty units or both. This law also suggests a stringent penalty for an aggravated form of repetition of such offenses. Also, engaging in prohibited or restricted activities in the protection zone attracts a substantial penalty, which may be enhanced if it is in aggravated form. An engagement is regarded as aggravated if the engagement relates to an intentional activity for obtaining a commercial gain, which may impose imprisonment for seven years or 420 penalty units or both.

The 1996 Act of New Zealand prescribes civil liability for violation of its law. It prescribes a hefty monetary fine for damaging cables that may not extend 250,000 dollars. A breach of its prohibited activities concerning the protected area is an offense under this law that imposes fines, which may not exceed 100,000 dollars. There may be less punishment if it is not committed to obtaining commercial gain. Failure to cooperate and extend assistance on the part of the vessel owner with the protection officer is also an offense that may incur liability, extending to 10,000 dollars. This law extends to the interferences with the maritime surveillance equipment, and failure to

Table 4.1 Submarine cable safety zones across the jurisdictions

Country/parameter	Australia	New Zealand	China	Indonesia	Japan	France	Argentina	Columbia	Uruguay	Ghana
Length of the restricted areas	1852 m either side of the cable	Not mentioned	Oceanic protection zones, natural protection zones which ranges from 50 to 500 m of the either sides of submarine cables	Cable corridor 3500 m, Distance between cables 500 m	50–1000 m underwater cable protected area	NIL	NIL	Security areas are established along the lines of submarine cables safety zones extending 500 m on either side of the submarine cables	Specified area that comprises with one nm of each side of submarine communications cables	Submarine cable protection area fifty meter on either side of the centerline of the specified cable

(continued)

Table 4.1 (continued)

Country/ parameter	Australia	New Zealand	China	Indonesia	Japan	France	Argentina	Columbia	Uruguay	Ghana
Prohibited activities/ restrictive activities	A list suggesting detailed activities as prohibited A list suggesting detailed activities as restricted	Only fishing equipment and anchoring without its further detail	Dig sand, drill, drive a pile into the ground, lay in anchor, drag anchor, fish, net, breed or other sea operations	Anchorage, dredging, mining or other underwater activities	Anchoring, engaging in fishing with a bottom dragnet or digging and gathering earth and sand or moor a boat or rafting to the landmark	Anchorage and using fishing gear or nets and refusal to withdraw such fishing gears	Prohibits fishing in the places where submarine cables or facilities exists prohibits those methods of fishing that can cause damage	Anchoring of any kind of ship and trawling and according to this provision any performance of maritime activity that wholly or partly maintains contacts with the seabed is also barred	Restriction on use of fishing gear fishing activities that have even partial contact with the seabed and the use of anchors within this specified area	Fishing operations with fishing vessels and anchoring within the subsea cable protection area

remove cable ceased to be used and may impose a fine, which may not exceed 5000 dollars.

Thus, both of these legislations have prescribed stringent penalties. Schedule 3A is way ahead in imposing severe punishments, which may extend to several years of imprisonment or fine or both. In this regard, the 1996 Act of New Zealand prescribes a monetary fine only. However, it has also imposed significant monetary liabilities for its violations, in particular for cable damage.

Both of the legislations provide for an exception to the offenses. However, Schedule 3A provides extra grounds of defense that are not available to the 1996 Act of New Zealand. In addition to the life or ships saving effort and reasonable exercise of skill of crews, Schedule 3A acknowledges efforts to keep submarine cables and preventing pollution as a ground of defense to the offenses.

The legislation of both countries provides compensation and indemnities as determined by the courts. The Schedule provides provisions for claims, indemnity, and compensation if the marine users meet losses concerning the submarine cable operation. Further, the Schedule provides provisions for claiming compensation that includes claims by one who has suffered a loss due to the acquisition of property/rights concerning cables by the cable owner. It suggests that the claimants may settle such claims on an amount mutually or determined by the court.

An array of provisions on the protection or enforcement officer is an essential aspect of implanting the 1996 Act of New Zealand. An officer under this law monitors the protected area and collects evidence about the alleged violations. He may ask the alleged vessel to assist him in obtaining such pieces of evidence. He also has the authority to seize the suspected property. Thus, it suggests procedures for the prosecution of an offense under it. Australian Federal Police is the implementing authority of the Schedule.

Regarding jurisdictions of the legislations, the 1996 Act of New Zealand applies to New Zealand's subjects. Its extraterritorial jurisdiction extends to a New Zealand citizen or a person ordinarily resident of New Zeeland. A New Zealand flagship also comes under the purview of the legislation. However, it prescribes for consultation with the Attorney-General if a proceeding involves a foreign subject for his alleged violation within New Zealand's EEZ. On the same line, the Schedule prescribes for consultation with the AGD before its enforcement authority initiates any proceeding against a foreign national or ship that is allegedly involved with violation of this law in Australia's EEZ. Thus, both legislations maintain the general rule of criminal jurisdictions concerning any offenses under it, and its extraterritorial application to foreign nationals has limited application.

The Schedule prescribes strict liability for breaking cables and interfering with restricted or prohibited activities concerning the protection zone. Other offenses under this Schedule follow the general rule of criminal liability. The Federal Court of Australia is the appropriate forum of the Schedule. For New Zealand, it is the District Court or the High Court.

Another essential part of this analysis is the relation between these legislations and UNCLOS concerning a submarine cable as stated in the second chapter of this study, the law of the sea has acknowledged the principles of spatial measures for ocean management. Under UNCLOS, States' rights and jurisdictions are specific. In this water, coastal States may take measures to advance their economic interests, and environmental issues adopt a law regulating fisheries and other activities concerning exploration and exploitation of resources. It is a legal arrangement that sought to strike a balance between coastal States' economic interest and other States' freedoms in the particular laying of submarine cables.

In this connection, a pertinent question relates to the basis of a coastal State's submarine cable protected areas or protected zones within its EEZ. The question refers to the legality of a national law that intends to control a foreign vessel in a protection zone within its EEZ unless UNCLOS affirms it. Beyond the TW, coastal States have no explicit basis for establishing submarine cable protection zones/areas.[94]

However, a declaration of such a protection zone may prescribe certain restrictions and warnings to the vessel without sovereign immunity. Such vessels may be asked to avoid the zones or permitted certain compliances such as immediate reporting about its whereabouts, description of cargos, etc. A non-compliance may subject the erring vessel to inspection.[95] In particular…

> In the context of pipelines and cables, it may be appropriate to revisit the proposal originally considered by the ILC in the 1950s and permit the creation of prohibited areas for anchoring. These would not restrict navigation but would prevent vessels from loitering in the immediate vicinity of a pipeline or cable. The width of such a zone could be relatively modest and probably be no more than 500 meters at best. States were reluctant to accept such a concept in 1958, and it is likely that they would still be reluctant over fears of harm to freedom of navigation.'[96]

In the late 1950s, the satellite system gained priority over the submarine cables as a means of communication that continued to mid of the 1980s when UNCLOS was concluded. Thus, restriction on navigation freedom for the safety of submarine cables might have been deemed unnecessary. A consideration on the said 1950s ILC proposal on 'permit the creation of prohibited areas for anchoring' is more relevant today given the critical nature of the submarine cable to the present and coming decades. Modest restrictions of this kind may not amount to the breach of navigation freedom; however, they will become effectual means of limiting cable vulnerabilities.

---

[94]Kaye [22].

[95]Ibid., *at* 421–22, '…If widening a safety zone is not an option, then widening the zone for certain purposes might produce a more acceptable balance of interests. A zone of three nautical miles width acting as a warning zone, rather man a navigation exclusion zone, might present a way forward. Vessels without sovereign immunity could be advised to avoid such zones, and upon entry render themselves obliged to report detailed information concerning their intentions, cargo, and destination. Failure to report would render the vessel liable to be boarded. The non-application of this to sovereign immune vessels, principally warships, might help allay concerns over freedom of navigation.' '…These would not restrict navigation, but would prevent vessels from loitering in the immediate vicinity of a pipeline or cable'.

[96]Kaye [22], *at* 422.

Coastal States may adopt a set of limited reasonable restrictions for submarine cable safety zone beyond the outer limits of TW, which would be short of navigation exclusion zones. Such restricted measures may be within 'the interests of the coastal States,' and all States shall have due regard to such restrictions in exercising freedoms under Article 87. Thus, if a coastal State adopts a set of modest, reasonable, and limited restrictions and the creation of a cable safety zone for the interest of the safety of their critical submarine cables beyond the outer limits of the TW may conform with Article 87 paragraph 2.[97] Such restrictions may not be regarded as an unnecessary restriction on the freedom of navigation—an effective means of reconciliation between the protection of submarine cables in the cable safety zone and other legitimate activities beyond the outer limits of the TW.

Therefore, the extension of the 1997 Act and 1996 Act to its EEZ raises a question. Even more, the 1997 Act of Australia intends to apply to the Australian water, which includes the extended limit of its continental shelf margin that is even beyond its EEZ.

However, both legislations are aware of such potential inconsistencies. Both the 1997 Act of Australia and the 1996 Act of New Zealand prescribe for mandatory consultations with the AGD of Australia and Attorney-General of New Zealand before prosecuting a foreign national or ship in relation to cable protection zone/area beyond its TW, respectively. Schedule 3A also provides for consultation with AGD before declaring and protection zone, installation permits, and protected or restricted activities beyond Australia's TW. Therefore, these laws in practice are restricted to their subjects only. However, it is still doubtful whether a national law that establishes protection or protected zones complies with UNCLOS.

The legislation on submarine cables of Australia and New Zealand is claimed to be model submarine cable legislation. Still, there is a scope of strengthening these legislations further. Significant areas of improvements include streamlining of cable installation permits, etc., for the 1996 Act of New Zealand, and enhancing monitoring system Australia, and for both legislation-building-wide cooperation among the marine users, identification of alleged vessels and a robust vessel registration system, conferring extensive authority on the enforcement agencies in preventing and enforcing offenses, etc. Such an improvement process may stress carrying navigational charts, which may help vessels within a cable protection zone comply with prohibitory or restrictive activities.[98]

Finally, both legislative schemes assuming protection zone or protected areas have relied on the spatial ocean management approach—an essential approach to marine governance. They have adopted an integrated system of cable governance to comprehensively deal with issues and challenges concerning the laying and protection of submarine cables.

---

[97] Article 79, paragraph 2 UNCLOS 1982 provides 'These freedoms shall be exercised by all States with due regard for the interests of other States in their exercise of the freedom of the high seas, and also with due regard for the rights under this Convention with respect to activities in the Area'.

[98] Submission to the ministerial advisory committee on oceans policy on behalf of telecom New Zealand limited as a representative for the owners of international submarine cables which come ashore in New Zealand.

Both of the principles of freedom of laying of submarine cables and other associated activities related to such cables and the protection of submarine cables together with the compensation, indemnity for loss or sacrifice, have been the cardinal principles of these legislations.

In particular, both the 1996 Act of New Zealand and the 1997 Act of Australia have adopted the sovereignty principle since its jurisdictions extend to every incident in relation to cables within the TW. Regarding penal jurisdictions, both of the legislations affirm the principle of extraterritorial jurisdictions too. Such extraterritorial jurisdictions apply primarily to these countries' subjects and foreign nationals or ships in exceptional cases.

Further, Schedule 3A suggests a regulatory mechanism for the protection zone on submarine cables explicitly. It prescribes a streamlined system for declaration of a protection zone and installation permits, etc. In this matter, New Zealand relies on the Minister. Thus, both countries concerning cable governance intend to offer a single-window mechanism.

Regarding liability, Schedule 3A has adopted the principle of strict liability concerning the protection zone. Regarding the procedure, the evidential onus of proof under it rests on the accused. It relies on both civil and criminal liability, which may prescribe fine or imprisonment or both. In this respect, New Zealand depends on civil liability and prescribes monetary punishment. Both of these legislations have adopted the rule of imposing severe deterrence as a means to control human-made risk to submarine cables.

Further, these legislations also appreciate cooperation among marine users such as carriers, fishing communities, other marine users, structures like pipelines, etc. They encourage a claim, compensation, or indemnity for losses to avoid cable damage or interferences to cable operation. The 1996 Act of New Zealand, in particular, suggests the deployment of monitoring and surveillance assets as a cables safety mechanism.

The fundamentals of these legislations will be most conveniently summarized in the accompanying table (Table 4.2):

Table 4.2 Submarine cable regimes of Australia and New Zealand—comparative chart

No.	Parameters	Australia	New Zealand	Comments
1	Scope of the law	EEZ plus water up to the extended continental shelf	Beyond TW apply only to the New Zealand subjects	Australia's Act has *ambitious jurisdiction*
2	Definition	Cable plus other devices, both international and domestic cables	Simply cable lie beneath the water	Both focus on telecommunication cables. *Application on the power cable doubtful*
3	Length of the restricted areas	1852 m either side of the cable	Not mentioned	Demarcation of safety zone needed
4	Prohibited activities	A list suggesting detailed activities as prohibited	Only fishing equipment and anchoring without its further detail	Targeted activities should be clarified
5	Restrictive activities	A list suggesting detailed activities as restricted	NIL	Potential threats needed to be prevented
6	Strict liability	The burden on the accused	A general rule of liability	Australia prescribes strict liability concerning cable protection zone

(continued)

Table 4.2 (continued)

No.	Parameters	Australia	New Zealand	Comments
7	Applicable procedure	Both criminal and civil	Civil	Need for speedy remedial process
8	Quantum of penalty	Intentional breaking/injury-imprisonment for 10 years/600 penalty unit or both Negligent breaking/injury imprisonment for three years/180 penalty units or both Violation for commercial gain-7 years/420 penalty units or both Violation of protection zone requirements—5 years/300 penalty units or both	Monetary fine not exceeding the following limit- Damage of cable 250,000 dollar Violation of prohibited activities 10,000 to 100,000 dollar Failure to remove the vessel from protected zone-10,000 dollar Failure to identify alleged vessel-5000 dollar Failure to produce document-5000 dollar Resisting or obstructing protection officer-10,000 dollar Violation of maritime surveillance equipment-5000 dollar Failure to remove the cable, not in use-5000 dollar	The intention is to establish severe deterrence
9	Indemnity/compensation/claims	Determined on mutual agreement or by court	Determined by court	Rest on specialized dispute resolution forum
10	Installation permit measures	Streamlined permit procedure under a dedicated regulatory body (ACMA)	Does not provide detailed procedure (Minister)	A clear and streamlined installation permit procedure for cable operation is desirable

(continued)

Table 4.2 (continued)

No.	Parameters	Australia	New Zealand	Comments
11	Enforcement officer	No designated post-rest on Australian Federal Police	Detailed on the protection and enforcement officer from The New Zealand Police and Royal Navy	Enforcement officer-wide power to issue order for vessels to produce documents, suspend operation, etc., seize equipment
12	Proceedings concerning an offense	Not detail however	Detail about the proceedings	Enforcement agency should have detailed guidelines to establish the guilt
13	Jurisdictions-extraterritorial	Unless the AGD's permission, it does not apply to foreign subjects and limited to Australian subjects	Unless the Attorney General's permission it does not apply to foreign subjects and limited to the New Zealand subjects	Jurisdictions must be on the line of UNCLOS
14	Grounds of defense	*Force majeure* plus a saving of cable plus prevention of pollution	Force *majeure* (saving life and ship)	Australia provides the additional ground of defense
15	Protection zone/protected area in EEZ and beyond and UNCLOS	Controversial as extraterritorial claims and exercise of national authority—a potential of inconsistencies to international law	Controversial as extraterritorial claims and exercise of national authority—a potential of inconsistencies to international law	More extensive coordination among marine users may be achieved under IMO

(continued)

Table 4.2 (continued)

No.	Parameters	Australia	New Zealand	Comments
16	Criticism	Ambitious Extraterritorial jurisdictions include the EEZ and beyond–contrary to UNCLOS	Extraterritorial jurisdictions limited to New Zealand's EEZ	More extensive consultations and cooperation among States under UNCLOS and carriers, other marine uses is desirable
17	A potential area of improvement	Monitoring and surveillance, vessel identification number, the vessel registration process for both commercial and Recreation, inadequate patrolling and infrastructure, failure to ensure to carry a navigational chart	Vessel identification number, the vessel registration process for both commercial and recreation, inadequate patrolling and infrastructure, failure to ensure to carry a navigational chart	

4.6 Summary

The chapter undertakes a comparative analysis between the national legislations on the submarine cable of Australia and New Zealand. It reveals that these legislations suggest several provisions concerning laying and protecting cables that include provision for cable protection zones, prohibited activities, monitoring and surveillance, liability for breach, claims, compensation, indemnity, enforcement agencies, and implanting procedures, regulatory mechanisms installation permits, etc. These provisions and the basic structure of these legislations are developed on several fundamental principles and approaches. They are spatial and integrated ocean management approach, the principle of laying and protection of cables along with claims, compensation, and indemnity, sovereignty, extraterritorial jurisdictions, strict liability, civil liability or criminal liability or both, stringent punishment of fine or imprisonment/both, reliance on the regulatory mechanism, surveillance, etc.

It appears that the regulators and the policymakers of Australia and New Zealand have appreciated the critical nature of the submarine cable system and prescribe measures to deal with issues of laying and the protection of submarine cables comprehensively. This analysis underscores that both Australia and New Zealand's cable regimes have significant potential to contribute to the jurisprudence of national law on cables.

It also reveals that with several exemplary cable-friendly measures, these legislations have limitations too. Establishing a protection zone or protected area in the international waters, i.e., EEZ or even beyond, may raise a potential concern regarding its consistency with UNCLOS unless addressed mutually. Both of the legislations have remained silent on human aggression on cables. Both legislations are also lagging in providing dedicated dispute settlement mechanisms, cable ship safety measures and vessel registry systems, institutional role in building cooperation, promoting awareness among the stakeholders, etc.

Lastly, in comparison to Australia, New Zealand's cable law falls short in providing specific measures for cable installation permits, etc. New Zealand deals with its enforcement agency's power and procedure elaborately, not provided by Australia. Therefore, the basic structure and fundamental parameters and limitations of these legislations may provide an essential basis for any effort in developing a model set for national instruments on submarine cable.

References

1. Takie, Y. (2012). Law and policy for international submarines cables: An Asia-Pacific perspective. *Asian Journal of International Law, 2*, 205–233.
2. Raha, U. K., & Raju, K. D. (2018–19). Critical telecommunication cable infrastructure under the law of the sea convention (UNCLOS 1982). *National Capital Law Journal, 17*, 65–75.
3. Act No. 61 of 1963. Submarine Cables and Pipeline Protection Act 1963 (Act No. 61 of 1963) of Australia. See https://www.legislation.gov.au/Series/C1963A00061. Accessed April 06, 2020.

4. No. 47, 1997. The Telecommunication Act 1997 (No. 47, 1997) of Australia. See https://www.legislation.gov.au/Series/C2004A05145. Accessed March 30, 2020.
5. No. 45, 2005. The Australian Communication and Media Authority Act 2005 (No. 45, 2005). See https://www.legislation.gov.au/Details/C2005A00044. Accessed March 30, 2020.
6. 1996 No. 22. The Protection of Submarine Cables and Pipelines Act 1996 (1996 No. 22) of New Zealand.
7. Coffen-Smout, S, & Herbert, G. J. (2000). Submarine cables: A challenge for ocean management. *Marine Policy, 24*, 441–448.
8. Explanatory Memorandum to the Bill 2013. See also "Explanatory Memorandum to the Telecommunications Legislation Amendment (Submarine Cable Protection) Bill 2013" (herein after the Explanatory Memorandum to the Bill 2013) *at* 6. See Australian Government, Federal List of Legislation, See https://www.legislation.gov.au/Details/C2013B00200/Download. Accessed March 30, 2020.
9. National Bandwidth Inquiry 1999. National Bandwidth Inquiry: Report of the Australian Information Economy Advisory Council, Commonwealth of Australia, 1999.
10. Explanatory Memorandum to Bill 2005. See Explanatory Memorandum and introduction of Schedule 3A to the Telecommunications Act 1997 to the Telecommunications and Other Legislation Amendment (Protection of Submarine Cables and other Measures) Bill 2005.
11. The Amendment Bill 2005. The Telecommunications and Other Legislation Amendment (Protection of Submarine Cables and other Measures) Bill 2005. See https://www.legislation.gov.au/Details/C2005B00133/Download. Accessed April 7, 2020.
12. Schedule 3A. Act 1997 (No. 47, 1997).
13. ACMA Act 2005 (No. 45, 2005).
14. ACMA Review Report 2010. "Report on the Operation of the Submarine Cable Protection Regime—A Report on Five Years' Operation of Schedule 3A of the Telecommunications Act 1997, the Submarine Cable Protection Regime, September 2010 (the ACMA Review Report 2010)." It was a statutory review report under clause 89 of the Schedule 3A to be prepared by the ACMA to review the operation of Schedule 3A within five years after this Schedule commenced. The ACMA required to publish it and report to the Minister Communications. This report made several recommendations for further evaluation of the Schedule 3A.
15. The Amendment Bill 2013. Australian Government, Federal List of Legislation. See https://www.legislation.gov.au/Details/C2013B00200/Download. Accessed March 30, 2020.
16. ACMA. https://www.acma.gov.au/zone-protect-sydney-submarine-cables. Accessed December 5, 2020.
17. Sydny Protection Zone A. https://www.legislation.gov.au/Details/F2007L02216/Download. Accessed December 5, 2020. See Sudny Protection Zone B https://www.legislation.gov.au/Details/F2007L02217/Download. Accessed December 5, 2020. See https://www.aph.gov.au/parliamentary_business/committees/senate/environment_and_communications/submarine_cable_protection/report/c01. Accessed December 5, 2020.
18. Australia's Criminal Code 1995.
19. Public Act 1996 No. 22. Submarine Cables and Pipelines protection Act 1996 (Public Act 1996 No. 22). See http://legislation.govt.nz/act/public/1996/0022/latest/DLM375803.html. Accessed April 6, 2020.
20. 1966 No 5. Submarine Cables and Pipelines Protection Act 1966 (1966 No. 5) of New Zealand.
21. New Zealand's 2011 No. 81. The Criminal Procedure Act 2011 (2011 No. 81).
22. Kaye, S. (2009). The protection of platforms, pipelines and submarine cables under Australian and New Zealand Law. In N. Klein (Ed.), *Maritime security international law and policy perspectives from Australia and New Zealand* (pp. 186–201, 191)

Chapter 5
Conclusion and Suggestions

The issues relating to the laying of underwater seabed cables, other associated activities, and submarine cables' protection have remained pressing matters for the telecommunication industry since its inception. To tackle these issues through the UN deliberations and formulation of the law of the sea has not produced expected results, and the matter is lingering for quite a long time. This study analyzes and points out the ambiguities, gaps, and merits in the cable regimes under international law, cable-related instruments in the selected jurisdictions, and the dedicated national legislation addressing issues relating to submarine cables. This research aims to look into all relevant sources on submarine cable regimes, which could form the basis for developing a common minimum framework for the formulation or drafting of national instruments to deal with issues relating to submarine cables.

This study set about four objectives that seek to tackle the problems at hand with respect to submarine cables. For that matter, this study raised four research questions; three of them have been discussed and addressed in the previous chapters by answering one related research question. This concluding chapter addresses its fourth objective and research question and outlines the research findings and suggestions. Finally, it proposes a model legal framework on submarine cable, which countries may consider adopting such provisos in their national instruments for strengthening the submarine cable regime.

The first chapter of this study introduces the topic, gives an overview of the issues, and undertakes the literature review on submarine cable regimes. It identifies the gap in the existing literature and the research problem and, finally, defines the objectives and formulated research questions. The second chapter discusses the study's first objective and answers the international regime on submarine cable. This research probes through an analytical method on the international regime on submarine cables set out in UNCLOS. The findings help the researcher identify essential principles and parameters and the limitations of the current regime.

It is noted that the customary principle of freedom of the sea, which includes laying of the submarine cables and the treaty laws, has a vital role in the promotion of international communication. UNCLOS Articles 58, 79, and 87 represent the codified

U. K. Raha and Raju K. D., *Submarine Cables Protection and Regulations*,
https://doi.org/10.1007/978-981-16-3436-9_5

treaty principles on the international regime on laying of submarine cables. It defines the concept of freedom of laying cables and confers states the rights of laying cables with due regards. UNCLOS also recognizes the principle of the protection of cables. It urges States to adopt legal measures against the breaking or injuring of cables beyond the territorial waters (TW).[1] It also upholds the principle of sovereignty within the States' TW; thus, the administration and regulatory measures for laying and operation of cables rest upon States' regulatory authority. However, it is submitted that the international cable regime remains inadequate for several reasons.

It is evident that UNCLOS is the constitution of the ocean and does not deal with every issue of the submarine cables in detail and urges States and international organizations to develop detailed rules on submarine cables within its guiding principles. Regarding the institutional role of this cable regime, it is submitted that the international institutions are yet to pay attention to these issues as stressed by the principles and provisions of UNCLOS. The development of this international cable regime by global authority remains a distant reality.

UNCLOS does not impose obligations on States to address cables' susceptibility to damage within TW following the sovereignty principle. Thus, the submarine cable governance within TW rests on States' discretion. It is observed that cable protection in a State where cable breaking is not illegal is at stake. It is also opined that the provisions that define States' obligations on protecting cables within EEZ also prove ineffectual. Thus, the submarine cable system is exposed to intense security threats within the current UNCLOS regime.

The principle of the protection of cables is focused on addressing cables vulnerabilities pose by regular marine activities. It is also identified that UNCLOS does not provide any direction which could effectively mitigate or address the issue of cable theft and maritime terrorism. It is a severe security lapse and an alarming threat to the stability of the cable system. The international cable choke points may become lucrative targets for a terrorist attack. Thus, it is cautioned that such a gap in the international submarine cable regime is likely to significantly adversely affect the submarine cable network's stability—a siren song to the—dependent telecommunication world.

Further, the Cable Convention 1884 prescribes cable ships' safety measures, limiting interference to cable operation and enforcement procedures. These measures prescribe (i) serving prior notice for withdrawal of other marine activities during cable operation, (ii) maintaining a minimum distance between cable ships and other vessels, (iii) rights of inspection officer to board the vessel in case of suspicion and for collection of evidence on alleged cable damage, etc. COLREGS 1972 urges all vessels to use appropriate lights and signal and maintain minimum distance, etc., to avoid a collision. The States must consider these arrangements giving necessary clues on the safety of vessels, cables, and enforcement procedures such as the collection of evidence of cable damage.

[1] Articles 113, 114 and 115 of UNCLOS [1].

Several States impose conditions and restrictions on cable operation in the EEZ, further stress on the freedom of laying submarine cables. Coastal States' continuous temptation for territorialization is a problem. According to the coastal States, such conditions and restrictions comply with the principles of reasonableness under UNCLOS. UNCLOS suggests two principles on procedures, i.e., reasonableness and due regards. It is submitted that coastal States permit requirements on cable operation beyond its TW may not always conform to these principles. The said conditions, restraints, and interruptions are not always on the line of internationally lawful uses of the ocean as provided in the law of the sea.

It is submitted that all of the said principles and specific parameters of the international cable regime, notwithstanding their limitations and implementation issues, provide the basis for a proposed legal framework for national instruments on cables. Besides these guiding principles of international law, other sources of principles and parameters on cables are the extraction of cable-related instruments, firstly, from the selected jurisdictions and secondly, from Australia and New Zealand.

The third chapter deals with submarine cable instruments from selected jurisdictions and addresses the second objective of this study. It discusses and identifies the commonalities and gaps of these cable instruments. It answers whether the existing regulatory instruments on cable in India and other jurisdictions are adequate to deal with challenges associated with the security and reliability of the submarine cable system through a comparative legal analysis. It highlights the relations between these instruments and international cable regimes and identifies the instruments' essential parameters.

It reveals that many of these jurisdictions have not enacted specific laws for submarine cables in the line of UNCLOS. However, they have adopted several administrative instruments, such as notifications, orders, directives, and regulations. They also offer policy instruments such as maritime policy, environmental policy, and other marine and coastal habitat conservation measures over cable operations and protection.

Notably, the submarine cable regulations in China, the UK, the USA, Ghana, Colombia, etc., indicate a lead agency for issuing permits for laying cables. France, one of the pioneer campaigners for cable protection, has adopted stringent provisions with severe liability for breaking cables (deliberate damage may meet imprisonment for five years or fine of 3750 Euros or both). It is also noted that many countries have prescribed for cable protection zones or corridors where certain marine activities are either prohibited or restricted and imposed punishment for their violations. Respective jurisdictions follow different standards for such cable safety zones, restrictions, liabilities, enforcement, etc. The area of cable safety zones varies from 50 to 3500 m and beyond. Countries like Singapore and Vietnam have issued guidelines that prescribe to promote awareness and knowledge about the critical nature of cables. These guidelines, however, do not fall under the category of legal instruments.

European Union (EU) legal framework, attracting OSPAR & ESPOO, prescribes additional standards concerning Maritime Protected Areas and Environment Impact Assessment for laying cables. England's cable regime comprises marine policy statements, pollution standards, conservation directives on water, waste management, habitat, a special area of conservations, etc., on cable operation. It is noted that Canada prefers the integrated ocean management approach for laying cable. It prescribes civil liability based on the principle of due diligence for awarding damages on cable breaking incidents. Thus, cable governance standards vary from jurisdictions to jurisdictions representing individual States' political will and interests in marine spaces. The cable operators meet immense difficulties in complying with such a different standard across the jurisdictions. It is also evident that instruments on cables in many countries bear significant drawbacks.

A few countries like India and China offer onerous permit regimes for cable operation even in their EEZ. In many jurisdictions, obtaining cable installation permits involves several government departments that provide multifaceted and cumbersome cable regulation. Such onerous permit regimes are linked with these countries' vital interests, including national security, immigration, customs, economic interests, safety and environmental concerns, etc. In contrast, countries including India, Indonesia, Japan, Canada, Argentina, etc., have not yet designated a lead agency for cable installation permits, etc. The cable operators, in many cases, also face difficulties in identifying necessary procedures and application routes for approvals. There are jurisdictions, including the USA, which have criminalized the incident of cable breaking. However, they have not updated their outdated laws, which provide minimal incentives to their enforcement agencies against its violation. Thus, many countries remain negligent in adopting clear legal and policy measures for existing and emerging challenges concerning the cable system. Indeed, the available cable-related instruments across these selected jurisdictions are suffering from complexities, inconsistencies, and inadequacies in providing measures on breaking cables; silence on human aggressions of cables theft and terrorist activities; and the lead agency for cables, in many countries.

Regarding the State practices on disputes, it is evident that the judicial precedents on submarine cables are rare. In one such latest case, the France court finds the fishermen guilty for their act of refusal to withdraw their fishing nets and gears for cable operation. In another example, the Supreme Court of Canada finds that the incident of cable cut by a fisherman is willful misconduct and awards a monetary fine. In this connection, it is also notable that submarine cable committees, particularly the ICPC and some international academic institutions, are pressing on developing a set of standards and adopting marine spatial planning for cables. They emphasize the promotion of awareness about the critical nature of cables and building coordination and cooperation among the cable operators and other marine users besides local and regional authorities.

In precise, it is submitted that present analysis on cable instruments in the selected jurisdictions, however, becomes helpful in identifying several parameters such as:

- imposing control on certain marine activities that may cause interference with laying of submarine cables and its breakage or injury;
- prescribing liabilities to discourage activities that may cause interference with laying of cable and its breakage or injury;
- indicating the existence of the lead agency, if any, at the national level;

- declaration of submarine cable protection zone or corridors;
- promotion of awareness program on submarine cable operation and its protection;
- the cooperative mechanism among the marine users' *inter se* and coastal authorities.

These parameters supply the basis for a model legal framework for the governance of submarine cables. Further, they also represent diversity in their scope and enforcement procedures. Such diversity could become helpful in determining the scope of the proposed parameters of the legal framework. A draft model also needs to ascertain the licensing terms and conditions, authority, functions, responsibilities of a lead agency appointed for the administration of submarine cable, standards for declaration of a cable safety zone, restricted activities within such zones, the quantum of liability, enforcement procedures, etc.

It is also observed that the submarine cable instruments of the selected jurisdictions, in many cases, do not deal with obligations in detail and remain obscure on its enforcement procedures. Many of the penal provisions on cables have become outdated. It is cautioned that these instruments' deterring elements have been compromised. Thus, it is opined that these measures' potentials are expected to be realized and enhanced further through appropriate actions. In that direction, the submarine cable regimes in Australia and New Zealand have shown the way forward.

The fourth chapter undertakes comparative legal research on the relevant legal and institutional frameworks in Australia and New Zealand and answers whether the submarine cable regimes of these countries facilitate laying and protecting cables. Schedule 3A of the Telecommunications Act 1997 (the 1997 Act of Australia), together with the Australian Communication and Media Authority Act 2005, comprises Australia's cable regime. For New Zealand, it is the Protection of Submarine Cables and Pipelines Act 1996 (the 1996 Act of New Zealand). This chapter's comparative analysis reveals that these legislations have made detailed provisions regarding the principles on submarine cables set out in UNCLOS.

It is observed that these legislations comprise essential parameters. The legislators have explicitly made it clear that both legal and institutional frameworks under it would support laying and protecting cables. They prescribe for dedicated authorities, which shall facilitate granting license for laying cables and promoting cable protection by establishing a submarine cable protection zone and restricting certain marine activities followed by effective enforcement mechanisms. It is also noted that these laws prescribe exemplary liability against cable breaking. New Zealand prescribes hefty fines (not exceeding 250,000 dollars only), and Australia imposes punishment (10 years of imprisonment/and fine). Australia, in particular, prescribes a detailed list of prohibited or restricted activities concerning the cable protection zone. It specifies installation permit and installation conditions, environment and heritage standards, one's acquiring rights on cables, and its violations are also punishable offenses. Interference with New Zealand's submarine cable enforcement or protection officer, who enjoys significant authority over cable protected area for its implementation, may meet with a fine not exceeding 10,000 dollars apart from seizures and forfeiture of property. This 1996 Act of New Zealand also prescribes a fine not exceeding 5000 dollars for damaging its surveillance equipment standards. Both of these laws also provide indemnity for the sacrifice of fishing gears or the cost of repairing a damaged cable. The national courts determine the indemnity and costs.

These legislations, however, are not free from criticisms. Some criticisms are distinct from the legislation. The 1996 Act of New Zealand remains silent on parameters, including the delineation of cable protected areas, detailed procedures, and mechanisms obtaining installation permits, a list of activities, preventive measures for potential threats to cables, etc. It is also silent on marine environment standards and heritage conservations. The 1997 Act of Australia does not provide for the enforcement agency's power and functions in detail. It is also silent on the maritime surveillance system.

The first one among the common demerits of these legislations relates to the extraterritorial jurisdictions. Both legislations affirm the establishment of a protection zone or area beyond their TW. Therefore, these legislations may apply to foreign nationals or flagships EEZ, the international water—a possible inconsistency between the sea's national law and international law. However, both of the States are aware of its jurisdictional extensions. Their enforcement agencies need to make a consultation with their respective Attorney-General before they initiate any proceeding against a foreign national or ship allegedly involved with contravening activities beyond their TW. Then, both of the legislations are silent on human aggression to cables in the form of piracy and terrorisms.

Both Australia and New Zealand do not provide for measures that include dedicated dispute resolution forum and reporting centers, vessel registration canters, institutional role in promoting knowledge and awareness about the critical nature of cables, etc. It is also submitted that these legislations also do not deal with essential parameters concerning maintaining the minimum distance between cable ship and other vessels and their marine uses, showing signals, etc.

It is opined that Australia and New Zealand's laws have potentials for developing national submarine cable instruments' jurisprudence. It is submitted that these submarine cable regimes contain loopholes, which are the barriers to effective cable governance and expected to be corrected through definite actions. The essential features of both merits and limitations of these legislations have been considered in this work, which could be used by States wishing to adopt similar laws on submarine cables in their respective jurisdictions. Indeed, these parameters provide a strong basis for a proposed national legal framework on submarine cables.

Throughout the study, the process of analysis reveals fundamental elements of submarine cable regimes across jurisdictions. The international submarine cable regime's provisions do not suggest enough arrangements on individual incidents of negligent or willful cable injuries by marine users. They are significantly weak in addressing premeditated human aggression on the cable system. States' actions and negligence further constrain the principle of freedom of laying cables. International organizations are also ignored reviewing the cable regimes toward development. The essential parameters of this regime include the freedom of laying cables, other associated activities—internationally lawful use of the ocean, due regard toward other States, protection of cables, indemnity for the sacrifice of fishing nets, gears and cost of cable repairing, enforcement procedure on the breaking of cables, maintaining minimum distance and showing signals for the protection of cables and cables ships, etc.

A specific national law on submarine cable is far and few in many jurisdictions. However, they have adopted several secondary instruments, which possess several drawbacks that include lack of provision on the lead agency for cables and adequate arrangements for the protection of cables' susceptibility to breakage. Nevertheless, some instruments in these jurisdictions prescribe distinguished parameters for cables such as the indication of the lead agency, protection, and cable protection zones/corridors, use of buoys for cable route, environmental and conservation standards, publication, awareness, and education on cables' critical nature and cooperation among stakeholders.

An integrated approach to ocean management resulted in dedicated national legislation on submarine cables in Australia and New Zealand. The specific cable regimes of these countries intend to deal with the issues of cable governances comprehensively. The essential features of these laws include the establishment of the institutional framework for laying of cables and other associated activities; declaring cable protection/protected zone; exercising control on marine activities; pronouncement of the stringent liability (*Strict Liability in Australia);* and establishment of competent enforcement mechanisms.

The study finds that many countries follow both civil and criminal procedural laws on procedural aspects, and some countries rely on civil procedure only in enforcing cable-related laws. It also finds that extraterritorial jurisdictions under both Australia and New Zealand's cable regimes attract criticisms. However, the countries are cautious about the prosecution of a foreign subject.

5.1 Suggestions

It is suggested that a dedicated national legal framework on submarine cables shall remove many of the misgiving, doubt, and unreasonable delay in laying cables, in particular, the time-sensitive cable repairing to the interference with cable operation and ensure better protection of these cables. Moving forward and appreciating the national submarine cable regimes of both Australia and New Zealand, this study proposes other States consider the following suggestions in their initiatives strengthening national submarine cables regimes in the line of UNCLOS:

1. adoption of integrated ocean management approach concerning submarine cables;
2. establishment of lead agency in the respective jurisdiction and enforcement mechanism at the national levels;
3. defining clear procedure and single-window approval process for cable installation permits, etc.;
4. establishing and maintaining a national vessel registry;

5. installing a surveillance and reporting system for cable routes and vessels;
6. establishment of submarine cable protection zone or corridor;
7. prescription of prohibitions, restrictions, and preventions on activities concerning the specified submarine cable protection area;
8. publication of the cable chart, concerning the submarine cable protection zones and their compliances, etc.;
9. maintaining minimum distance and showing signals for the protection of cables and cables ships;
10. building cooperation among submarine cable operators, other marine users, coastal authorities, local and regional fishing, shipping organizations, etc.;
11. notifying the marine users, including the fishing vessels, etc., in advance about the area of cable operation, ensuring former a reasonable opportunity to withdraw their vessels, fishing nets, gears, etc.;
12. providing indemnification against the sacrifice of fishing nets, gears, etc., recovery of the cost of cable repairing, and compensation for loss concerning cable operation;
13. creating a fund to be supported by cable operators to meet expenditure incurred by the lead agency and its associated agencies on cables;
14. prescribing environmental and conservation standards;
15. promotion of awareness, coordination among the stakeholders on cables;
16. adoption of the principle of strict liability for cable protection;
17. prescribing enforcement procedure;
18. defining the offense and lay down the punishment;
19. defining threats of terrorist attacks following national law on maritime terrorism addressing incidents of a deliberate attack on the cable system or any act likely to cause such attacks.

Thus, the given principles, approaches, parameters, and procedures become the basis for a proposed draft model legal framework on national submarine cables.

5.2 Draft Model Law on National Instrument on Submarine Cable

5.2.1 Executive Summary

Submarine cable infrastructure facilitates the transmission of data and telecommunication. It supports the Internet, a driving factor of the global economy and a strategic tool in every State's national security. Modern society, in general, may not be aware of issues relating to submarine cables and their vulnerability; as a result, governments remain unresponsive toward their legal governance. Legal measures for laying and protecting cables within the national jurisdictions are under stress to accommodate competing interests among growing cable operations and other marine activities.

The cables are becoming more vulnerable at both ends, and most cable damage is reported within the national marine jurisdictions.

Further, in many States, submarine cable operations are not supported by dedicated regulatory regimes. There, a time-sensitive cable repairing operation gets delayed-an obstacle in immediate relinking of telecommunications. Still, many States remain lackadaisical in adopting legal and policy measures for laying and protecting cables. Hence, laying cables and quick relinking of telecommunication connections have become critical, making timely approval from local authorities to facilitate cable operators and repair ships to mobilize and accomplish their tasks. Though very crucial, yet it remains mostly unattended to in many jurisdictions. There is a clear need for a dedicated national instrument to deal with issues relating to the laying and protection of submarine cables. In response to their obligations concerning cables beyond TW, as set out in UNCLOS, the States require to adopt a precise national instrument. Though States are not obliged to adopt adequate measures for the regulation of cables within their TW, however, they have committed to promoting international communications, including submarine telecommunications—the interests common to all. Therefore, States hold the responsibility to adopt appropriate legal and administrative measures to facilitate in laying and protection of submarine cables. A prospective national submarine cable law should address the following:

1. Facilitating the laying of cables by a specialized national agency;
2. Protection of cables;
3. Penalty;
4. Additional Regulations to deal with procedural aspects.

UN General Assembly resolution[2] and the ICPC Draft Convention for Protection and Repair of Submarine Cable Infrastructure 2008, together with the provisions from submarine cable law and other instruments and guidelines across the jurisdictions, form the basis for this draft model law. States may peruse this proposed model law. It may consider a policy and basis to further build upon framing a similar instrument for the governance of submarine cable guidelines and a basis to further build upon framing a similar instrument for submarine cable governance.

5.2.2 *Purpose of the Model Law*

The proposed draft model legal framework suggests a set of standards and guidelines for administering a specific submarine cable regime by States. It also takes into account:

- to prevent and protect cables from human activities, either intentional or negligent act;
- to strengthen the regime of protection of submarine cable system;

[2] '*… calling upon States to take measures to protect fiber optic submarine cables and to fully address issues relating to these cables* [2].'

- to avoid unnecessary interference with the laying of cables and related activities;
- to foster integration measures, such as interaction, consultation, cooperation, and coordination among various institutions within the State and institutions across the nations *inter se;*
- to promote national interest in submarine cable network—critical communication infrastructure and power cables and to enhance its goal to achieve prominence in cyber-power;
- to promote awareness and knowledge about the global telecommunication system and submarine networks.

5.2.3 Guiding Principles of the Model Law

A set of measures concerning submarine cables at the national levels to be developed within the spirit of broad principles laid down in the law of the sea, such as (i) the principle of freedom of the sea, including the freedom of laying submarine cables, (ii) the principle of high sea, (iii) the principle of territorial sovereignty, (iv) the principle of the protection of submarine cables and penalty, (v) the principles of compensation claims and indemnity, and vi) the principle of spatial ocean management.

The international law of the sea aims to promote international communication, and it is acknowledged as the privilege of States *inter se*. Freedom of laying submarine cable is the extension of that privilege. It encompasses freedom of laying of the submarine cables and all other associated activities such as the cable route survey, repair, and maintenance. All privileges come with obligations; thus, the States' obligation is to protect submarine cables within their national jurisdictions. It also recognizes the principles of indemnity, claims, and compensation concerning cable damage, breakage, and injury.

The present draft model law on submarine cables follows the zonal management approach and the integrated ocean management approach. While the former State the spatial distribution of national jurisdictions and later States on international cooperation between States. Thus, the coexistence of both zonal and integrated management approaches becomes the basis of the national instruments on submarine cables while relying on relevant principles embodied in the sea and national laws.

In defining liability concerning submarine cable protection zones standards, the proposed instrument assumes the principle of *strict liability*. Countries like Australia also rely on the principle of strict liability on cable damage, infringement of prohibited or restricted activities, and cable installation without permit concerning the submarine cable protection zones. The study anticipates that submarine cable protection zone standards supported by strict liability would significantly deter the marine users. The proposed liability scheme concerning the submarine cable protection zone is to be developed on the principle of strict liability. It may follow the general rule of liability in dealing with the submarine cable non-protection zone standards.

Lastly, UNCLOS [1], by Article 79, states that *all States* are entitled to laying submarine cables on the continental shelf. It also imposes obligations on States to adopt measures to protect cable beyond TW (Articles 113–115). The phrase *all States* includes cable carriers who enjoy such rights on behalf of their States. However, the exercise of such rights and cables' protection relies on States' cooperation and supervision. Moreover, prevailing legal standards on principle suggest States assume a more significant role toward the functioning of governmental or non-governmental (private) entities, i.e., cable carriers. The States are supposed to facilitate cable carriers in the laying and protection of cables. A State may do so by extending a clear cable operation approval mechanism (authorization and licensing) and continued supervision. Such States' actions must be in conformity with their national legal frameworks and commitments toward submarine cable communication infrastructure—a system of common interests.

5.2.4 Structure of the Model Law

The draft framework begins with preliminary provisions on the scope and interpretation. It prescribes a lead agency conferred with extensive administrative powers for framing guidelines, providing licenses and permits, set standards, cable installation procedures, etc. This lead agency was also authorized to declare cable safety zones and specify restrictions on certain protected zones' activities. The next part deals with the safety of cable ships and interference with the cable operation. The following section deals with the reporting center, indemnity, cost of repairs, and environmental measures for cables. The final part of the framework deals with the implementation procedures, dispute settlement, and offenses. This framework ends with the provisions on penalties. States can adopt these proposed draft provisions with necessary modifications as per their suitability and interests in their marine spaces.

5.3 Proposed Draft Model Framework

5.3.1 Proposed Measures and Procedural Guidance for the Implementation of National Instrument on Submarine Cable

5.3.1.1 Part I: Short Title

This proposed model may be cited as the Law for Laying and the Protection of Submarine Cables.

Comment: This draft model law may be known as 'The Law for Laying and the Protection of Submarine Cables,' or the State may customize, upgrade it, and frame it into comprehensive legislation.

5.3.1.2 Part II: Application

This law shall apply to any act or omission by a person within the internal water, territorial water of AB. It may be extended and limited to the nationals and flagships of AB within the exclusive economic zone and the continental shelf.

Comment: AB denotes the representing country considering this model law in enacting submarine cable law. It may apply this law based on a person's nationality or an artificial person like the flagships, fishing vessels, etc.

5.3.1.3 Part III: Definition

In these regulations, unless the context otherwise specifies

(a) 'Submarine Cable' means an undersea cable system landing in two or more States or between a State and an island of that State.[3]
(b) 'Laying of the Cable' includes route survey, the laying of cable, and the repairing and maintenance of cables.
(c) 'Cable Ship' means a vessel that is equipped to lay and repair submarine cables.[4]
(d) 'Submarine Cable Agency' is an agency set up to dealing with the laying of submarine cables and associated activities and the protection of submarine cables within the national marine jurisdictions.
(e) 'Submarine Cable Protection Zone or Protected Area' is an area within national jurisdictions of the marine spaces established to facilitate submarine cables' laying and protection.
(f) 'Advisory Committee' is a committee consisting of experts in relevant areas of marine governance to be set up under the Submarine Cable Agency to support the latter in decision making.
(g) 'Enforcing Officer' is an officer in command of a ship designated by the marine security force under Part XIII.
(h) Internal Water, territorial waters, and EEZ denote the marine spaces as defined in UNCLOS (under Articles 8, 1, and 55, respectively).

Comment: This list is not exhaustive, and national authority may add terminologies as per their requirement.

[3]Article 1(1) (d) of the International Cable Protection Committee Draft on 'Convention for the Protection and Repair of Submarine Cable Infrastructure' 2008 (ICPC restricted access).

[4]Article 1(1) (c) of the International Cable Protection Committee Draft on 'Convention for the Protection and Repair of Submarine Cable Infrastructure' 2008 (ICPC restricted access).

5.3.1.4 Part IV: National Submarine Cable Agency: Power and Function

(a) The State shall designate or establish a National Submarine Cable Agency comprising the governmental departments' representatives for this law.
(b) The National Submarine Cable Agency shall be responsible for providing a single-window mechanism for laying cables and other associated activities in consultation with the Advisory Committee.

Comment: The State parties to UNCLOS 1982 that acknowledge the freedom of laying the submarine cables are expected to adopt appropriate measures for facilitating in laying and protecting cables. This part prescribes AB for establishing a National Submarine Cable Agency (the agency) for cable with the necessary legislative competence to implement this law. It will be regarded as a competent agency or lead agency of the States to lay submarine cables. This agency comprises members representing the Department of Defense; foreign affairs; telecommunication; energy, fishing, shipping, trade, industry, and tourism; natural resource and environments, coastal zone management and conservation authorities, etc. This agency may issue guidelines for laying, repair, and maintenance addressing vital interests, including national security, immigration, customs, economics, safety, environmental concerns, pre-approval, etc. The issues are akin to the best practices on permits.

The agency must be competent to prescribe a streamlined procedure and prescribed application forms (application) for cable installation permits and approval for cablc route survey, repair, maintenance, etc. It may specify the information that includes information regarding the eligibility of the applicant (cable operators); proposed cable operation; marine environment and the location of operation; means, resources involved; stipulated time and the method of cable operation; the purpose of such cables; details on the person intending to carry out the laying of cables; and impose fees for this license.

To dispose of the said application before it, this agency must have a response procedure addressing issues including examination of the application, conducting the hearing of applicants followed by a consultation with its members, and the Advisory Committee, tracking of application's status and time limit for a decision, etc. It needs to be a competent authority to decide on this application, prescribes the license duration, and the conditions of its renewal, suspension, revocation, etc. For the continuation and renewal of license granted by it, the agency may require the licensee to notify of any change in cable operation, extend cooperation with inspection, and monitor operation by the security officers employed under this law. It must have the authority to consult on sensitive issues, e.g., an application by cable operators requesting for treating the submarine cable repairing the ship as an 'ambulance' for the earliest clearance to initiate the immediate cable repairing process.

5.3.1.5 Part V: Arrangement for Non-protection Zones

The National Submarine Cable Agency shall adopt an appropriated procedure to grant the application of submarine cables beyond the designated submarine cable protection zone or protected area.

Comment: The agency may provide a different arrangement for laying of cables beyond the cable protection or protected area.

5.3.1.6 Part VI: Submarine Cable Protection Zone

With due consultation with the Advisory Committee, the National Submarine Cable Agency shall declare a submarine cable protection zone in marine space within the national marine jurisdiction.

Comment: The agency shall be the competent authority to declare any area as the cable protection zone/cable protected area and prescribe for restrictions on marine activities. Such marine activities may include fishing, anchoring, shipping, and its methods, etc., and any other marine activities as it deems fit for the protection of cables concerning cable protection zone/cable protected area and shall notify it on the government gazette of AB. This protected area may be within the internal water, territorial waters, and EEZ as it happens in Australia. It is noted that the establishment of such a protected area in EEZ is not on the line of UNCLOS provisions. Several countries have prescribed cable corridors extending 50–500 m around a cable route.

5.3.1.7 Part VII: Restrictions and Prohibitions

The National Submarine Cable Agency shall declare that certain marine activities within the designated submarine cable protection zones are either prohibited absolutely or restricted.

Comment: The agency shall be the competent authority to consult with the Advisory Committee to identify and declare marine use prohibited or restricted within this protected area. These activities include anchoring, dredging, trawling gear, mining, etc. The restrictive activities include anchoring in a protection zone, lowering, raising, or suspending a hotline from a ship, using an explosive or explosive device, etc. Identifying the number of activities, these laws rest on AB make the other marine users known about such mandates.

5.3.1.8 Part VIII: Signaling and Mantinea of Minimum Distance Between Vessels

The cable ships and other marine vessels shall maintain a distance set by the National Submarine Cable Agency to avoid interference by other marine uses and collisions between ships.

Comment: Under Articles 18 and 27 of the Convention on the International Regulations for Preventing Collisions at Sea 1972, the vessels must show appropriate lights and signals, maintenance of distance (one nautical mile) between cable ships and other vessels, including fishing vessels.[5]

5.3.1.9 Part IX: Withdrawal of Marine Uses

On receiving prior notice from the cable operators, the National Submarine Cable Agency shall ensure that the other vessels and fishing nets, etc., of the place of cable operation, are withdrawn.

Comment: For prevention of interference from other marine activities to cable operation, the Cable Convention 1884 prescribes for withdrawal of marine activities on prior information. The agency, based on a previous notice by the cable operators regarding repair and maintenance of submarine cables process, shall ensure that the fishing and other vessels and fishing gears be removed from the specified palace of cable operation (as mentioned in the said notice) for a definite period as requested by the cable operators. The agency on receiving such requests shall communicate the marine force (Coast Guard) unit of AB to make necessary communication to the local fishing associations to control fishing vessels accordingly.

5.3.1.10 Part X: Surveillance and Reporting

Any marine user who comes across any violation of this law or has reason to believe that there was an attempt to break cable exists at a specific location shall report the discovery to the nearest port at the earliest.

Comment: The agency may not be able to make effective surveillance and monitoring on cables that are laid on the seabed of the vast marine spaces due to scarcity of resources. However, mandatory reporting requirements for marine users may help the agency obtain information to act upon accordingly. Such reporting shall be used for further proceedings, including collecting evidence, awarding indemnity for the sacrifice of fishing gears, etc. The policymakers of AB are to deal with the challenging task of the implementation of such reports. It also fixes maritime surveillance equipment

---

[5]See also Article V of the Cable Convention 1884 [3] states

'Vessels engaged in laying or repairing submarine cables shall conform to the regulations as to signals which have been, or may be, adopted by mutual agreement among the High Contracting Parties, with the view of preventing collisions at sea.

When a ship engaged in repairing a cable exhibits the said signals, other vessels which see them, or are able to see them, shall withdraw to or keep beyond a distance of one nautical mile at least from the ship in question, so as not to interfere with her operations.

Fishing gear and nets shall be kept at the same distance.

Nevertheless, fishing vessels which see, or are able to see, a telegraph-ship exhibiting the said signals, shall be allowed a period of 24 h at most within which to obey the notice so given, during which time they shall not be interfered with in any way.

The operations of the telegraph-ships shall be completed as quickly as possible.'

for instant reporting. This agency may also be a component authority for coordination among the cable operators, other marine users, and other coastal authorities, including ports and vessel registration offices. It may cooperate with other organizations across the borders to prevent and suppress hostile attacks on submarine cables.

5.3.1.11 Part XI: Breaking or Injury by Owners of a Submarine Cables

The owner of a cable ship that causes breaking or injury of the cable shall bear the cost of the repairs.

Comment: Article 114 UNCLOS provides that the owner of a submarine cable subjected to the AB in laying of cables if breaks another cable is to bear the cost of repairs.

5.3.1.12 Part XII: Indemnity for Sacrifice of Fishing Gears, Etc.

Anyone engaged with the marine activities, including fishing, shall report to the National Submarine Cable Agency through the port authority about the loss of sacrificed anchor or fishing gear within 24 h of such incident to claim for indemnity.

Comment: Article 115 of UNCLOS prescribes the States to adopt a law awarding indemnity to the owner who sacrifices an anchor, a net, or any other fishing gear to avoid injuring a submarine cable. The agency needs the authority to award such indemnity in coordination with the port authority to whom the owner shall first report such loss. This law shall not compensate for the cost of the expected catches but fishing gears. The agency, in coordination with the relevant cable operators, may create an '*Indemnity Fund*' supported by the cable operators that may be utilized in meeting such indemnity and loss occurs due to withdrawal of marine activities during cable operation.

5.3.1.13 Part XIII: Terrorist Activities on Submarine Cables

The provisions of maritime legislation of the States' may apply to the terrorist activities on cables.

Comment: AB may deal with the threat of terrorist attacks on cables on the line of legislation on maritime terrorism. It also encourages cooperation among coastal authorities within a State and across the States in the prosecution of accused.

5.3.1.14 Part XIV: Environmental Standards

The laying of cables shall comply with coastal States' marine environment standards.

Comment: AB may impose its marine environmental and conservation standards on laying cables.

5.3.1.15 Part XV: Enforcing Mechanism and Proceedings

The law of procedure shall follow the general rules of procedural law.

Comment: Article 10 of the Cable Convention 1882 provides for a detailed procedure for the collection of evidence of breaking or injury of cables, disruption, sabotage, or destruction or any attempt of that kind, of submarine cables, significantly beyond the territorial waters by vessels of war or a vessel specially commissioned for that purpose.[6] AB may designate the law enforcement officer from Coast Guards, Navy, and Marine Police. It shall empower such officer the authority to board on a vessel in suspicious for the inspection and access into necessary documents such as logbook, containers for obtaining information and cessation of and forfeiture of property or escort the vessel for inspection. This officer must be liable to produce such information to establish the guilt before a dispute settlement forum in AB. This mechanism must have the responsibility to coordinate with the reporting centers under this law and vessel registration authority in AB.

5.3.1.16 Part XVI: Duty to Cooperate with the Enforcing Officer

The suspected vessel owner and other marine users operating within the national jurisdiction of AB shall have the duty to cooperate with this inspection and comply with the law.

Comment: The other vessels operating within the national authority of AB need to bring under a duty to cooperate with the inspection officer and other coastal authorities under this law, such as the agency, vessel registration center, and the reporting center.

[6]Article X of the Cable Convention 1884 [3] provides 'Offences against the present Convention may be verified by all means of proof allowed by the legislation of the country of the court. When the officers commanding the ships of war, or ships specially commissioned for the purpose by one of the High Contracting Parties, have reason to believe that an infraction of the measures provided for in the present Convention has been committed by a vessel other than a vessel of war, they may demand from the captain or master the production of the official documents proving the nationality of the said vessel. The fact of such document having been exhibited shall then be endorsed upon it immediately. Further, formal statements of the facts may be prepared by the said officers, whatever may be the nationality of the vessel incriminated. These formal statements shall be drawn up in the form and in the language used in the country to which the officer making them belongs; they may be considered, in the country where they are adduced, as evidence in accordance with the laws of that country. The accused and the witnesses shall have the right to add, or to have added thereto, in their own language, any explanations they may consider useful. These declarations shall be duly signed.' See also Article 9 of the International Cable Protection Committee Draft on 'Convention for the Protection and Repair of Submarine Cable Infrastructure' 2008 (ICPC restricted access).

5.3.1.17 Part XVII: Dispute Settlement

Any dispute regarding the interpretation and any breach of this law shall subject to the national dispute settlement mechanism.

Comment: A dispute relating to the submarine cable shall be subjected to the national forum and be dealt with summarily. This forum shall have jurisdictions to award indemnity for loss and penalty against violations relating to the protection of cables and permit requirements. The evidence collected by the enforcing agency may be admissible to this forum.[7]

5.3.1.18 Part XVIII: Offense

Any activity that carries out or attempts to carry out in the infringement of the obligations set out in the present law is a punishable offense except *force majeure*, the saving of cables, and the environment.

Comment: Infringement by any person of the provisions under this model law on the protection of cables, the protection of submarine cable zones and its prohibitions and restrictions, and conditions of the license is an offense.

5.3.1.19 Part XIX: Penalties

(a) Any intentional breaking or injury of cable is punishable with a fine not lower than (XX) dollars and imprisonment of (YY) years or both.
(b) The cable breaking for commercial gain by other marine users, including cable operators, is punishable with a fine not lower than (x) dollars.
(c) Any violation in the cable protection zone is punishable with a fine not lower than (x) dollars and imprisonment of (y) years or both.
(d) Any repetitive violation set out in this model is punishable with a fine not lower than (W) dollars or imprisonment (Z) years.
(e) Any violation of licensing provision in Part II of this law is liable to the revocation/suspension of the license of laying or renewal of cables.

Comment: Article 113 of UNCLOS imposes an obligation on State parties to adopt measures prescribing liability against breaking or injuring cable beyond territorial water. Breaking or injury of submarine cables under this law is strict liability.

[7] See Article 9 of the International Cable Protection Committee Draft on "Convention for the Protection and Repair of Submarine Cable Infrastructure' 2008. (ICPC restricted access)—'Evidence obtained in accordance with Article 10 of the Paris Convention can be introduced in national courts or in proceedings provided for in Article 12.' Article 12 of the Paris Convention or Cable Convention 1884 provides that The High Contracting Parties engage to take or to propose to their respective legislatures the necessary measures for insuring the execution of the present Convention, and especially for punishing, by either fine or imprisonment, or both, those who contravene the provisions …".

Some States have prescribed liability on intentional or negligent acts of breaking or injuring cable within national jurisdictions or any attempt as an offense punishable with fine/imprisonment. The quantum of punishment denoting the minimum and maximum limit rests on AB, who may prescribe severer punishment for repeated violations under this model law.

Many of the national submarine cable regimes are expected to be strengthened by adopting effective measures. Such measures may adopt a spatial ocean management approach, dedicated regulatory authority, a competent enforcement agency, competent enforcement agency, and strict liability with exemplary punishment on its violations. Coastal States may consider a common minimum framework in implementing initiatives toward adopting a robust law and policy for reliability, resiliency, and security of the cable system. Finally, this draft model law is a beginning, and it can be improved further by States. A coastal State can adopt these proposed draft provisions, as it is or with modification, to suit their respective interests in marine spaces.

References

1. UNCLOS. (1982). The United Nations Convention on the Law of the Sea December 10, 1982, 1833 UNTS 3.
2. G.A. Res. 65/37, 121 (December 7, 2010).
3. The Cable Convention 1884. Convention for the Protection of Telegraph Cables 1884.

Bibliography

Books

1. Burnett, D. R. (Eds.). (2014). *The submarine cables: Law and policy* (1st ed.). Martinus Nijhoff.
2. Starosielski, N. (2015). *Introduction, The undersea network* (1st ed.). Duke University Press.
3. Lagoni, R. (1999). *Legal aspects of submarine high voltage direct current (HVDC) cables* (pp. 1–120). Lit Verlag.
4. Kwiatkowska, B. (1989). *The 200 mile exclusive economic zone in the new law of the sea* (pp. 1–397). Martinus Nijhoff.
5. Rutkowski, A. M., & Codding, G. A. (1988). *International telecommunication union in S changing world* (pp. 1–432). Artech House.
6. Churchill, R. R., & Lowe, A. (1999). *The law of the sea* (3rd ed.). Manchester University Press.
7. Rothwell, D. R. (Ed.). (2015). *The oxford handbook of the law of the sea* (1st ed.). Oxford University Press.
8. Drew, S., & Hopper, A. G. (2009). *Fishing and submarine cables—Working together* (2nd ed.). International Cable Protection Committee.
9. Shaw, M. (2005). *International Law* (5th ed.). Cambridge University Press.
10. Worzyk, T. (2009). *Submarine power cables: Design, installation, repair, environmental aspect*. Springer.
11. Tanaka, Y. (2012). *The international law of the sea* (1st ed.). Cambridge University Press.

Journal Articles

12. Friedman, A. (2017). Submarine telecommunication cables and a biodiversity agreement in ABNJ: Finding new routes for cooperation. *The International Journal of Marine and Coastal Law,* 32, 1–35.
13. Sugadev, A. (2016). India's critical position in the global submarine cable network: An analysis of Indian law and practice on cable repairs. *Indian Journal of International Law, 56*, 173–200.
14. Aillson, A. L. (1992–1993). Meeting the challenges of change: The reform of the international telecommunication union. *The Federal Communications Law Journal, 45*(3), 491–339.
15. Kotera, A. (1991). Deregulation of the international telecommunications business in Japan. *Japanese Annual International Law, 34*, 1–20.
16. Oxman, B. H. (1996). The rule of law and the united nations convention on the law of the sea. *European Journal of International Law*, *7*, 353–351.

U. K. Raha and Raju K. D., *Submarine Cables Protection and Regulations*,
https://doi.org/10.1007/978-981-16-3436-9

17. Clark, B. (2016). *Undersea cables and the future of submarine competition. Bulletin of the Atomic Scientists, 72*(4), 234–237.
18. Burnett, R., & Carter, L. (2017). *International submarine cables and biodiversity of areas beyond national jurisdiction—The cloud beneath the sea* (Vol. 1, No. 2, pp. 1–75). Brill Research Perspectives in the Law of the Sea.
19. deF. Chandler, C. (1922). *Submarine telegraph cables* (Vol. 127, No. 2, pp. 91–92). Scientific American.
20. Plaidy, C., Wellstein, L. M., Wakhariya, S., Papandrea, J., Worlton, A., Yoo, C., Paoletta, P. (2002). Telecommunications law and policy around the world. *The International Lawyer, 37*(2), 457–471.
21. Burnett, D. (2010). Recovery of cable repair ship cost damages from third parties that injure submarine cables. *The Tulane Maritime Law Journal, 35*, 105–122.
22. Burnett, D. R. (2013). Submarine cables on the continental shelf. In M. H. Nordquist (Eds.), *The regulation of continental shelf development* (Vol. 17, pp. 53–70). Center for Oceans Law and Policy.
23. Burnett, D. R. (2006). International law considerations for owners and operators of cabled and buoy observatories. *IEEE Journal of Oceanic Engineering, 31*.
24. Burnett, D. R. (2011). *The 1884 international convention for protection of submarine cables provisions not in UNCLOS deserve attention now* (pp. 1–12). Squire, Sanders & Dempsey.
25. Headrick, D. R., & Griset, P. (2001). Submarine telegraph cables: Business and politics, 1838–1939. *The Business History Review, 75*(3), 543–578.
26. Kroon, D. (2018). Due regard in the high seas: The tension between submarine cables and deep seabed mining. *Australian International Law Journal, 24*, 35–57.
27. Schuster, D. B. (2015, June). International telecommunication union—150 years of history: Adaptation to change and the opportunity for reform. *IEEE Communications Magazine—Communications Standards Supplement*, 10–15.
28. Winseck, D. (2017). The geopolitical economy of the global internet infrastructure. *Journal of Information Policy, 7*, 228–267.
29. Langlet, D. (2014). Transboundary transit pipelines: Reflections on the balancing of rights and interests in light of the nord stream project. *International and Comparative Law Quarterly, 63*(4), 977–995.
30. Brown, E. D. (1992). The significance of a possible EC EEZ for the law relating to artificial islands, installations, and structures, and to cables and pipelines, in the exclusive economic zone. *Ocean Development and International Law, 23*, 115–144.
31. Pope, E. L., et al. (2017). Which earthquake triggers damaging submarine mass movements: Insights from the global submarine cable breaks? *Marine Geology, 384*, 131–146.
32. Wagner, E. (1995). Submarine cables and protections provided by the law of the sea. *Marine Policy, 19*, 127–136.
33. Malecki, E. J., & Wei, H. (2009). A wired world: The evolving geography of submarine cables and the shift to Asia. *Annals of the Association of American Geographers, 99*(2), 360–382.
34. Andrulewicz, E., Napierska, D., & Otremba, Z. (2003). The environmental effects of the installation and functioning of the submarine SwePol link HVDC transmission line: A case study of the polish marine area of the Baltic Sea. *Journal of Sea Research*, 49, 337–345.
35. Feketekuty, G., & Aronson, J. D. (1984). Restrictions on trade in communication and information services. *Michigan YBI Legal Studies, 5*, 145–167.
36. Nugroho, H. B. (2012). Law of the sea aspects of Indonesian National Legislation on submarine telecommunications cable. In *Maritime border diplomacy*. Center for Oceans Law and Policy (Vol. 16, pp. 79–105).
37. White, H. M., Jr., & Lauria, R. (1995). The impact of new communication technologies on international telecommunication law and policy: Cyberspace and the restructuring of the international telecommunication union. *California Western Law Review, 32*(1), 1–30.
38. Hayes, J. (2008). A history of transatlantic cables. In M. Schwartz (Ed.), *IEEE Communications Magazine* (pp. 42–48).

39. Ashley Roach, J. (2014). *Today's customary international law of the sea. Ocean Development and International Law, 45*(3), 239–259.
40. Ruiz, J. B., & Barnett, G. A. (2015). Who owns the international internet networks? *The Journal of International Communication, 21*(1), 38–57.
41. Crispin, J., Cummins, J. M., Emus, R., & Reyna, J. (1985). Satellites versus fibre optic cables. *International Journal of Satellite Communications, 3*, 217–220.
42. Jayakar, K. (1998). Globalization and the legitimacy of international telecommunications standard-setting organizations. *Indiana Journal of Global Legal Studies*, **15**(2), 711–738.
43. Rauscher, K. F., Krock, R. E., & Runyon, J. P. (2006). Eight ingredients of communications infrastructure: A systematic and comprehensive framework for enhancing network reliability and security. *Bell Labs Technical Journal, 11*(3), 73–81.
44. Rauscher, K. F. (2004). Protecting communications infrastructure. *Bell Labs Technical Journal, 9*(2), 1–4.
45. Ekwere, K. (2016). Submarine cables and the marine environment: Enhancing sustainable and harmonious interactions. *China Oceans Law Review*, 2016(1), 129–186.
46. Carter, L., & Burnett, D. R. (2015). *Subsea telecommunications from: Routledge handbook of ocean resources and management routledge* (pp. 349–365).
47. Wrathall, L. R. (2010–2011). The vulnerability of subsea infrastructure to underwater attack: Legal shortcomings and the way forward. *The San Diego International Law Journal, 12*, 224–247.
48. Trautman, L. J. (2016–2017). Is cyberattack the next Pearl Harbor? *North Carolina Journal of Law & Technology, 18*, 233–289.
49. Marra, L. J. (1989). Sharkbite on the SL submarine lightwave cable system: History, causes, and resolution. *IEEE Journal of Oceanic Engineering, 14*(3), 232–237.
50. Kordahi, M. E. (2016). Global trends in submarine cable system faults. *Emerging Subsea Networks, SubOptic* (pp. 1–7).
51. Ross, M. (2014). Understanding interconnectivity of the global undersea cable communications infrastructure and its implications for international cyber security. *SAIS Review of International Affairs, 34*(1), 141–155.
52. Mudric, M. (2010). Rights of states regarding underwater cables and pipelines. *ARELJ, 29*, 235–256.
53. Green, M. P., & Burnett, D.R. (2008). Security of international submarine cable infrastructure: Time to rethink? In: *Legal challenges in maritime security* (Vol. 12, pp. 557–584). Center for Oceans Law and Policy.
54. Agarwala, N. (2018). Green cables—Development, opportunities and legal challenges: Part I. *Maritime Affairs: Journal of the National Maritime Foundation of India, 14*(2), 49–62.
55. Agarwala, N. (2019). Green cables—Development, opportunities and legal challenges: Part II. *Maritime Affairs: Journal of the National Maritime Foundation of India, 15*(1), 93–107.
56. Higgins, P. (1921–1922). Submarine cables and international law. , 2.
57. Bannon, R., &, Burnett, D. (2003). Submarine cable infrastructure defense against terrorist aggression. *Sea Technology*, 4, 1850–1861.
58. Rapp, R. J., et al. (2012). India's critical role in the reliance of the global undersea communications cable infrastructure. *Strategic Analysis*, 375–383.
59. Zeuschner, R. (2011). Pipelines and cables—The offshore transportation of oil, gas and renewable energy. *International Energy Law Review, 8*, 311–326.
60. Beckman, R., & Davenport, T. (2012). The EEZ regime: Reflections after 30 years, securing the ocean for the next generation. In *LOSI Conference Papers* (pp. 1–41).
61. Coffen-Smout, S., & Herbert, G. J. (2000). Submarine cables: A challenge for ocean management. *Marine Policy, 24*, 441–448.
62. Kaye, S. (2006–2007). International measures to protect oil platforms, pipelines, and submarine cables from attack. *Tulane Maritime Law Journal, 31*, 377–421.
63. Kaye, S. (2009). The protection of platforms, pipelines and submarine cables under Australian and New Zealand law. In N. Klein (Ed.), *Maritime security international law and policy perspectives from Australia and New Zealand* (pp. 186–201).

64. Roberts, S., Secor, A, & Zook, M. (2011). *Critical infrastructure: Mapping the leaky plumbing of US hegemony, antipode* (pp. 1–6).
65. Shackelford, S. J., & Andres, R. B. (2010–11). State responsibility for cyber attacks: Competing standards for a growing problem. *Georgetown Journal of International Law, 42*, 971–1016
66. Davenport, T. (2012). Submarine communications cables and law of the sea: Problems in law and practice. *Ocean Development and International Law, 43*(3), 201–242.
67. Davenport, T. (2013). The installation of submarine power cables under UNCLOS: Legal and policy issues. *German Yearbook of International Law, 56*, 107–148.
68. Davenport, T. (2013). Submarine communications cables and science: A new frontier in ocean governance? In H. N. Scheiber (Eds.), *Science, Technology, and New Challenges to Ocean Law* (209–252). A Law of the Sea Institute Publication.
69. Davenport, T. (2018). The high seas freedom to lay submarine cables and the protection of the marine environment: Challenges in high seas governance, symposium on governing high seas biodiversity. *AJIL Unbound, 112*, 139–143.
70. Davenport, T. (2015). Submarine cables, cybersecurity and international law: An intersectional analysis. *Catholic University Journal of Law and Technology, 24*, 57–109.
71. Mensah, T. A. (2015). Submarine cables and the international law of the sea. In L. del Castillo (Eds.), *Law of the sea: From grotius to the international tribunal for the law of the sea* (pp. 725–749). Liber Amicorum Judge Hugo Caminos.
72. Treves, T. (2019). 'Due Regard' obligations under the 1982 UN convention on the law of the sea: The laying of cables and activities in the area. *The International Journal of Marine and Coastal Law, 34*(2), 167–194.
73. Foster, W. F. (1970). New Zealand's coastal jurisdiction. *California Western International Law Journal, 1*(1), 1–20.
74. Takie, Y. (2012). Law and policy for international submarines cables: An Asia-Pacific perspective. *Asian Journal of International Law, 2*, 205–233.
75. Van Logchem, Y. (2014). Submarine telecommunication cables in disputed maritime areas. *Ocean Development & International Law, 45*(1), 107–122.
76. Sun, Z. (2018). Protection of cable ships engaged in operations for submarine telecommunication cables. *Ocean Development and International Law,* 49(2), 118–133.
77. Keyuan, Z. (2002).Disrupting or maintaining the marine legal order in East Asia? *Chinese Journal of International Law, 1*(2), 449–497.

Online Sources

78. Beckman, R. (2010). Submarine cables—A critically important but neglected area of the law of the sea. In *7th international conference on legal regimes of sea, air, space and Antarctica (ISIL Conference)*, January 2010, New Delhi. See https://cil.nus.edu.sg/wp/wp-content/uploads/2010/01/Beckman-PDF-ISIL-Submarine-Cables-rev-8-Jan-10.pdf. Last updated January 7, 2017.
79. Beckman, R., & Davenport, T. (2012). The EEZ regime: Reflections after 30 years, securing the ocean for the next generation. In *LOSI conference papers* (1–41). See https://www.law.berkeley.edu/files/Beckman-Davenport-final.pdf. Last updated May 7, 2017.
80. Burnett, D. R. (2006). The importance of the United Nations law of the sea convention to the cable industry. *Submarine Telecoms Forum, 26*, 22–24. See https://www.unclosdebate.org/citation/1349/importance-united-nations-law-sea-convention-cable-industry. Last updated April 14, 2017.
81. *Threats to Undersea Cable Communications* (2017). See https://www.dni.gov/files/PE/Documents/1---2017-AEP-Threats-to-Undersea-Cable-Communications.pdf. Last updated January 09, 2018.

82. Commander Matis, M. (2012). *The protection of undersea cables: a global security threat*. See https://apps.dtic.mil/dtic/tr/fulltext/u2/a561426.pdf. Last updated January 09, 2018.
83. Simcock, A. (2016). *Chapter 19. Submarine cables and pipelines*. See https://www.un.org/Depts/los/global_reporting/WOA_RPROC/Chapter_19.pdf. Last updated February 2, 2018.
84. *Fishing and submarine cables working together* (2009). International Cable Protection Committee (2nd ed., pp. 1–54).
85. Sechrist, M. (2012). *New threats, old technology vulnerabilities in undersea communications cable network management systems* (pp. 6–22). See https://www.belfercenter.org/sites/default/files/files/publication/sechrist-dp-2012-03-march-5-2012-final.pdf. Last updated February 2, 2018.
86. Perez-Alvaro, E., Unconsidered threats to underwater cultural heritage: Laying submarine cables. *Rosetta, 14*, 54–70. See http://www.rosetta.bham.ac.uk/issue14/perezalvaro.pdf. Last updated February 2, 2017.
87. Discussion Paper Series on Problems and Challenges in Transit Connectivity Routes and International Gateways in Asia, Discussion Paper series 2014/1, Economic and Social Commission for Asia and the Pacific ICT and Development Section, ICT and Disaster Risk Reduction Division (pp. 1–25). See https://www.unescap.org/sites/default/files/Discussion%20Paper-Transit-Connectivity_0.pdf. Last updated January 11, 2017.
88. Submarine Cables and BBNJ Preparatory Committee established by General Assembly resolution 69/292: Development of an internationally binding instrument under the United Nations Convention of the Law of the Sea on the conservation and sustainable use of marine biological diversity of areas beyond national jurisdiction. The International Cable Protection Committee. See https://www.un.org/depts/los/biodiversity/prepcom_files/ICC_Submarine_Cables_&_BBNJ_August_2016.pdf. Last updated March 12, 2017.
89. Meißner, K., Schabelon, H., Bellebaum, J., & Sordyl, H. (2016). Impacts of submarine cables on the marine environment—A literature review, 1–88. See http://www.naturathlon.eu/fileadmin/BfN/meeresundkuestenschutz/Dokumente/BfN_Literaturstudie_Effekte_marine_Kabel_2007-02_01.pdf. Last updated March 18, 2017.
90. Characteristics and Common Vulnerabilities Infrastructure Category: Cable Landing Stations (2004) (pp. 1–14). See https://info.publicintelligence.net/DHS-UCL-CV.pdf. Last visited March 26, 2018.
91. Alazri, A. S. (2018). The threat and vulnerabilities of submarine cables in information security and telecommunication. *International Journal Multimedia and Image Processing, 8*(3), 432–437. See https://infonomics-society.org/wp-content/uploads/ijmip/published-papers/volume-8-2018/The-Threat-and-Vulnerabilities-of-Submarine-Cables.pdf. Last updated November 28, 2019.
92. Wacker, M. R. (2014). *Cyber infrastructure: The forgotten vulnerability* (pp. 1–68). See https://pdfs.semanticscholar.org/36d6/2c1a30cde84f5973a33b87d246c5ab09637c.pdf. Last updated April 19, 2017.